DISCOVER THE WEALTH WITHIN YOU

Also by Ric Edelman

What You Need to Do Now

Ordinary People, Extraordinary Wealth

The New Rules of Money

The Truth About Money

DISCOVER THE WEALTH WITHIN YOU

A Financial Plan for Creating a Rich and Fulfilling Life

RIC EDELMAN, CFS, RFC, CMFC, CRC

HarperBusiness
An Imprint of HarperCollins*Publishers*

Presentation of performance data does not imply that similar results will be achieved in the future. Rather, past performance is no indication of future results and any assertion to the contrary is a federal offense. Any such data is provided merely for illustrative and discussion purposes; rather than focusing on the time periods used or the results derived, the reader should focus instead on the underlying principles.

None of the material presented here is intended to serve as the basis for any financial decision, nor does any of the information contained within constitute an offer to buy or sell any security. Such an offer is made only by prospectus, which you should read carefully before investing or sending money.

The material presented in this book is accurate to the best of my knowledge. However, performance data changes over time, and laws frequently change as well, and my advice could change accordingly. Therefore, the reader is encouraged to verify the status of such information before acting.

HarperCollins books may be purchased for educational, business, or sales promotional use. For information please write: Special Markets Department, HarperCollins Publishers Inc., 10 East 53rd Street, New York, NY 10022.

Designed by Ric Edelman and Suzi Fenton

First HarperBusiness Paperback Edition
ISBN 0-06-000833-4

Library of Congress Cataloging-in-Publication Data has been applied for.

03 04 05 06 07 QW 10 9 8 7 6 5 4 3 2 1

This book is dedicated to

Tom Bresnahan
John Butler
Jim Gallant
Janice Ockershausen

and Brent Byers.

I am forever grateful for the opportunity they have given me.

Benefit from Ric's Unique Advice

★ **You Can Create a Financial Plan**
It's not complicated or difficult when using Ric's easy-to-understand recipe.

>> turn to page 141

★ **Too Many Americans Own Too Much Employer Stock**
The Enron mess was predictable and easily avoidable. Let Ric show you how to protect yourself.

>> turn to page 226

★ **The First Real Consumer Guide to Morningstar** — The ranking system that virtually all mutual fund investors rely on to invest trillions of dollars — and almost no one uses it correctly.

>> turn to page 259

★ **The 4 Steps to Successful Goal Setting**
Ric shows you the secrets to getting what you want out of life.

>> turn to page 25

★ **How to Pick Mutual Funds**
Learn the right way to pick the funds that are right for you.

>> turn to page 281

★ **Learn How to Invest Like a Professional**
Ric shows you how to adopt the secrets of America's biggest institutional money managers!

>> turn to page 220

★ **Why Owning Index Funds is a Bad Idea**
Learn about "The World's Dumbest Investor."

>> turn to page 331

1,384 Reasons to Read This Book

plus 242 ridiculous, amusing, and (sometimes) hugely insightful footnotes

Some of the Unique, Award-Winning Advice You'll Discover

To Learn About **Turn to Page**

Table of Contents

Introduction

No author, not even a best-selling one, would be so bold as to tell his readers that they are going to love his new book. That would be arrogant, self-centered and egotistical. So, no, I would never say you will love this book.

You're going to love half of it.

I just don't know whether you will love the first half or the second half. What I do know is that you'll prefer one much more than the other — and that you need both halves.

The first half — which is really less than 50% of the total, but who's counting — shows you how to choose fun, enriching and rewarding goals, and then reveals how to achieve those goals.

The second half is a detailed exploration of investing — showing you how to choose the mutual funds that can best help your goals become reality. Asset allocation, portfolio modeling and the like can be rather dull, so we'll instead talk about baking a cake. With luck, the analogy will make the topic easier for you to, uh, digest (sorry).

Like I said, you're probably going to like one half more than the other. You might find goal setting to be fun, inspiring and motivational, and mutual fund analysis to be drudgery. But you might just as easily love the detail you'll find in the second half. This is as true for readers who have never bought a mutual fund as it is for those who regard investing as a hobby.

Although you'll favor one half over the other, both are critically important. Without goals, you can't invest effectively. And if you don't invest effectively, you won't achieve your goals. That's why this book contains both halves — it's really two different books — and why I urge you to devote your attention to the half you're enjoying least (because that's the part you probably need most).

As you turn the pages, you'll discover that the secret to attaining wealth is not found in the business section of the daily newspaper. It's not revealed on financial talk shows, and it's not in your rich uncle's will. No, the secret to attaining wealth is in the one place you haven't looked. You'll discover that all the wealth you could ever want is already within your grasp. So come along and discover . . . the wealth within you.

Acknowledgments

I am indebted to the many members of my staff who devoted many hours to reading the manuscript at its various stages. Their blunt comments — such as Dutch's "This sentence makes absolutely no sense!" — were of tremendous help.

The Order of the Red Pen includes the financial planners of Edelman Financial Services, namely, Jim Baker, CPA, CFP®; Cindee Berar, MBA, RFC, CRC; Jack Bubon, CFP®; Kristine Duwar Chaze, RFC; Marty Corso, CFP®, CLU, ChFC; John Davis, RFC; Mary Davis, CFP®, CRC; Pat Day, CFP®; Joe Gilmore, RFC, CRC; Diane Jensen, MS, CFP®; Jan Kowal, CPA, CFP®; Andrew Massaro, CFP®, CFS, CRC; Ed Moore, CFP®; Betty O'Lear, MBA, CFP®, CRC; Doug Rabil, CFP®, CRC; Rey Roy, CFP®; Kelsey Williams, RFC, CRC; and Tom Wood, CFP®, CLU, ChFC, as well as EFS staff members Mike Attiliis, CFS, Brenda Carter, Will Casserly, Brandon Corso, AAMS, CMFC, Sharon Deaver, Suzi Fenton, Dutch Fox, Lisa Korhnak, Dawn Lanphier, Andrea Major, Bruce Mattare, Colleen Parker, Donna Piwetz, Carol Roberts, Evy Sheehan, Mary Jane Spradlin, Dale Tison, Pam Wallin, and Rosa Zediker. Thanks to their comments, the book you hold in your hands bears little resemblance to the drafts they reviewed.

Kudos go to the EFS Communications Department — to Suzi Fenton and Will Casserly for their outstanding layout and design, to Rodel Berber for his charts, to Adrian Reilly for his artwork and to Jerry Mason for his research assistance.

I also want to thank Don Phillips of Morningstar for his invaluable assistance and Kevin Fryer of Overlap for his cooperation.

Appreciation also goes to Dave Conti and the gang at HarperCollins, and to my agent, Gail Ross.

As always, my most heartfelt and important thank-you goes to my wife, Jean, who unceasingly tolerates my absence and inattention while I engage in projects such as this. I am incredibly lucky and most undeserving of her affections, which are exceeded only by mine for her.

With all the people involved, this book must be perfect. But it's not, and all its errors and failings are solely mine.

Answer These Two Questions

Circle below the percentage
of your long-term investments that you are willing
to place into stocks and/or stock mutual funds:

0% 10% 20% 30% 40% 50% 60% 70% 80% 90% 100%

Over the next 20 years, on an overall basis,
what return do you expect your investments to earn,
on average per year?

_______%

For now, set aside your answers. Later in the book, we'll return to them.

PART 1

The Pursuit of Happiness

CHAPTER 1

Does the Cabbie Know Where You Want to Go?

CHAPTER 1

Does the Cabbie Know Where You Want to Go?

Have you ever gotten into a cab but refused to tell the driver where you want to go? Of course not. The whole point of hailing a cab is to have the driver help you get to your destination. You tell him your goal, and the cabbie both develops the plan for getting you there and implements it for you.

Financial planning operates the same way. Thus, if you don't have goals, the planning effort is as pointless as asking a cabbie to drive you around town,[1] with no destination in mind.

I bet you can tell me what surveys reveal are the top three reasons people save money.[2] They are:

- To buy a home[3]
- To pay for college
- To afford a comfortable retirement

[1] "And step on it!"
[2] Listed here chronologically rather than by priority.
[3] Or two.

If you were to expand this list, you could add:

- ✦ wedding costs
- ✦ capital expenses, such as a car
- ✦ celebrations, such as a couple's 50th anniversary
- ✦ vacations
- ✦ major medical expenses
- ✦ elder care costs
- ✦ and, ultimately, leaving your money to your kids and/or other heirs.

Each of the above is a common reason why people save and invest. Each requires or constitutes a set of goals. And when combined, each fits into an overall financial plan.

"I want to walk the length of the Great Wall of China in 2016."

~Jill Johnson, 49, Sr. Procurement and Contracting Specialist

But one thing bothers me about this entire list. And I imagine it bothers you, too. You know what the problem is?

Simple: The entire list is boring.

I mean, really boring. Yeah, I'll grow up. Buy a car. Get married. Have kids. Pay for college. Maybe foot the bill for a wedding or two. Retire. Wither away in some old-age home. Die.

And to make this even *more* fun, I'm supposed to pay some financial planner to tell me I can't afford it.

There's more to life than this, isn't there? Tell me there is! Please! Yes, there is much more to life than obligation and responsibility. There is also personal fulfillment and happiness. In fact, it's partly why our nation was founded.

By permission of Johnny Hart and Creators Syndicate, Inc.

In the Declaration of Independence, the founders of our nation recognized our right to "life, liberty and the pursuit of happiness."

The pursuit of happiness.

The document doesn't say anything about financial planning.

This is what makes the United States of America the greatest nation on earth. If anyone ever disputed that notion, no one has dared do so since September 11, 2001. On that day, our lives changed forever. At some point — was it days? weeks? I can't remember — I began wondering if this book's message would still be valid. So, I reread my manuscript, and discovered that you still need the message this book offers you, and that perhaps you need to hear this message even more so than before that horrible day.

That's because this book is all about setting and achieving goals. More than ever, you need to focus on your future. But as you read, you'll see that my emphasis on goal-setting is of a personal, and in many cases, materialistic nature. And in the aftermath of September 11, I suspect that many of us will have replaced many such goals with different, more fundamental ones. Where in the past goals might have pertained to beach houses, fancy cars and exotic vacations, people increasingly are considering goals that involve their communities, charities and families. All of this is healthy, and as you'll see as you read on, it is entirely consistent with my message.

Life is about the future. And our future is bright, thanks to the incredible foresight of our nation's founders. So, let's return to our nation's roots — and begin our journey, a journey in the pursuit of happiness.

CHAPTER 2

You Can't Tell the Cabbie What You Don't Know

Chapter 2

You Can't Tell the Cabbie What You Don't Know

Do you remember ever saying:

Before I die, I want to ____________________________.

Or this:

Before I retire, I'm going to __________________________.

Perhaps you said one or both of the above when you were a child. Perhaps you were a college student when you said it, or maybe it was just yesterday.

Do you remember how you filled in those blanks?

When you were a little kid, people used to ask you:

What do you want to be when you grow up?

Well, now you're all grown up! But have you fulfilled your dreams?

Many people think financial planning is boring. Maybe you do, too. And is it even necessary? After all, you'll retire one day, whether you plan for it or not. And who wants to focus on retirement, old age and death? Those things simply are not fun to think about.

So let's make planning fun. Let's make it exciting. I want you to do what most people fail to do: Think about the things that get you excited.

Perhaps you already have a financial plan you created with the aid of some software program or Web site. Or maybe you've had one prepared for you by a financial advisor. But no matter its source, I have one simple question for you:

Did getting your plan make you feel excited?

If not, you need to redo your plan, by setting the right kind of goals.

Meet Evelyn Vandermark

Evelyn is one of my firm's clients. To celebrate her 65th birthday, she jumped out of an airplane. In a letter to me, she wrote:

> It was a thrilling experience, somehow very liberating. Seniors are not what they used to be. I've managed to do ballroom dancing four nights, lift weights two nights, walk 2½ miles each morning before I leave for work, was just elected to the church council and sing in the choir. All this and working 50 to 60 hours a week and being a grandma who does sleepovers and bakes cookies.
>
> And as you know, more fun is on the way as I shift to part-time work, where I can choose when and how often I want to work. I truly believe that had I not gone skydiving I probably would not have had the courage to make the job change. It gave me a sense of freedom.

Photo Courtesy of Danovision Productions   To take the plunge call Air Adventures, 800-533-6151.

Now, *that's* exciting.

Yet, this didn't happen out of the blue.[4] Evelyn had to plan ahead for this event. She had to get herself psyched up. She had to anticipate what it would cost — in terms of time and physical exertion, not just financially. But could she really have anticipated the wonderful reward she gave her spirit?

Too many people ignore this kind of planning. Yet, this is exactly the kind of planning that keeps you young at heart and which makes life so exciting. That's what I want you to think about.

Chances are, it's been years — even decades — since you've thought of your childhood dreams. Were they pushed out of your consciousness by the obligations and hassles of daily life?

It's okay if that's what happened — it happens to almost everyone. Just think about those dreams and desires again. And because the thought of having a pony probably isn't as exciting to you as it was when you were four, allow yourself to dream new dreams.

Twenty years from now you will be more disappointed by the things you didn't do than by the ones you did do. So throw off the bowlines. Sail away from the safe harbor. Catch the trade winds in your sails. Explore. Dream. Discover.

~Mark Twain

As mentioned in Chapter 1, the September 11 Attack on America showed how unpredictable life can be, and how important it is to live life to the fullest. As a result of our nation's greatest tragedy, people are developing a new commitment to lead more fulfilling lives. It's one more example that terrorists can attack us, but they cannot defeat us.

[4] Though it did happen into the blue! Ha Ha . . . uh, sorry.

In my seminar on goal-setting and financial planning, I present a short videotape to help the audience see how people change over the years. It opens with interviews of second- and third-graders, moves on to high school sophomores, then twenty-somethings new to the workplace, and ends in conversations with retirees.

The video reveals something startling. The youngest kids, naturally, are full of dreams and hopes and visions of the future. Indeed, children consider themselves immortal. To them, everything is exciting; their entire life is in front of them. As a result, if you listen carefully, young children talk in "future-speak" — everything is about what they're *going to do.* When we asked the grade-schoolers their age, they consistently answered in terms of their next birthday, as in, "I'm going to be seven," or "I'll be eight next month."

Even the high-schoolers did this: They're always talking about the driver's license they're going to get, the college they're going to attend. They talk in future-speak — who they're going to be, what they're going to do — because their life is not about where they are, but about where they're going.

> There are three ages of man — youth, age, and "you're looking wonderful."
>
> ~Francis Spellman

The newly minted graduates, early in their careers, have the same enthusiasm. For the first time in their lives, they have their own money — more of it than ever before. And they're beginning to get a sense of what they really can do with their lives. Result: They're very excited.

But you can notice an important change in their conversation: They are speaking in the present tense. When I asked them their ages, they all answered plainly. "I'm 24," "I'm 26," and "I'm 32." They talked about current events and current conditions — how things are at the moment. Compared to the children, these 20- to 30-year-olds talked less about the future and more about the present.

And when we shift to the senior citizens — people in their 60s, 70s and 80s — we find that they talk in the past tense. They talk about where they used to live, what they used to do, the children they raised, and the places they've been. Instead of revealing how old they are, they tend to cite ages younger than they really are — like the women who half-jokingly insist they're 29.[5] They talk mostly about the past and very little about the future. Much of their conversation, in fact, is about their laments and regrets — the things that they didn't do that they wished they'd done.

And, as you'd expect, the two most often-cited reasons why they aren't doing the things they'd always envisioned are lack of money and poor health.

Meet Lillian Brown

And then my video introduces Lillian, another client of ours. Let me share with you her on-camera comments:

> I will be 87 in August and have been on my own, the head of the household for 20 years. I was on the faculty of George Washington University for 10 years, and then joined American University for another 10 years. After 20 years, one can get retirement benefits, so I retired. Then I walked over to Georgetown and asked if they needed somebody like me. I've now been there for another 20 years.
>
> I think the most exciting place I've ever been is Machu Picchu in Peru. The second most exciting place is Ephesus. Both are wonderful historical places. I've been to Norway and traced the Old Norse language down through Scotland, where I also go a lot — this year I'm going to Orkney because there's a Scottish castle there that belongs to some of my relations. It's on an old Viking settlement, so that's going to be very interesting.
>
> Next week, I'm going to my 70th high school reunion in Ohio. Then I'll be going to Yale to lecture at the Women's Campaign School. After that, I'm going to Denver to speak at the Mayo Clinic. Then it's off to Teaneck, New Jersey, to talk to the folks at Lockheed. And so forth.

[5] It's half-serious, too. The unspoken message is that they lament their current age, and they much prefer to look back at younger times than look forward to the future, when they'll be even older than they are now.

> I intend to do a lot of traveling. I intend to teach as long as they want me to. I intend to do a lot of consulting. I want to go to the opera more. I want to finish my book. I think you always have to be open to new opportunities that come along. But I think you also have to see that you're financially secure so that you can live a beautiful life.

Did you notice how Lillian referred to her age? She said, "I will be 87 in August" — phrasing it the same way as the 5-year-olds. When we taped Lillian, her birthday wasn't for another four months, but she was already talking about it, and looking forward to it with eagerness. Think about that: She didn't say, "I'm 86." She said, "I will be 87" — even though that date was a third of a year away.

"I would like to travel to all 50 states and collect ceramics/pottery to go with my existing collection of 2000+ pieces. By age 75."

~Mattie McKnight, 49, Systems Engineer

During the interview, in a portion of the tape that we edited out, I asked Lillian, "Where have you just been?" because (as is obvious) she travels all the time.[6] But Lillian couldn't immediately remember the places she's been in the past year — not because of any "senior moment" but because she was so focused on where she's about to go. Indeed, when I posed the question, she gave me a look that said, "What difference does it make where I've been? Let's talk about where I'm going!"

[6] She's a public image and makeup consultant. She was television's first makeup artist and served six U.S. presidents, from Kennedy to Clinton. She's well known in the broadcasting field.

To Lillian, where she's been doesn't matter nearly as much as where she is going next. That's why she is so easily able to cite her list of upcoming speeches. She mentioned on the tape that she's writing her next book; what she didn't say is she has already published three. And when I asked her when she would finish her new book, she promptly gave me her deadline.

In other words, Lillian not only knows what she wants to do, she has dates for when she'll achieve each of them. That's why she's so happy: She is focused on achieving her goals, and the journey is as much fun for her as the achievement.

Within Lillian Brown lies the secret to successful goal-setting.

So, here's what I want you to do: Think about and choose your goals. Pick just one if you like, or choose several or even many. If you have a spouse or partner, do this by yourself, and then create another, separate list as a couple.

You must begin this process individually because goal-setting is a very personal experience. To do this successfully, you must think about the ideas, places, people, subjects and events that make up your dreams. You might not have thought of these in 20 or even 40 years. You might never have voiced them to anyone, even to your spouse. You might not even have been willing to admit to yourself that you have them.

You now have permission to do so.

That's why you must begin this exercise by yourself. Don't worry what others might think. You're not doing this for your friends, your family, your co-workers or your spouse. You're doing it for you. Each goal you select must inspire you. It must motivate you. It must excite you. If your goal is merely something that (you think) others would want you to have or do or be, you won't achieve it. In fact, you'll eventually resent it — and them.

Don't create a list of things that you think others want you to have or do. Your list is highly personal, and it need please no one other than yourself.

Take plenty of time to identify your goals. Some goals might pop into your head immediately; others will surface only after considerable time.

Although this seems to be a simple exercise, many people find it to be remarkably difficult.

As you've begun to notice, this book is peppered with the goals of ordinary people, people just like you. I collected this information by giving a questionnaire to everyone who visited my office over a two-month period.

In the beginning, few gave me the information I sought. The answers I got included:

> **"be able to retire and maintain my current lifestyle"**
> **"maybe have money to give to the kids"**
> **"have enough income for the rest of our lives"**
> **"retirement planning so we can retire by 62"**
> **"enough income for a comfortable retirement"**
> **"to not be a burden to my children"**
> **"to have a decent retirement income"**
> **"achieve a portfolio that will provide us a comfortable retirement"**
> **"accumulate wealth"**
> **"retire comfortably"**

You get the idea. Virtually no one was able to tell me what they'd actually do with the money they say they want to accumulate. I figured the fault lay in the way I was asking the question, so I changed the questionnaire to read:

> When stating a goal, do not refer to financial planning; that is a given. Instead, talk about something specific lifestyle-wise. It doesn't have to be dependent on money (such as learning to play with a yo-yo), although most goals do require wealth (such as buying a beach house).

I still didn't get the answers I was looking for. People kept talking generically and vaguely about retirement, travel, college and kids. Was it possible that no one has any goals?

I refused to believe that. Instead, I think people simply are unused to the idea of setting specific goals. So I modified the questionnaire yet again, this time saying:

> For the purposes of this exercise, the following goals are *not acceptable*:

1. have financial security
2. retire comfortably
3. have a decent retirement income
4. have travel money (too vague)
5. put kids through college
6. not be a burden to my children
7. be able to retire
8. not run out of money
9. have $5 million
10. pay for daughter's wedding
11. send kids to private school

Also not acceptable is anything pertaining to:

12. accumulation of wealth (instead, tell me what you'd do with that wealth)
13. your desire to retire
14. paying for children's educations
15. paying for daughters' weddings
16. providing elder care for parents
17. elimination of debt

Each of these is a given. Tell me instead about personal dreams, goals, ambitions, and desires.

Ahhhh — now, they got it. I'm convinced that our society has been conditioned to think of money and financial planning in terms of obligation and security. Somewhere, somehow, someone has taken all the fun out of it! But when I overtly and forcefully gave my clients permission to think creatively and (let's admit it) selfishly, the ideas flowed freely. You see the results throughout this book.

Set yourself free. It's a wonderful experience.

Open your mind to the possibilities, and let the ideas come. Choosing goals isn't something you do once. It's something you'll do for the rest of your life. And once you have a goal in place, you'll be ready to begin achieving it.

If you have a spouse or partner, set additional goals together, after you've established your own goal(s). See if you have in common any individual goals; if so, you can work on them together.

Problem is, most of us haven't set a goal in decades. To set a goal, you've got to make a decision, and that's probably something you haven't done in a very long time.

Think about it: When was the last time you made a decision — a *real* decision?

"I want to learn to fly an airplane by December of this year."

~Michael Lechner, 26, Tech Manager

Well, if you're still working, your job determines:

- when you're going to get out of bed. You think you're the one who decided what time the alarm clock will ring? Nah — your boss made that decision for you.

- what you're going to wear. If you're a lawyer due in court, your wardrobe is pre-established. Ditto for the construction worker.[7]

- where you're going to drive. The location of your home relative to your place of employment determines your route.[8]

- how you're going to spend your day. Your job has predetermined what you'll be doing all day — all you've got to do is do it. In fact, your job dictates when you're going to eat, where you'll eat, and quite likely who you're going to eat with. It might even determine what you're going to eat.[9]

So, c'mon. Admit it. The last time you really made a decision was probably the day you decided to take that job. That, indeed, was a very big decision — because its impact on all the above is so clear.

[7] Oh, yeah, sure, you get to pick the tie or select the jeans. But that's not a decision, that's the process of elimination!
[8] Yes, you can vary it slightly. But you never do, do you?
[9] And please, don't pretend that selecting a banana instead of an apple is a decision.

What other decisions have you made in your life? You can cite them as well as I:

- **who to marry (and for many, whether to divorce)**
- **what college to attend**
- **what career to pursue**
- **where to live**
- **whether to have children, and if so, how many to have and when to have them**

Those are big decisions, but for someone who's going to be on this planet for maybe 80 or 90 years, this is a remarkably short list.[10, 11, 12, 13, 14]

Thus, most of our daily activities really are not decision-oriented. Instead, our day is prescribed for us by the decisions we've previously made. Which brings up a good point: You're a lousy tennis player.[15]

I mean, you play tennis what, once or twice a week, maybe not once in the past year? How can you expect to be good at something you never[16] do? Ditto with goal-setting. If the last time you made a decision was three years ago, then clearly you aren't going to do it very well.

This explains why you never get a good deal when buying a car. You buy a car maybe once every three or four years. But the guy you're buying it from sells a car once every three or four hours. He's going to win that negotiation because he's had a lot more practice than you. And when he's done with you, he asks his finance manager to further pummel you.

---

[10] It's even more amazing when you consider that most of these decisions are packed into a single decade — your twenties — a time when your ability to make good decisions is highly debatable. That's why so many of us experience regret.

[11] Regret and your efforts to avoid it (which cause you to make bad investment decisions) are covered in greater detail in my third book, *Ordinary People, Extraordinary Wealth.*

[12] $14.99, at bookstores everywhere.

[13] And with these footnotes, I welcome back footnotes to footnotes. Actually, I just set a new personal record — four footnotes in a single usage! Beat that, Stephen King!

[14] Not to mention the return of my usual shameless self-promotion. But this time, it's different. No, really. You see, my prior books covered a variety of topics but none of them in huge detail; this one (as you'll discover) covers only two topics but delves deeply into them. (Picture a field measuring 10x10 that's only two feet deep, versus a field that's 2x2 but 10 feet deep. That's the difference between my prior books and this one.) In this book, for example, you'll learn how to analyze, sort, select and monitor mutual funds. This forces me to assume that you know what a mutual fund is and how it works. For a lot of people, that's a silly assumption. Therefore, I have two choices: Either I provide that important-yet-fundamental background in this book, or tell you — in case you need it — where you can find that information (by referring you to the appropriate chapter of my previous books). In most cases, I chose the latter, because if I didn't, this book would be a whole lot longer than it already is, and it would be largely redundant to my prior books. So, I'll skip my tradition of referencing my prior books humorously, and just make the references as appropriate, and I'll let you decide whether I'm offering information of value, or merely hawking my other books to make a quick buck. And this makes five footnotes.

[15] Good segue, huh?

[16] Or only rarely.

Yet, proper and effective goal-setting is the key to financial planning — just as giving the correct address to the cab driver is key to getting you to the proper destination. Unfortunately, few financial planners ever talk about goal-setting with their clients. Too often, the only thing planners talk to their clients about is retirement.

If you've been to a planner, you know the drill. They ask two questions. The first is, "When do you want to retire?"

Are you able to answer that question?

The second question is, "How much income do you want to have at that time?"

Are you able to state the amount of income you want in retirement?

I am not suggesting that these questions are unimportant. Quite the contrary: It's critical that you be able to talk with confidence about these issues.

Which is why I just posed them to you.

But focusing on retirement, and retirement alone, creates two problems. First, as we've already shown, this stuff is boooooooooooor*ing*.[17] Second, if all we focus on is retirement, you could end up working longer than you otherwise would. Let me explain.

© 2001 Thaves. Reprinted with permission. Newspaper dist. by NEA, Inc.

[17] Put a little jingle in your voice as you say that word, please. It'll work better.

Meet Penny Dawson

Penny, 52, is a schoolteacher and has been for 24 years. Her husband, Neal, is a very successful chiropractor who operates three clinics. Thanks to their substantial combined incomes, excellent savings habits and recent inheritances, the Dawsons[18] have amassed $2 million.

> ***"Own a beach home by age 65."***
>
> **~Tom Conlan, 56, Prep School Teacher**

Penny once loved to teach. But her school system has changed significantly over the years ("and so have the kids," she tells me). Thus, she does not find teaching to be as rewarding or fulfilling as she once did. So, her goal is to teach for another six years, at which time she'll have put in 30 years, making her eligible for a pension. She has even pondered whether to work a few years beyond that, because her pension benefits rise with each extra year she works.

I was dismayed when she told me this.

Penny's goal is a traditional one: To work until retirement. And I have no doubt she can achieve that goal. There's only one problem: She no longer likes her job; she's working solely for the money.

But does she really need the money? If she quits teaching now, she'll get no pension. But to get the pension, she'll have to work six more years. By then, her health might not be as good, her husband's health might not be as good, and her children will be six years older.

She thinks she's working because she'll need the pension. She thinks the question is, "Will I be able to retire in six years?"

But the truth is that she can afford to quit now: Her assets easily can replace her paycheck, and she'll never even notice — let alone miss — the fact that she's not getting a pension.[19]

---

[18] Not their real name.

[19] It's true: Although Penny earns $70,000 as a teacher, her investments could provide her with an annual income of more than $140,000 — right now. So why work for six more years to get a pension that will be less than half of what she can receive from her investments today?

So here's the real question: If she quits, what will she do with all her newfound time?

You see, like you, 12 hours of Penny's day are work-related.[20] This explains the *real* reason Penny is still working: S*he has not envisioned anything else to do with all that time.*

Clearly, money isn't the problem. For her — and maybe for you, too — *time* is the problem.

You can solve that problem by creating new goals. Whereas up until this point your primary[21] goal was filling your time by filling your wallet, your challenge now is to fill your time by filling your spirit. *Let's focus on the exciting stuff!*

And here's how to do it.

During a recent review meeting with another couple, the husband mentioned that he planned to retire in two years. When I asked why he wasn't retiring now, he just shrugged.

When I told them that they had enough money saved to support themselves for life, they were shocked.

"You mean he could stay home all the time?" the wife asked, wide-eyed and smiling.

I nodded.

"You mean he'd be able to help me, by doing things around the house, and run errands, and such?" she asked, now grinning.

I nodded again.

"This is wonderful!" she said. "It'd be great to have a wife!"

He's a real nowhere man, sitting in his nowhere land,
Making all his nowhere plans for nobody.

Doesn't have a point of view, knows not where he's going to,
Isn't he a bit like you and me.

Nowhere Man, please listen,
You don't know what you're missing,
Nowhere Man, the world is at your command.

~John Lennon and Paul McCartney

---

[20] It's a myth that people work an 8-hour day. If you spend 1 hour getting ready for work, 45 minutes commuting each way, and 30 minutes "decompressing" after you get back home, you're really spending 12 hours a day in work-related activities. No job means you now have 12 hours of new time available.

[21] Sole?

The First Step to Successful Goal-Setting: Set a Positive Goal

You must use phrases your brain can process. You see, the human brain has difficulty processing negativity. To demonstrate this, try this example:[22]

Stretch out your arm with your palm facing down.

Now, as quickly as you can, follow this instruction:

Do not keep your fingers outstretched.

> ***"Starting in four years, I'll spend more time with my hobby of building museum-quality 19th-century ships and models. I also want to design and build tools to aid ship modelers."***
>
> **~Philip R. Eddy, 57, Architect**

Wasn't very easy, was it? Well, let's try again. Once again, as you did before, stretch out your arm with your palm facing down. And again, as quickly as you can, follow this instruction:

Bend your fingers.

What did you notice? You were able to execute the second instruction much more quickly than the first. You see, when the brain is presented with a negative, we throw it out, leaving us with the positive.

This is why you got wrong[23] all those double-negative test questions in school. You find those questions confusing[24] because human brains aren't programmed to handle negatives.

[22] And don't just sit there reading — actually do this! (I promise — it won't hurt.)
[23] Okay, I got wrong.
[24] Okay, I find them confusing.

I told you to "not keep your fingers outstretched" and your brain, confused by this instruction, tossed out the "not" — leaving you with your fingers outstretched. After additional thought, you finally closed your fingers into a fist.

But you were able to execute the positive instruction — fold your fingers — much more quickly. That's because the brain had less to process.

Did you ever tell children, "Don't do that!" and then wonder why they did? Try telling them what you want them to do instead of what you don't want them to do. "Stay here" is more effective than "Don't go there."[25]

Here are negative words that cause people to fail:

Not - as covered above, the brain dismisses the word, so you internalize the very sentiment you seek to eliminate.

Don't, Won't, Shouldn't, Can't - all derivations of "not." Don't tell me what you don't do, won't do, shouldn't do or can't do. Tell me instead what you want to do.

Ever go on a diet and tell yourself that you "will not eat"? Now you know why you always fail: Your brain can't process "not," so it dismisses it, leaving you with "will eat."

So, state a diet goal that's positive, not negative.

How about, "I will fit in a size 'x' dress" or "I will be able to run four miles." Guess what? When you fit in that dress, you'll be the weight you desire. By running that distance, you'll be the weight you desire. Those are positive goals. Telling yourself you will "stop eating ice cream" is a negative goal, and all you're doing is filling your mind with the things you don't want to do.

[25] Sometimes, when you're dining out, the waiter bringing your food says, "Don't touch the plate — it's very hot." What's the first thing you do?

Stop - you'll stop when you're dead. Until then, keep on going!

Avoid - although it seems positive — avoid fatty foods — your brain knows better: It will focus on whatever it is you've told it to "avoid."

Impossible and **Never** - the worst words of all.

Here are dangerous words that, although not negative, nonetheless belittle your efforts:

Little - there's no such thing as succeeding a little bit. Either you do or you don't.

Later - the motto of procrastinators. My first book, *The Truth About Money,* shows why procrastination is the #1 cause of financial failure.[26]

Will - smokers often say that they "will quit tomorrow." And they say this every day of their lives. How about, "I have already quit."

Try - people who "try" always succeed — at trying. But they also always fail to finish. Do you want to "try to save for a new car" or do you want to "save for a new car"?

Should - you know what you "should" be doing. It's more important that you focus on what you "are" doing.

Start - almost as bad as "later" and "will." Don't start your journey — be underway with it.

Possible - an incredibly meaningless word that, to some, seems to convey more than it does.

[26] $14.99, bookstores everywhere. Oops, sorry, I said I wouldn't do that.

You've learned that the human brain cannot process negatives. Now learn that the brain cannot tolerate conflicts, either.

Say you want to plan for retirement but you can't decide how much income you want at that time. Your brain will resolve this conflict, using one of many tools that psychologists have known about for years.

Ideally, you'll resolve the conflict through what they call assertive coping; you'll take a positive action directly aimed at resolving the conflict. By assertively coping with retirement, you'll evaluate your income needs.

Even if you are unable to resolve your conflict assertively, you will resolve it nonetheless. That's a scary revelation, so I hope you digest that statement slowly and carefully. Even if you are unable to resolve your conflict assertively, you will resolve it nonetheless. If you are unable to decide how much money you want in retirement, your brain will force you to make a decision, and it will do this by using one or more of the many destructive methods available to it. These include:

***Aggression*, either direct or displaced. Through direct aggression, you'll never retire. Through displaced aggression, you'll kick the dog. But either way, the conflict remains: You haven't created your retirement plan. Although getting angry is perhaps the most common emotion exhibited by people in conflict, it's also the least useful, because while you were merely conflicted before, now you're conflicted — and angry.**

***Depression and apathy*. You become unhappy with your dilemma, so much so, in fact, that you lose all interest in retiring. The conflict is unhappily resolved.**

***Withdrawal*. You abolish your goal and retreat into yourself to make the conflict go away. Thus, you never retire (you've failed to achieve your goal), but at least the conflict is resolved.**

***Vacillation*. You consider one income, then another, then another, and your brain keeps you playing this game. In the meantime, you keep going to work.**

***Stereotyped behavior.* You examine your expenses. Then you re-examine them — several dozen times. You repeat this even though there's no useful purpose.[27]**

And then, of course, there are the six defense mechanisms identified by Sigmund Freud. Each of these involves some amount of self-deception and distortion of reality. They are:

[27] People do this all the time: They attempt to start their car a zillion times after discovering they have a dead battery.

Rationalization. You convince yourself that you really didn't want to attain the goal you had laid out. Unable to decide how much income you want in retirement, you decide you don't want to retire, anyway.

Repression. Your conscious mind completely forgets about the goal. By not remembering that you want to retire, you avoid regret[28] when you fail to achieve it.

Sublimation. The conversion of an unacceptable behavior into one that is tolerated by society. Freud said that Michelangelo turned forbidden sexual urges into artistic creativity. Freud also said that people with the desire to control others become schoolteachers, and that those with hostility or cruelty in their dispositions channel those emotions by becoming surgeons or prosecuting attorneys.[29]

Identification. Freud says we become who we want to be, like Trekkies who dress up as Captain Kirk.

Reaction formation. You engage in a behavior that is the exact opposite of what you really want. You keep working even though you don't want to.

Projection. You accuse others of feeling the way you actually feel. The worker blames his or her inability to retire on his or her spouse.

Did you see yourself in any of these descriptions? Be on your guard against them, for they can interfere with your ability to achieve your goals.

As you concentrate on your goals, state them in a positive way (no negatives) that avoids conflict. This means that you need to change the way you talk to yourself. It's the first step toward positive goal-setting.

The best words to describe yourself are:

I Am - who are you? Are you someone who is "saving to buy a car" or someone who is not?

I Do - either you are working on your goal, or you're not. It's that simple.

Always - inherent in the above two; easily and powerfully inserted in any sentence.

So, set a goal, and make it a positive goal.

"By the age of 50, I would like to travel to England, Australia, France, and New York City and watch all four of the major Grand Slam tennis tournaments."

~Matthew Strait, 28, Drug Scientist

[28] See footnote 11 on page 21.
[29] Hey, gimme a break. Freud said this, not me.

The Second Step to Setting a Goal: Set a Date

A goal becomes a goal only when you put a date on it.

Why do many women say that the only time they achieved their weight-loss goal was on their wedding day?

Simple: They had set a date for achieving their goal.

Meet Steve Nichols

In my goal-setting seminar, I ask members of the audience if they have any goals. In one session, Steve, 32, said to me, "I've always wanted to go to Turkey." He was quite ahead of most members of my audiences, whose minds tend to go blank when I ask them to think of a goal. And you could tell by the way he phrased it that Steve[30] had thought about going to Turkey for a long time.

But then, I stumped him. "When do you want to go?" I asked. Without hesitation, he replied, "I have no idea."

That's a problem.

My wife, Jean, and I have lived in the Washington, DC, area for more than 20 years, and I've never been inside the Washington Monument. I've always wanted to go there, and I fully believe that, one day, I will. So, how come I've never done it?

For one simple reason: Because I haven't set a date. When tourists visit the nation's capital, one of the first things they do is visit the monument. Why have so many of them seen it while I haven't — and I've been here for 20 years?

Because they had set a date, and I haven't.

Wanting to visit Turkey is fine, but if you don't set a date, the trip won't happen. Instead, you'll lament that you'd always wanted to go, but that you never have.

[30] Not his real name.

Don't let that happen to you. Choose your goal, and immediately set a date for it.

Two Rules for Setting Dates

Rule One: Make an Appointment

The date must be exactly that: A date. Saying you'll retire at 65 does not count. Saying you'll see Disney's *The Lion King* on Broadway by the end of the year is not valid. For your date to count, it must be an actual, specific date.

"I'm going to retire on September 30, 2017."

"I'm going to see *The Lion King* in New York on March 18, 2003."

False date-setting has prevented many goals from ever getting achieved. Have you ever said anything similar to the list below?

"I'll do it...
... this month."
... next year."
... by the time I'm 40."
... not until the honeymoon."[31]
... before I graduate."
... after I graduate."
... before we have kids."
... after the kids are born."
... when the kids are older."
... when I get that promotion."
... when the dog dies."
... after Mom dies."
... when you die."[32]

"I want to spend at least part of each winter in a warm location, preferably on a cruise."

~James Cleven, 55, Audit Director

In casual conversation, each of those phrases appears to be specific. They certainly convey intent, and they place the topic within conversational parameters.

[31] Just kidding.
[32] Just kidding on that one, too.

Unless you're having a conversation with a three-year-old.

> It's kind of fun to do the impossible.
>
> ~Walt Disney

There's no way that a child who wants ice cream will tolerate such nonsense as, "later." They want to know *exactly* when they are going to get their ice cream. And once you tell them the date,[33] they will do everything in their power to reach that target. And woe to everyone in sight if the kid's goal is not fulfilled.

So . . . when are you going to achieve your goals?

Rule Two: Get Real

The date must be realistic. It doesn't do you much good to say you'll reach your goal by the time you die. How could that be motivating?

Setting a date is easier to do than it appears. It's also something you're more used to than you realize. After all, you deal with deadlines all the time, and you achieve most of them.

Think about it. Your boss gives you specific dates to complete assignments. Your family gives you specific dates for everything from school activities and homework assignments to family celebrations, holidays and vacation schedules. You've even got dates for when the plumber is coming and when *The Wizard of Oz* will next air on TV.

It's also ridiculous to say you'll achieve your goal by tomorrow, for you'll never accomplish that. Thus, setting an unrealistic target is certain to lead to failure. Consequently, you'll become demoralized and you won't set a new target. Instead, you'll wallow in your current circumstance. And the only thing worse than wallowing is wallowing while feeling bad about wallowing.

So, your date not only must be attainable, it must be motivational. That means making it realistic.

So, go ahead, set a date for each of your goals.

[33] Or, more accurately, the time, since kid calendars are printed in minutes, not months.

The Third Step to Setting a Goal: Write it Down

It's easy to get distracted, and people frequently put their goals aside as they tend to urgent everyday matters. This is why you must put your goal(s) on paper.

It's also why your third-grade teacher forced you to write one hundred times "I will not pull Tammy's hair."[34] Repetition helps you memorize, assimilate, comprehend and internalize. You must live, eat and breathe your goal. It must become a part of you, something as natural to you as tying your shoelaces.

To do this, write your goal on a piece of paper. But don't merely say, "I want to go to Turkey on October 15, 2006." That's not good enough, because that's an intellectual statement. If you were about to embark on one of the most important journeys of your life, something you've dreamed of for years, don't you think you'd be a little *emotional* about it?

Sure you would. But how do you become emotionally involved? That takes us to our fourth and final step.

"I want to lead a national movement to restore careful (safe) recreational use of firearms by training school children. The campaign will launch Q3, 2002."

**~Edward M. Sybert, 56,
Program Manager**

The Final Step to Setting a Goal: Stay Focused

Start fulfilling that goal right now. Since Steve wants to go to Turkey, I told him to begin planning the trip. Start reading magazines about Turkey. Go to the Turkish government's Web site. Contact their embassy or tourist office here in the United States for information about the country. Contact the U.S. State Department for information about Turkey. Look up Turkish-American organizations and meet people who are from Turkey. Learn about the country, its history, its culture, its economy, its environment, and its people.

[34] Okay, my third-grade teacher.

I told him to start making travel plans. Get a passport. Contact a travel agent, and find out how he'll get there. How long a trip will it be? Any medical or safety precautions to take? Where will he stay? What will be his itinerary? And of course,[35] *figure out how much it will cost.*

Are you sure you're sincere about wanting to achieve your goal? To test Steve's seriousness, I asked him one question:

"Do you have a passport?"

He didn't. This showed me that Steve's goal wasn't real to him. Going to Turkey sounded intriguing — a trip to some exotic, far-off land. And getting a passport seems to be a rather pedestrian step — after all, there's nothing exotic about going to the post office to fill out a form. Yet that's what achieving goals is all about: Turning big ideas into ordinary steps. Because those ordinary steps make your goal real.

You can apply this "realism" strategy to any goal. Want to own a home? Read *Architectural Digest, Better Homes and Gardens* magazine and dozens of others like them. Talk with builders, architects, Realtors®, developers and mortgage lenders. Look at blueprints and floor plans. Constantly tour homes for sale. Get immersed in your goal, and keep it in your mind all the time. Don't worry if you won't be buying a home for five years. Build your anticipation, and get excited about it! Five years will be here before you know it!

This process is called dreaming, and not only will it help you reach your goal, it's a ton of fun.

Make your goal real, as though you were living it today. By doing this, your enthusiasm will rise, your focus will intensify, and you'll be able to stick with your goal. And sure enough, one day, you will make it happen. Because you'll have made it important to you, vitally important.

You must keep your goal in front of you. Put pictures of your goal on the refrigerator door, on the bathroom mirror, on your PC monitor at the office, and on the steering wheel of your car.

Why is it that dieters place a scale in the bathroom? Nobody eats in the bathroom! If you want to lose weight, put that scale in the kitchen doorway! By focusing on your goal at exactly the time you need to be focused on it, you'll achieve it.

[35] Lest you forget that this is a book about financial planning.

And then, when you return from Turkey, the first thing you need to do is . . . set another goal. Life, in short, is the never-ending pursuit and achievement of personal goals. It is, as our nation's founders said, the pursuit of happiness.

Many people struggle with choosing a goal. They're not sure that the goal they've considered would be truly fulfilling to them. They fret they are thinking more of fantasies than goals (fantasies are fun to envision but are not things you'd really do).

For example, one client told me he always wanted a motorcycle but his wife forbade him (too dangerous, she said). But a few years later, she got the idea of riding cross-country. Suddenly faced with the opportunity to get his wish, he changed his mind. It turned out that the fantasy of riding a motorcycle was of greater enjoyment to him than actually riding one. And he was depressed to have discovered this. "I really thought I always wanted a motorcycle," he told me. "I never really had to think too hard about it because it never appeared that it might ever become a possibility."

So, how can you know that the goal you've established will prove to be truly fulfilling? Try this: Instead of selecting one goal, establish one hundred of them.

"Learn to paint, first by charcoal/pencil, then acrylics and finally watercolor, while reading the 100 classics — between ages 65 and 70."

~Hal Tickle, 60, Business Solutions Consultant; Retired Navy Officer

Create for yourself a list of 100 goals. Use the process psychologists call "free association" — where you write down goals as you think of them. Don't try to order your thoughts, just let the ideas flow.

You'll find the effort itself to be a fascinating experience, because it's easy to come up with the first five or ten (most people start with travel ideas[36]).

After the first half-dozen or so, you'll find yourself really challenged to fill out your list. Indeed, it will take you some time to finish, often involving more than one session. Take your time. Add to your list whenever an idea pops into your head. Review your list often. That's part of the fun.

[36] But forget I said that, because I don't want to interfere with your effort to associate freely.

Figure 2-1 shows the list created by one of my firm's clients. The flow of topics reflects her random thinking.[37] Her list is highly personal[38, 39] and it contains a wide variety of ideas. And by going through her list, she will be able to identify which are the most important to her — and those are the ones she'll focus on first.

One Client's Goals

1. Tour Australia
2. Tour Africa
3. Tour Ireland
4. Tour Scotland
5. Tour Germany
6. Tour Italy
7. Tour Alaska
8. Tour the Ukraine
9. Travel in outer space
10. Learn to change a tire
11. Meet Dave Matthews
12. Ride an elephant
13. Go white water rafting
14. Learn to dive
15. Drive an Indy car
16. Learn to play the drums
17. Meet Oprah
18. Buy a house
19. Own a beach house
20. Have a live-in maid
21. Hike the Grand Canyon
22. Own a dog
23. See an Olympic event in person
24. Learn to ski well
25. Vacation on a charter boat
26. Go to the Super Bowl
27. Go to Mardi Gras
28. Go to the Grammy Awards
29. Go to the Oscars
30. Have a scholarship in my name at my alma mater
31. Save someone's life using CPR
32. See Mt. Rushmore
33. Learn to snorkel
34. Learn to arrange flowers like a pro
35. Learn to golf well
36. Hit a hole in one
37. Hike Mt. Washington
38. Go skydiving
39. Visit the top of the Sears Tower
40. Receive a blessing from the Pope
41. Tour India
42. Tour Egypt
43. See the Pyramids
44. Swim with dolphins
45. Learn my blood type
46. Be able to give blood without fainting
47. Go whale watching
48. Learn to fly a plane
49. Have a baby
50. See my grandchildren get married
51. Become fluent in French
52. Do field announcements during a Redskins game
53. Have a walk-on in a network TV show
54. Make the final cut of a major motion picture
55. Ride in a helicopter
56. Ride in a hot air balloon
57. See an erupting volcano
58. Go to Santorini
59. Spend a week at a spa
60. Meet Matt Lauer
61. Have a makeover on "Fashion Emergency"
62. Own more than 1 car
63. Have an interior designer do my home
64. Run a marathon
65. Get an honorary degree
66. Hug a chimp
67. Visit my ancestral home
68. Trace my family tree
69. Orchestrate a great wedding ceremony/reception
70. Learn to ride a horse
71. Have a successful vegetable garden
72. Become more computer-savvy
73. Learn how to remember people's names
74. Get into great physical shape
75. Originate a fad
76. Learn to design jewelry
77. Learn to knit
78. Learn Pilates
79. Learn to make bread
80. Be interviewed on national TV
81. See my picture on a billboard
82. Win big $ on a game show
83. Relearn the principles of photography
84. Learn to rock climb
85. Learn to sail
86. Keep a journal
87. Have plastic surgery
88. Learn Tae-Kwan-Do
89. Go parasailing
90. Go deep-sea fishing
91. Learn to surf
92. Find a really valuable antique at a garage sale
93. Learn different swim strokes
94. Donate a large sum of money to a charity
95. Learn to yo-yo

Figure 2-1

[37] Notice what's missing? Dates.
[38] So I thought I'd share it with everyone!
[39] Don't worry, I've eliminated identifying goals — which is why you see only 95 instead of 100.

If you'd like help getting some ideas, visit Discovery.com's Travel Channel. It once offered a list of "101 Things to Do Before You Die," which I've summarized for you in Figure 2-2. For information on these and other ideas, visit Discovery.com. Or get a course catalog from a local college or university. Hundreds of programs are offered online, too.

101 Things to Do Before You Die

ADVENTURE:

1. Learn to survive in the wilderness.
2. Skydive in a spectacular place, such as Auckland, New Zealand.
3. Visit an active volcano.
4. Visit a nude beach.
5. Bare it all at a nudist colony.
6. Scuba dive the Great Barrier Reef.
7. Climb Mt. Everest, Kathmandu, Nepal.
8. Race in Alaska's Iditarod.
9. Learn how to be a clown.
10. Eat fugu.

ANIMAL WATCHING:

1. Go on a safari.
2. Take a swamp tour and learn how to wrestle an alligator.
3. Swim with sharks.
4. Learn to ride a bull.
5. Get close to a wild animal that could kill you.
6. Run with the bulls in Pamplona.
7. Swim with dolphins.
8. See the Monarch butterfly's annual migration.
9. Go whale watching.
10. Witness the wildebeest migration.

EXPAND YOUR MIND:

1. Go to a writer's retreat and work on your novel.
2. Learn to paint a landscape like Van Gogh.
3. Read *Anna Karenina*.
4. Attend a Shakespeare festival.
5. Participate in a powwow with Native Americans.
6. Explore the NY Public Library.
7. Spend a week at Burning Man, Reno, Nevada, Labor Day weekend.
8. Visit Michelangelo's David.
9. Sample the goods at Hershey's Chocolate factory.
10. Visit Alcatraz.
11. Volunteer to help others.

GREAT CITIES:

1. Ride a cable car in San Francisco.
2. Watch the changing of the guard at Buckingham Palace.
3. Skate through the streets of Paris at night.
4. Go to Graceland.
5. Enjoy NYC at Christmas.
6. Get a taste of high fashion in Milan.
7. Learn to tango in Buenos Aires.
8. Sip tea in a traditional tea garden in Kyoto, Japan.
9. Dance a waltz at the Vienna Opera Ball.
10. Visit the world's first public art museum: The State Hermitage Museum, St. Petersburg, Russia.

HISTORY AND CULTURE:

1. Visit the Vietnam Wall in Washington, D.C.
2. Visit a former concentration camp.
3. Explore the routes of America's underground railroad.
4. Visit the Crazy Horse monument in South Dakota.
5. Walk the Great Wall of China.
6. See the ruins of Pompeii.
7. Visit the Athenian Acropolis.
8. Participate in a traditional Tet celebration.
9. Celebrate the Day of the Dead in Mexico.
10. Relive America in the 1950s: Go to a drive-in movie theater with your sweetie, Carthage, Missouri.

MYSTERIOUS PLACES:

1. Sleep in a haunted castle, Comlongon Castle, Scotland.
2. See Stonehenge.
3. See the Great Pyramid.
4. Visit Machu Picchu.
5. Visit a magnificent temple: Sri Meenakshi temple, Madurai, India.
6. Visit a spiritual place: Church of St. Suplice, Paris, France.
7. Kiss the Blarney stone, Blarney Castle, Cork, Ireland.
8. Visit the mysterious Blue Grotto in Capri.
9. Bathe in the Blue Lagoon: Near Reykjavik, Iceland.
10. Witness the Thaipusam Festival in Singapore.

Figure 2-2

INDULGENCE:

1. Eat a meal with a world-class master chef.
2. Tour a vineyard and sample a good bottle of wine.
3. Stay at the world's fanciest five-star hotel.
4. Enjoy the Oscars like the movie stars do.
5. Vacation like James Bond.
6. Live like a rock star for a day.
7. Crash a Hollywood studio.
8. Rent your own private island.
9. Spend a weekend in Vegas.
10. Bask in the sun on a beach in Rio.
11. Soak in the mud and waters of the Dead Sea.

SCIENCE AND NATURE:

1. See the southern sky.
2. Rediscover evolution the Darwin way in the Galapagos Islands.
3. Help dig for dinosaur bones.
4. See a tornado or hurricane and live to tell your grandkids.
5. See the northern lights.
6. Visit the Amazon rainforest.
7. Float along the Nile.
8. See the sunrise from Maui's Mt. Haleakala.
9. See the birth of a baby — human or animal.
10. Volunteer to help save the environment.

ULTIMATE RIDES:

1. Take a train ride on the Orient Express.
2. Ride a Harley across the U.S.
3. Ride the biggest, meanest roller coaster in the world.
4. Raft down a world-class river.
5. Ride a gondola in Venice with the love of your life.
6. Ride a mule through the Grand Canyon.
7. Test drive a Ferrari.
8. Take a steamboat cruise down the Mississippi.
9. Take a ride at the Pushkar Camel Fair.
10. Train like an astronaut at space camp.

SPORTS FANTASY:

1. Ride a leg of the Tour de France.
2. Be a basketball star: Sports Legends Fantasy Camp.
3. Hit the links at St. Andrews, the birthplace of golf.
4. Drink a mint julep at the Kentucky Derby.
5. Take in the Indy 500, Indianapolis, Indiana.
6. Run, or walk, in the New York marathon.
7. Try to hit a major-league fastball.
8. Climb Mount Olympus.
9. Watch the sumo wrestling championships in Japan.

Reprinted with special permission of King Features Syndicate.

Don't Feel That You Must Create a Big List

Some people find it easy to create a list of 100 goals; others find it impossible. If you find it a challenge, don't despair. After all, it's as acceptable to have one goal as it is to have one hundred.

In fact, you might find it more effective to think of goals within categories. For example, you might choose one or more goals for each of these areas of your life:

- Career/Professional
- Educational
- Family
- Health
- Material
- Mental
- Physical
- Political
- Recreational
- Religious
- Social

You may prefer to choose goals that vary in scope. For example, pick a goal that you can reach within:

- One hour
- One day
- One week
- One month
- One year
- One decade
- One career
- One lifetime

Or choose goals that use money as a benchmark, goals that cost:

- $1
- $100
- $1,000
- $10,000
- $100,000
- $1,000,000
- $10,000,000

A journey of a thousand miles begins with a single step.

~Chinese Proverb

Once you get started, you'll be able to create your own parameters, too. Indeed, deciding to set goals is itself a goal!

Your Goals Can't Be Too Big

It's highly unlikely that all of your goals will require massive amounts of money or require huge amounts of time, like walking the entire Appalachian Trail. You'll discover that some of your goals are simple, even ordinary by some standards, and require no financial effort at all.

> The man who removes a mountain begins by carrying away small stones.
>
> ~Chinese Proverb

Still, you may discover that the goals that motivate you most are very big-picture indeed. Things like getting a college degree.

So, let's talk about that. With an undergraduate or graduate degree easily costing $50,000 to $100,000, and taking years to complete, there are few goals that require more money, time or effort. Yet many people cite their desire to "go back to school."

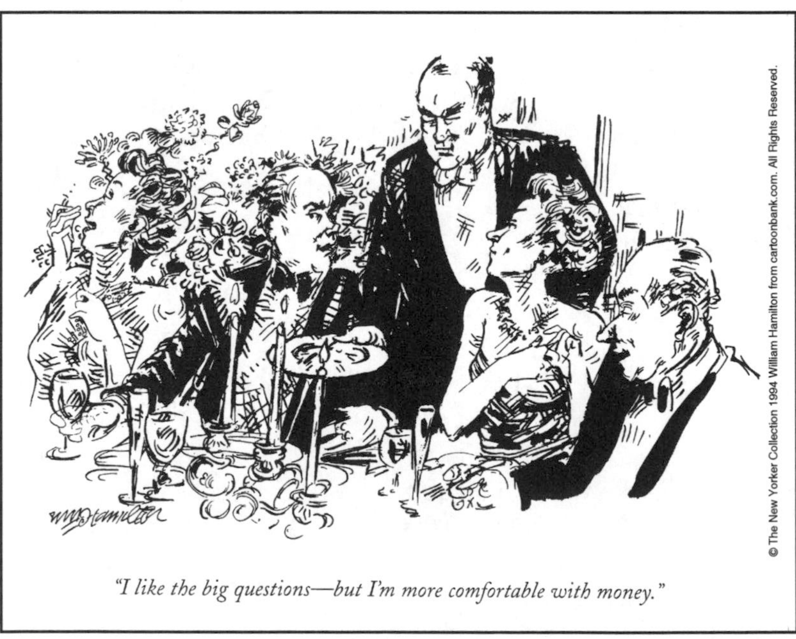

"I like the big questions—but I'm more comfortable with money."

But few of them ever do. Why is that? Perhaps it's because "going to college" is a huge undertaking, like using a knife and fork to eat an entire elephant. So, how can you effectively tackle the job?

Simple: One bite at a time.

If you have a big goal, break it down into smaller goals. Getting a degree is not something you can do today. But requesting the course catalog is something you can do today. And through a series of small steps, you can achieve big things.

The secret of getting ahead is getting started. The secret of getting started is breaking your complex overwhelming tasks into small manageable tasks, and then starting on the first one.

~Mark Twain

You'll also find this to be much more effective at maintaining your motivation. Give yourself one small assignment today — order the course catalog — and reward yourself for accomplishing that goal. Give yourself another assignment — select the course — and reward yourself for accomplishing that, too.[40]

"GOOD FRIENDS AND FRESH MUD! IT DOESN'T GET ANY BETTER THAN THIS!"

You'll discover that any goal can be broken into dozens of tiny baby-goals, all of them oriented toward winning the ultimate prize.

[40] The reward should be commensurate with the accomplishment. For doing something as easy as ordering a course catalog, the reward might be a candy bar, a café latte, or a hot bath.

Want to go to Turkey? That 10-day trip in five years is a big event, too far off to have much impact on your life today. But let's convert it into smaller pieces, like this:

ACTION	SET YOUR ACHIEVEMENT DATES
1) Get a passport	
2) Obtain three magazine articles about Turkey	
3) Read the first article	
4) Read the second article	
5) Read the third article	
6) Visit the Turkish government's Web site	
7) Contact the Turkish Embassy in the United States	
8) Contact the American Embassy in Turkey	
9) Contact the U.S. State Department for information about Turkey	
10) Find a Turkish-American organization and arrange to meet some of its members	
11) Determine all costs, including air fare, accommodations, meals and so on	
12) Evaluate medical and safety precautions	
13) Begin to identify itinerary possibilities	
14) Book the trip	
15) Buy needed clothing and travel items	
16) Head to the airport!	

Even though the trip might be years away, creating manageable assignments with current deadlines not only makes the trip real, it keeps it inspiring and motivating. And it's the only way I know to eat an elephant.

There's another side benefit to all this: By focusing all your energy and attention on your goals, you won't even notice that you've stopped other destructive behavior, such as spending money at the mall. Instead of saying, "I won't spend money," you'll be saying, "I'm saving my money to buy something I really want."[41]

[41] For more on how goal-setting can get you out of debt, see Chapter 51 of *The Truth About Money*. Was that pitch low-key enough for you?

Ready to set some goals of your own?

Turn the page and change your life . . .

① What would excite you? What were your visions and dreams and fantasies when you were a kid? What are they right now? List at least five of your long-held dreams, visions and fantasies:

1. ______________________________

2. ______________________________

3. ______________________________

4. ______________________________

5. ______________________________

Who are the people you would like to meet?

✦ In academia — such as science, medicine, law or education?

1. _________________________

2. _________________________

3. _________________________

✦ In the performing arts — Hollywood, television or theater?

1. _________________________

2. _________________________

3. _________________________

✦ In the visual arts — painters, sculptors, architects?

1. _________________________

2. _________________________

3. _________________________

- In media — authors, journalists, publishers?

 1. ______________________________

 2. ______________________________

 3. ______________________________

> Imagination is more important than knowledge.
>
> ~Albert Einstein

- In government — the legislative, judicial or executive branches?

 1. ______________________________

 2. ______________________________

 3. ______________________________

- In religion — clergy and leaders from your faith or others?

 1. ______________________________

 2. ______________________________

 3. ______________________________

PETER SOUZA

This is Stacy Brosnahan, my executive assistant, meeting the Pope.

✦ In sports — athletes, coaches, sportswriters and broadcasters?

1. ______________________________

2. ______________________________

3. ______________________________

✦ In business — Fortune 500 CEOs, entrepreneurs or regulators?

1. ______________________________

2. ______________________________

3. ______________________________

✦ In humanities — environment, public health or education?

1. ______________________________

2. ______________________________

3. ______________________________

✦ In family — long-lost or distant relatives?

1. ______________________________

2. ______________________________

3. ______________________________

If you can see yourself in possession of your goal, it's half yours.

~Tom Hopkins

② What events would you like to witness?

Some examples:

- ✦ the eruption of a volcano
- ✦ the last performance of a person or show
- ✦ a solar eclipse
- ✦ the aurora borealis
- ✦ a birth
- ✦ surgery
- ✦ a sport's championship game
- ✦ the swearing-in of a president

It's better to live rich than to die rich.

~Samuel Johnson

List below three events you would like to witness:

1. ______________________________

2. ______________________________

3. ______________________________

③ In what events would you like to participate?

Some examples:

- ✦ the running of the bulls in Pamplona, Spain
- ✦ the taking of the U.S. Census
- ✦ an archaeological discovery

List below three events in which you would like to participate:

1. ______________________________

2. ______________________________

3. ______________________________

 What subjects would you like to study?

Below are six groups of subjects, listed in random order. From each group, pick one subject that you'd like to study:

Mathematics
Finance
Marketing
Urban Studies
Telecommunications
Classical Studies
Communications
Dance
Engineering
Public Policy
Chemistry

____
This is a subject you'll study

Geology
English as a Second Language
Political Science
Reading Education
Women's Studies
Economics
Education
Religion
History
Counseling
Nursing

____
This is a subject you'll study

Literature
Social Work
Accounting
Biotechnology
Languages
Data Analysis
Special Education
Medicine
Computer Science
African American Studies
Archaeology

____
This is a subject you'll study

Linguistics
Information Systems
Cultural Studies
Forensic Biosciences
English
Medical Technology
Physical Education
Art
Law
Financial Planning
Government

____
This is a subject you'll study

Earth Science
Business
Public Administration
Management
Philosophy
Environmental Science
Statistics
Music
Science
Art History
Forest Service

____
This is a subject you'll study

Anthropology
Geography
Theater
Instructional Technology
Folklore
Gerontology
Astronomy
Military Science
Health Education
Psychology
Biology

____
This is a subject you'll study

Because the above subjects are listed in random order, you might prefer several subjects from one list and none in another. Feel free to select from the above subjects however you wish. What's important is that you find subjects that interest you; how you find them is not important.

5 What hobbies would you like to pursue?

This is a multistep exercise. Start here by choosing from the following random lists the one hobby within each list that most appeals to you:

Trains and Railroads
Theme Parks
Electronics
Darts
Stained Glass
Automobiles
Video Games
Knotting
Floral Arrangements
Candle and Soap Making

Hosting Parties
Composing
Cross-Stitch
Trivia
Weaving/Spinning
Reading
Humor
Amateur and Ham Radio
Woodworking
Crossword and Other Puzzles

Arts & Crafts
Model Railroading
Jewelry Making
Card Games
Beachcombing
Treasure Hunting
Motorcycles
Internet Games
Pyrotechnics
Miniatures

____
This is Semi-Finalist #1

____
This is Semi-Finalist #2

____
This is Semi-Finalist #3

From your Semi-Finalists 1-2-3 above, pick the one you most want to pursue.

____
This is Finalist "A"

Pick another hobby from each of the following three groups:

Shopping
Toy Collecting
Needlepoint
Beekeeping
Ceramic Arts
Landscaping
Computers
Crochet
Mime
Pin Collecting

Hot Air Ballooning
Board Games
Fireworks
Antiques
Fortune Telling
Fantasy Sports Leagues
Calligraphy
Puppetry
Drawing/Sketching/Painting
Photography

Game Designing
Radio Controlled Vehicles
Sewing
Rockets
Go-kart Racing
Arcade Games
Comic Book Collecting
Gardening
Billiards/Shooting Pool
Book Collecting/Bookbinding

____
This is Semi-Finalist #4

____
This is Semi-Finalist #5

____
This is Semi-Finalist #6

From your Semi-Finalists 4-5-6 above, pick the one you most want to pursue.

____
This is Finalist "B"

Repeat the process with the next three lists.

Singing
Contests and Sweepstakes
Murder Mystery Games
Designing
Chess/Checkers
Astrology
Kite Flying
Collecting
Cigars
Pets

Pottery
Urban Exploration
Dungeons and Dragons
Rug Making
Dolls and Dollhouse Collecting/Making
Martial Arts
Stereo and Audio
Aquariums
Sports Fan

Knitting
Bonsai
Sports Trading/Card Collecting
Costume Jewelry
Video/Home Theater
Juggling
Interactive Fiction
Marbles and Pebble Games
Playing Musical Instruments
Poetry
Whale Watching

____
This is Semi-Finalist #7

____
This is Semi-Finalist #8

____
This is Semi-Finalist #9

From your Semi-Finalists 7-8-9 above, pick the one you most want to pursue.

____
This is Finalist "C"

Do it again one last time!

Magic and Illusion
Quilting
Model Making
Locksmithing
Beadwork
Wordplay
Guns
Astronomy
Decorating/Interior Design
Gambling

Role Playing Games
Glassblowing
Roads and Highways
Beer/Home Brewing
Kaleidoscopes
Languages
Writing
Boating
Baking/Cooking
Flea Markets

Genealogy
Historical Reenactment
Origami
Graphic Design
Bird-Watching
Rocks, Gems, and Minerals
Aviation
Handwriting Analysis
Basketry/Basket Weaving
Ping-Pong/Table Tennis

____
This is Semi-Finalist #10

____
This is Semi-Finalist #11

____
This is Semi-Finalist #12

From your Semi-Finalists 10-11-12 above, pick the one you most want to pursue.

____
This is Finalist "D"

Record your four finalists:

A ____________________

B ____________________

C ____________________

D ____________________

Of the four hobbies on the left, choose:

the hobby you'll start this month: ____________

the hobby you'll start in one year: ____________

the hobby you'll start in three years: ____________

the hobby you'll start in five years: ____________

 What sports or physical activities would you like to watch as a spectator?

Pick one sport from each group of 10 below:

Water Skiing
Track & Field
Cycling
Snow Boarding
Dance
Equestrian
Stickball
Kickball
Squash
Roller Blading

Racewalking
Luge
Windsurfing
Snorkeling
Lacrosse
Lumberjacking
Auto Racing
Water Polo
Badminton
Ironman

Martial Arts
Climbing
Figure Skating
Billiards/Shooting Pool
Surfing
Table Tennis
Ice/Roller Hockey
Polo
Disc Sports
Paddleball

________________ This is Semi-Finalist #1

________________ This is Semi-Finalist #2

________________ This is Semi-Finalist #3

From your Semi-Finalists 1-2-3 above, pick the one you most want to watch:

________________ This is Finalist "A"

Repeat the process below:

Baton Twirling
Boxing
Ultimate Frisbee
Canoeing
Marathon/Biathlon/Triathlon
Ice Skating
Handball
Cricket
Yoga
Archery

Bocce
Racquetball
Rafting
Field Hockey
Football
Motocross
Diving
Body Building
Fishing
Hunting

Rugby
Fencing
Skydiving
Basketball
Farming
Baseball
Skiing
Cross Country
Weight Lifting
Volleyball

________________ This is Semi-Finalist #4

________________ This is Semi-Finalist #5

________________ This is Semi-Finalist #6

From your Semi-Finalists 4-5-6 above, pick the one you most want to watch:

________________ This is Finalist "B"

Repeat the process one last time:

Tennis	Scuba Diving	Cheerleading
Softball	Golf	Paintball
Shooting	Walking	Paddleball
Wrestling	Bowling	Dog or Cat Showing
Kayaking	Curling	Croquet
Horseshoes	Rowing	Wallyball
Gymnastics	Spinning	Skateboarding
Sailing	Running	Shuffleboarding
Rodeo	Mountain Biking	Swimming
Soccer	Aerobics/Fitness	Bobsledding

______________	______________	______________
This is Semi-Finalist #7	This is Semi-Finalist #8	This is Semi-Finalist #9

From your Semi-Finalists 7-8-9 above, pick the one you most want to watch:

____
This is Finalist "C"

You have just selected three spectator sports. Get fan magazines, tune in to the games, and buy tickets to watch the hometown teams and your favorite players. As before, you might prefer several sports from one list and none from another.

2,400,000 Americans play the accordion – hopefully not at the same time.

~Inside of a Pepsi cap

7 What sports or physical activities would you like to pursue as a participant?

Pick one sport from each group of 10 below:

Volleyball	Bocce	Track & Field
Scuba Diving	Farming	Tennis
Soccer	Archery	Field Hockey
Surfing	Fishing	Racewalking
Dance	Weight Lifting	Martial Arts
Figure Skating	Body Building	Wallyball
Walking	Lumberjacking	Basketball
Shooting	Rodeo	Bowling
Football	Kickball	Water Skiing
Snorkeling	Fencing	Yoga

______________ This is Semi-Finalist #1

______________ This is Semi-Finalist #2

______________ This is Semi-Finalist #3

From your Semi-Finalists 1-2-3 above, pick the one you most want to play:

______________ This is Finalist "A"

Repeat the process below:

Luge	Windsurfing	Climbing
Racquetball	Water Polo	Squash
Bobsledding	Paddleball	Diving
Spinning	Polo	Mountain Biking
Auto Racing	Skiing	Motocross
Swimming	Ice Skating	Cricket
Skateboarding	Skydiving	Cross Country
Curling	Ironman	Sailing
Ultimate Frisbee	Cycling	Paddleball
Ice/Roller Hockey	Billiards/Shooting Pool	Rowing

______________ This is Semi-Finalist #4

______________ This is Semi-Finalist #5

______________ This is Semi-Finalist #6

From your Semi-Finalists 4-5-6 above, pick the one you most want to play:

______________ This is Finalist "B"

Repeat the process one last time:

Marathon/Biathlon/Triathlon	Wrestling	Roller Blading
Paintball	Hunting	Baseball
Equestrian	Running	Kayaking
Croquet	Disc Sports	Badminton
Canoeing	Aerobics/Fitness	Dog or Cat Showing
Handball	Stickball	Snow Boarding
Shuffleboarding	Baton Twirling	Rugby
Golf	Softball	Gymnastics
Horseshoes	Lacrosse	Cheerleading
Table Tennis	Rafting	Boxing

______________	______________	______________
This is Semi-Finalist #7	This is Semi-Finalist #8	This is Semi-Finalist #9

From your Semi-Finalists 7-8-9 above, pick the one you most want to play:

____
This is Finalist "C"

You have just selected three sports you want to play. Get fan magazines, buy the equipment, join a team or league, and hire a coach. As before, you might prefer several sports from one list and none from another.

What parts of the United States would you like to visit?

New England
Connecticut
Maine
Massachusetts
New Hampshire
Rhode Island
Vermont

If you want to see this part of the United States, go to page 58

Mid-Atlantic
Delaware
Kentucky
Maryland
New Jersey
New York
North Carolina
Pennsylvania
Tennessee
Washington, DC
West Virginia

If you want to see this part of the United States, go to page 59

South
Alabama
Florida
Georgia
Louisiana
Mississippi
South Carolina
Virginia

If you want to see this part of the United States, go to page 62

Midwest
Arkansas
Illinois
Indiana
Iowa
Kansas
Michigan
Minnesota
Missouri
Nebraska
Ohio
Oklahoma
Texas
Wisconsin

If you want to see this part of the United States, go to page 63

Southwest
Arizona
Colorado
Nevada
New Mexico
Utah
Wyoming

If you want to see this part of the United States, go to page 66

West
Alaska
California
Hawaii
Idaho
Montana
North Dakota
Oregon
South Dakota
Washington

If you want to see this part of the United States, go to page 67

For all sad words of tongue and pen,
the saddest are those "It might have been."

~John Greenleaf Whittier

What parts of the world outside the United States would you like to visit?

Scandinavia
Denmark
Finland
Netherlands
Norway
Sweden

If you want to see this part of the world, go to page 73

Canada
Montreal
Quebec
Toronto

If you want to see this part of the world, go to page 72

Eastern Europe
Armenia
Bulgaria
Hungary
Latvia
Poland
Romania
Russia
Slovakia
Ukraine

If you want to see this part of the world, go to page 73

Caribbean
Aruba
Bahamas
Barbados
Bermuda
Cayman Islands
Dominican Republic
Jamaica
Puerto Rico
Tobago
Trinidad
Virgin Islands

If you want to see this part of the world, go to page 71

Asia
China
Hong Kong
Japan
Malaysia
Singapore
South Korea
Taiwan
Thailand
Vietnam

If you want to see this part of the world, go to page 70

Central America
Belize
Costa Rica
El Salvador
Guatemala
Honduras
Mexico
Nicaragua
Panama

If you want to see this part of the world, go to page 72

Middle East
Israel

If you want to see this part of the world, go to page 72

South Pacific
Australia
Guam
Indonesia
New Zealand
Papua New Guinea
Philippines

If you want to see this part of the world, go to page 70

United Kingdom
England
Ireland
Scotland
Wales

If you want to see this part of the world, go to page 74

Northern Africa
Egypt
Liberia
Morocco
Sierra Leone

If you want to see this part of the world, go to page 71

Southern Africa
Angola
Botswana
Kenya
Namibia
South Africa
Tanzania
Zimbabwe

If you want to see this part of the world, go to page 71

South America
Argentina
Brazil
Chile
Ecuador
Peru
French Guiana
Venezuela

If you want to see this part of the world, go to page 70

Western Europe
Austria
France
Germany
Greece
Italy
Monaco
Portugal
Spain
Switzerland
Turkey

If you want to see this part of the world, go to page 73

What types of places would you like to visit?

New England

State	Attractions	Type
Connecticut	Mystic Aquarium	aquarium
Connecticut	Hillstead Museum	art
Connecticut	Wadsworth Atheneum	art
Connecticut	Gillette Castle State Park	castle
Connecticut	Mashantucket Pequot Museum	cultural
Connecticut	Project Oceanology & Lighthouse Program	education
Connecticut	Yale	education
Connecticut	Harriet Beecher Stowe Center	house
Connecticut	Mark Twain House	house
Connecticut	Mystic Seaport	village
New Hampshire	Currier Gallery of Art	art
New Hampshire	Robert Frost Farm	house
New Hampshire	Saint-Gaudens National Historic Site	house
New Hampshire	Crawford Notch State Park	scenic
New Hampshire	Franconia Notch	scenic
New Hampshire	Lake Winnipesaukee	scenic
New Hampshire	White Mountain National Forest	scenic
New Hampshire	Loon Mountain	ski
New Hampshire	Canterbury Shaker Village	village
New Hampshire	Weirs Beach	village
Maine	Portland Museum of Art	art
Maine	Jasper Beach	beach
Maine	Cole Land Transportation Museum	museum
Maine	Maine Maritime Museum	museum
Maine	Boothbay Railway Village	railroad
Maine	Acadia National Park	scenic
Maine	Monhegan Island	scenic
Maine	Vinalhaven Island	scenic
Maine	Sugarloaf	ski
Maine	Kennebunkport	village
Massachusetts	Museum of Fine Art	art
Massachusetts	Coast Guard Beach	beach
Massachusetts	Harvard University & Museums	education
Massachusetts	Freedom Trail	history
Massachusetts	House of Seven Gables Historic Site	house
Massachusetts	Concord Museum	museum
Massachusetts	Cape Cod National Seashore	scenic
Massachusetts	Deerfield	village
Massachusetts	Old Sturbridge Village	village
Massachusetts	Plymouth Plantation	village
Rhode Island	Museum of Art	art
Rhode Island	Breakers	castle
Rhode Island	Chateau-Sur-Mer	castle
Rhode Island	Elms	castle
Rhode Island	Touro Synagogue National Historic Site	history
Rhode Island	Rosecliff	house
Rhode Island	Block Island	scenic

Rhode Island	Norman Bird Sanctuary	scenic
Rhode Island	Jamestown	town
Rhode Island	Narragansett Pier	village
Vermont	Bennington Museum	art
Vermont	Wilson Castle	castle
Vermont	Billings Farm	house
Vermont	Hildene	house
Vermont	Green Mountains National Forest	scenic
Vermont	Lake Champlain Islands	scenic
Vermont	President Calvin Coolidge State Historic Site	scenic
Vermont	Killington	ski
Vermont	Shelburne Museum	village
Vermont	Woodstock	village

Mid-Atlantic Region

Delaware	Sewell Biggs Museum of American Art	art
Delaware	Rehoboth Beach	beach
Delaware	Nemours Mansion and Gardens	history
Delaware	Brandywine River Museum	museum
Delaware	Hagley Museum	museum
Delaware	Winterthur Museum Garden and Library	museum
Delaware	Fort Delaware State Park	scenic
Delaware	Delaware Agricultural Museum and Village	village
Delaware	Odessa	village
District of Columbia	Washington National Cathedral	architecture
District of Columbia	Corcoran Gallery of Art	art
District of Columbia	National Gallery of Art	art
District of Columbia	Capitol	history
District of Columbia	Holocaust Memorial Museum	museum
District of Columbia	Kennedy Center	music
District of Columbia	Library of Congress	history
District of Columbia	White House	history
District of Columbia	Lincoln Memorial	monument
District of Columbia	Thomas Jefferson Memorial	monument

District of Columbia	Vietnam Veterans Memorial	monument
District of Columbia	Washington Monument	monument
District of Columbia	National Air and Space Museum	museum
District of Columbia	Smithsonian Institution	museum
District of Columbia	National Zoo	zoo
Kentucky	Bernheim Arboretum and Research Forest	botanical
Kentucky	Mammoth Cave National Park	cave
Kentucky	Cumberland Gap National Historical Park	history
Kentucky	Locust Grove Historic Home	history
Kentucky	My Old Kentucky Home State Park	history
Kentucky	Shaker Village of Pleasant Hill	history
Kentucky	Kentucky Horse Park	museum
Kentucky	National Corvette Museum	museum
Kentucky	John James Audubon State Park	scenic
Kentucky	Churchill Downs and Derby Museum	sport
Maryland	National Aquarium	aquarium
Maryland	Baltimore Museum of Art	art
Maryland	Antietam National Battlefield	battlefield
Maryland	U.S. Naval Academy	education
Maryland	Fort McHenry National Monument	history
Maryland	Historic St. Mary's City	museum
Maryland	B&O Railroad Museum	railroad
Maryland	Assateague Island National Seashore	scenic
Maryland	Great Falls Tavern and Museum	scenic
Maryland	Baltimore Zoo	zoo
New Jersey	Atlantic City Boardwalk	amusement
New Jersey	Liberty Science Center	education
New Jersey	Edison National Historic Site	history
New Jersey	Morristown National Historical Park	history
New Jersey	New Jersey State Museum	museum
New Jersey	Old Barracks Museum	museum
New Jersey	Cape May	village
New Jersey	Waterloo Village	village
New Jersey	Wheaton Village	village
New Jersey	Cape May County Park and Zoo	zoo
New York	Empire State Building	architecture
New York	Rockefeller Center	architecture
New York	Metropolitan Museum of Art	art
New York	Museum of Modern Art	art
New York	East Hampton Beach	beach
New York	United Nations	education
New York	West Point	education
New York	New York Stock Exchange	education
New York	Statue of Liberty and Ellis Island	monument
New York	Greenwich Village	neighborhood
New York	Times Square	neighborhood
New York	Central Park	park
New York	Adirondack Park	scenic
New York	5th Avenue	shopping
New York	Holiday Valley	ski
New York	National Baseball Hall of Fame	sports
New York	Niagara Falls	waterfalls
New York	Bronx Zoo	zoo

North Carolina	Bald Head Island	beach
North Carolina	Biltmore Estate	castle
North Carolina	Oconaluftee Indian Village	cultural
North Carolina	Blue Ridge Parkway	drive
North Carolina	Discovery Place	museum
North Carolina	Cape Hatteras National Seashore	scenic
North Carolina	Grandfather Mountain	scenic
North Carolina	Great Smoky Mountains National Park	scenic
North Carolina	Tweetsie Railroad	railroad
North Carolina	Old Salem	village
Pennsylvania	Philadelphia Museum of Art	art
Pennsylvania	Longwood Gardens	botanical
Pennsylvania	Gettysburg National Military Park	history
Pennsylvania	Independence National Historical Park	history
Pennsylvania	Valley Forge National Historical Park	history
Pennsylvania	Hershey's Chocolate World	industry
Pennsylvania	Carnegie Cultural Complex	museum
Pennsylvania	Johnstown Flood Museum	museum
Pennsylvania	Landis Valley Museum	museum
Pennsylvania	Camelback Ski Resort	ski
Tennessee	Dollywood	amusement
Tennessee	Shiloh National Military Park	battlefield
Tennessee	Belle Meade Plantation	history
Tennessee	Hermitage	history
Tennessee	National Civil Rights Museum	history
Tennessee	Graceland	house
Tennessee	American Museum of Science and Industry	museum
Tennessee	Country Music Hall of Fame	museum
Tennessee	Opryland	music
Tennessee	Great Smoky Mountains National Park	scenic
West Virginia	Ogebay Park	botanical
West Virginia	Lost World Caverns	cave
West Virginia	Smoke Hole Caverns	cave
West Virginia	Harper's Ferry National Historical Park	history
West Virginia	Cass Scenic Railroad	railroad
West Virginia	Hawk's Nest Canyon Tramway	railroad
West Virginia	Blackwater Falls State Park	scenic
West Virginia	Monongahela National Forest	scenic
West Virginia	New River Gorge National River	scenic
West Virginia	Oglebay's Good Zoo	zoo

"To tour the United States by train, getting off to spend a day or two in each city, then continuing the journey. In four years."

~Anonymous, 54, Engineer, Construction Company, VP Operations

South

Alabama	Mobile Museum of Art	art
Alabama	Bellingrath Gardens & Home	botanical
Alabama	Alabama Shakespeare Festival	entertain
Alabama	Ave Maria Grotto	history
Alabama	Arlington Antebellum Home & Gardens	house
Alabama	Anniston Museum of Natural History	museum
Alabama	Carver Museum	museum
Alabama	U.S. Space & Rocket Center	museum
Alabama	Mobile's History Districts	neighborhood
Alabama	Old Alabama Town	village
Florida	Busch Gardens	amusement
Florida	Disney World	amusement
Florida	Seaworld Adventure Park	amusement
Florida	Universal Orlando	amusement
Florida	Fort Desoto Park	beach
Florida	St. George Island State Park	beach
Florida	Cypress Gardens	botanical
Florida	Kennedy Space Center Complex	museum
Florida	Everglades National Park	scenic
Florida	St. Augustine	town
Georgia	Six Flags Over Georgia	amusement
Georgia	Ocmulgee National Monument	archaeological
Georgia	Chickamauga & Chattanooga Military Park	battlefield
Georgia	Cumberland Island	beach
Georgia	Callaway Gardens	botanical
Georgia	Andersonville Historical Site	cemetery
Georgia	Little White House State Historic Site	history
Georgia	Martin Luther King Jr. National Historical Site	history
Georgia	Okefenokee Swamp Park	scenic
Georgia	Stone Mountain	scenic
Louisiana	Norton Art Gallery	art
Louisiana	Jungle Gardens	botanical
Louisiana	Rip Van Winkle Gardens on Jefferson Island	botanical
Louisiana	Longfellow-Evangeline State Historic Site	culture
Louisiana	Nottoway Planation	house
Louisiana	Preservation Hall	music
Louisiana	French Quarter	neighborhood
Louisiana	Jean Lafitte Historical Park & Preserve	scenic
Louisiana	Laurel Valley Village	village
Louisiana	Audubon Zoo	zoo
Mississippi	Mississippi Museum of Art	art
Mississippi	Vicksburg National Military Park	battlefield
Mississippi	Natchez Trace Parkway	drive
Mississippi	Beauvoir	house
Mississippi	Natchez Pilgrimage	house
Mississippi	Lynn Meadows Discover Center	kids
Mississippi	Mississippi Agriculture & Forestry Museum	museum
Mississippi	DeSoto National Forest	scenic
Mississippi	Florewood River Plantation State Park	scenic
Mississippi	Gulf Islands National Seashore	scenic

South Carolina	South Carolina Aquarium	aquarium
South Carolina	Gibbes Museum of Art	art
South Carolina	Kings Mountain National Military Park	battlefield
South Carolina	Kiawah Island	beach
South Carolina	Brookgreen Gardens	botanical
South Carolina	Magnolia Plantation	botanical
South Carolina	Middleton Place	botanical
South Carolina	East Battery, Charleston	history
South Carolina	Fort Sumter National Monument	history
South Carolina	Hilton Head Island	scenic
Texas	Seaworld	amusement
Texas	Six Flags Over Texas	amusement
Texas	Kimbell Art Museum	art
Texas	Padre Island	beach
Texas	Alamo	history
Texas	Lyndon B. Johnson National Historical Park	history
Texas	Sixth Floor	museum
Texas	Space Center	museum
Texas	San Antonio River Walk	neighborhood
Texas	Big Bend National Park	scenic
Virginia	Paramount's Kings Dominion	amusement
Virginia	Maymont	botanical
Virginia	Luray Caverns	cave
Virginia	Arlington National Cemetery	cemetery
Virginia	Blue Ridge Parkway	drive
Virginia	Carter's Grove	history
Virginia	Colonial Williamsburg	history
Virginia	Gunston Hall Plantation	history
Virginia	Jamestown Settlement	history
Virginia	Monticello	history
Virginia	Mount Vernon	history
Virginia	Yorktown Victory Center	history
Virginia	Museum of the Confederacy	museum
Virginia	Wolf Trap Farm for the Performing Arts	music
Virginia	Shenandoah National Park	scenic

Midwest

Arkansas	Blanchard Springs Caverns	cave
Arkansas	Ozark Folk Center	culture
Arkansas	Arkansas Post National Memorial	history
Arkansas	Mid-America Science Museum	museum
Arkansas	White River Scenic Railroad	railroad
Arkansas	Buffalo National River	scenic
Arkansas	Hot Springs National Park	scenic
Arkansas	Mammoth Spring State Park	scenic
Arkansas	Petit Jean State Park	scenic
Arkansas	Eureka Springs	village
Illinois	Six Flags Great America	amusement
Illinois	Sears Tower	architecture
Illinois	Art Institute of Chicago	art

Illinois	Starved Rock State Park	hiking
Illinois	Cahokia Mounds State Historic Site	history
Illinois	Lincoln's New Salem Historic Site	history
Illinois	Adler Planetarium & Astronomy Museum	museum
Illinois	Field Museum	museum
Illinois	Museum of Science and Industry	museum
Illinois	Lincoln Park	park
Illinois	Magnificent Mile	shopping
Indiana	Eiteljorg Museum	art
Indiana	Indianapolis Museum of Art	art
Indiana	Wyandotte Caves	cave
Indiana	Lincoln Boyhood National Memorial	history
Indiana	Spring Mill State Park	history
Indiana	Children's Museum of Indianapolis	kids
Indiana	Indiana Dunes National Lakeshore	scenic
Indiana	Indianapolis Motor Speedway	sports
Indiana	College Football Hall of Fame	sports
Indiana	Conner Prairie	village
Iowa	Adventureland	amusement
Iowa	Des Moines Art Center	art
Iowa	Herbert Hoover National Historic Site	history
Iowa	Bily Clock Museum	museum
Iowa	Humboldt County Historical Museum	museum
Iowa	Living History Farm	museum
Iowa	Pella Historical Village Museum	museum
Iowa	Boone and Scenic Valley Railroad	railroad
Iowa	Ledges	scenic
Iowa	Amana Colonies	village
Kansas	Spencer Museum of Art	art
Kansas	Boot Hill	history
Kansas	Eisenhower Center	history
Kansas	Fort Scott National Historic Site	history
Kansas	State Capital	history
Kansas	Frontier Army Museum	museum
Kansas	Kansas Space Center	museum
Kansas	Kauffman Museum	museum
Kansas	Old Cow Town Museum	village
Kansas	Sedgwick County Zoo	zoo

"I want to be a competitive grand prix dressage rider, and breed sport horses. I want to share my husband's enjoyment of the bay and boating. Within 10 years."

~Rita Riddle, 43, Telecommunications

Michigan	Curious Kids' Museum	kids
Michigan	Gilmore Classic Car Club Museum	museum
Michigan	Kalamazoo Aviation History Museum	museum
Michigan	Van Andel Museum Center of Grand Rapids	museum
Michigan	Isle Royale National Park	scenic
Michigan	Mackinac Island & Fort	scenic
Michigan	Pictured Rocks National Lakeshore	scenic
Michigan	Fayette Township	village
Michigan	Henry Ford Museum & Greenfield Village	village
Michigan	Detroit Zoological Park	zoo
Missouri	Six Flags	amusement
Missouri	Nelson-Atkins Museum of Art	art
Missouri	Missouri Botanical Garden	botanical
Missouri	Meramec Caverns	cave
Missouri	Onondaga Cave State Park	cave
Missouri	Shepherd of the Hills Homestead	farm
Missouri	Mark Twain Boyhood Home	history
Missouri	Gateway Arch	monument
Missouri	Branson	music
Ohio	Paramount's Kings Island	amusement
Ohio	Seaworld	amusement
Ohio	Cleveland Museum of Art	art
Ohio	Toledo Museum of Art	art
Ohio	Rainforest	botanical
Ohio	Perry's Victory and Peace Memorial	history
Ohio	Sauder Village	history
Ohio	Rock and Roll Hall of Fame	museum
Ohio	Cuyahoga Valley National Rec. Area	scenic
Ohio	Pro Football Hall of Fame	sports
Oklahoma	Philbrook Museum of Art	art
Oklahoma	Crystal Bridge at Myriad Botanical Gardens	botanical
Oklahoma	Fort Sill Military Reservation	history
Oklahoma	Oklahoma City National Memorial	history
Oklahoma	Jasmine Moran Children's Museum	kids
Oklahoma	National Cowboy Hall of Fame	museum
Oklahoma	Will Rogers Memorial Museum	museum
Oklahoma	Chickasaw National Recreation Area	scenic
Oklahoma	Wichita Mountains National Wildlife Refuge	scenic
Oklahoma	Oklahoma City Zoo	zoo
Minnesota	Valleyfair	amusement
Minnesota	Great Lakes Aquarium	aquarium
Minnesota	Walker Art Center	art
Minnesota	Minnesota Landscape Arboretum	botanical
Minnesota	Mystery Cave	cave
Minnesota	Soudan Iron Mine	education
Minnesota	Forest History Center	industry
Minnesota	North Shore Drive	scenic
Minnesota	Mall of America	shopping
Minnesota	Minnesota Zoo	zoo

Nebraska	Joslyn Art Museum	art
Nebraska	Arthur Bowring Sandhills Ranch State Park	history
Nebraska	Scotts Bluff National Monument	history
Nebraska	Lincoln Children's Museum	kids
Nebraska	Museum of Nebraska History	museum
Nebraska	Museum of the Fur Trade	museum
Nebraska	Plainsman Museum	museum
Nebraska	Stuhr Museum of the Prairie Pioneer	museum
Nebraska	University of Nebraska Museum	museum
Nebraska	Harold Warp Pioneer Village	village
Wisconsin	Mitchell Park Horticultural Conservatory	botanical
Wisconsin	Circus World Museum	kids
Wisconsin	Lumberjack Specila & Camp Five Museum	museum
Wisconsin	Wisconsin Maritime Museum	museum
Wisconsin	National Railroad Museum	railroad
Wisconsin	Apostle Islands National Lakeshore	scenic
Wisconsin	Devil's Lake State Park	scenic
Wisconsin	St. Croix National Scenic Riverway	scenic
Wisconsin	Old World Wisconsin	village
Wisconsin	Stonefield State Historic Site	village

Southwest

Arizona	Desert Botanical Garden	botanical
Arizona	Canyon De Chelly National Monument	cultural
Arizona	Casa Grande Ruins National Monument	cultural
Arizona	Walnut Canyon National Monument	cultural
Arizona	Montezuma Castle National Monument	cultural
Arizona	Monument Valley Navajo Tribal Park	cultural
Arizona	Tombstone	history
Arizona	Heard Museum	museum
Arizona	Grand Canyon National Park	scenic
Arizona	Petrified Forest National Park	scenic
Colorado	Denver Art Museum	art
Colorado	Mesa Verde National Park	cultural
Colorado	Air Force Academy	education
Colorado	Durango and Silverton Narrow Gauge Railroad	railroad
Colorado	Black Canyon of the Gunnison National Park	scenic
Colorado	Great Sand Dunes National Monument	scenic
Colorado	Pikes Peak	scenic
Colorado	Rocky Mountain National Park	scenic
Colorado	Aspen	ski
Colorado	South Park City Museum	village
Nevada	Lehman Caves	cave
Nevada	Lincoln Highway	drive
Nevada	Fleischmann Planetarium	education
Nevada	Las Vegas	entertain
Nevada	Mormon Station State Historic Park	history
Nevada	Lake Tahoe	lake
Nevada	National Automobile Museum	museum
Nevada	Great Basin National Park	scenic
Nevada	Lake Mead National Recreation Area	scenic
Nevada	Virginia City	town

New Mexico	Carlsbad Caverns National Park	caves
New Mexico	Aztec Ruins National Monument	cultural
New Mexico	Bandelier National Monument	cultural
New Mexico	Española Pueblos	cultural
New Mexico	Taos Plaza	cultural
New Mexico	Santa Fe Plaza	history
New Mexico	Cumbres Scenic Railroad	railroad
New Mexico	Capulin Volcano National Monument	scenic
New Mexico	Cloudcroft	skiing
New Mexico	Chimayo	village
Wyoming	Bradford Brinton Memorial Western Art	art
Wyoming	Buffalo Bill Historical Center	museum
Wyoming	Cheyenne Frontier Days Old West Museum	museum
Wyoming	Nelson Museum of the West	museum
Wyoming	Devils Tower National Monument	scenic
Wyoming	Grand Teton National Park	scenic
Wyoming	Yellowstone National Park	scenic
Wyoming	Jackson Hole	ski
Wyoming	Trail Town	village
Wyoming	Wyoming Territorial Park	village

West

Alaska	Alaska Native Heritage Center	cultural
Alaska	Alaska Highway	drive
Alaska	Klondike Gold Rush Historic Park	history
Alaska	Sitka National Historic Site	history
Alaska	Anchorage Museum of History	museum
Alaska	White Pass	railroad
Alaska	Denali National Park	scenic
Alaska	Glacier Bay National Park	scenic
Alaska	Kenai Fjords National Park	scenic
Alaska	Mendenhall Glacier	scenic
California	Disneyland	amusement
California	Knotts Berry Farm	amusement
California	SeaWorld	amusement
California	Hearst Castle	castle
California	Avenue of the Giants	drive
California	Highway One	drive
California	Napa Valley	drive
California	Huntington Library	education

"I strive to gain enough experience and training to enable me to audition for and land a part in a Broadway (or off-Broadway!) play in 5-7 years."

~Lisa Lander, 34, Labor/Employee Relations Specialist

California	Stanford University	education
California	Lake Tahoe	lake
California	Chinatown	neighborhood
California	Golden Gate Park	park
California	Catalina Island	scenic
California	Sequoia and Kings Canyon National Park	scenic
California	Yosemite National Park	scenic
California	Rodeo Drive	shopping
California	Squaw Valley	ski
California	San Diego Zoo	zoo
Hawaii	Honolulu Academy of Arts	art
Hawaii	Hulopoe Beach	beach
Hawaii	Wailea Beach	beach
Hawaii	Polynesian Cultural Center	cultural
Hawaii	Pu'uhonua O Honaunau National Park	history
Hawaii	USS Arizona Memorial	history
Hawaii	Bishop Museum and Planetarium	museum
Hawaii	Haleakala National Park	scenic
Hawaii	Hawaii Volcanoes National Park	scenic
Hawaii	Waimea Canyon State Park	scenic
Idaho	Idaho Botanical Garden	botanical
Idaho	Nez Perce National Historical Park	history
Idaho	Crystal Gold Mine	industry
Idaho	Coeur D'Alene Lake	lake
Idaho	Bonneville Museum	museum
Idaho	Discovery Center of Idaho	museum
Idaho	Hells Canyon National Recreation Area	rafting
Idaho	Boise National Forest	scenic
Idaho	Craters of the Moon National Monument	scenic
Idaho	Sun Valley	ski
Montana	Russell Museum	art
Montana	Little Bighorn Battlefield National Monument	battlefield
Montana	Lewis and Clark Caverns State Park	cave
Montana	Cathedral of St. Helena	church
Montana	Beartooth Scenic Highway	drive
Montana	Montana Historical Society Museum	museum
Montana	Museum of the Rockies	museum
Montana	Gates of the Mountains Recreation Area	scenic
Montana	Glacier National Park	scenic
Montana	Virginia City	village
North Dakota	Knife River Indian Villages National Site	archaeology
North Dakota	Chateau de Mores Historic Site	architecture
North Dakota	International Peach Gardens	botanical
North Dakota	Fort Abraham Lincoln State Park	history
North Dakota	Fort Union Trading Post National Historic Site	history
North Dakota	Dakota Dinosaur Museum	museum
North Dakota	North Dakota Heritage Center	museum
North Dakota	Lewis and Clark State Park	scenic
North Dakota	Theodore Roosevelt National Park	scenic
North Dakota	Sullys Hill National Game Preserve	zoo

Oregon	Historic Columbia River Highway	drive
Oregon	Oregon Shakespeare Festival	entertain
Oregon	Pendleton Roundup	entertain
Oregon	Oregon Museum of Science and Industry	museum
Oregon	Crater Lake National Park	scenic
Oregon	Silver Falls State Park	scenic
Oregon	Wallowa Lake State Park	scenic
Oregon	Washington Park	scenic
Oregon	Mount Hood	ski
Oregon	Oregon Zoo	zoo
South Dakota	Corn Palace	architecture
South Dakota	Redlin Art Center	art
South Dakota	Jewel Cave National Monument	cave
South Dakota	Homestake Gold Mine	industry
South Dakota	Crazy Horse Memorial	monument
South Dakota	Mount Rushmore National Memorial	monument
South Dakota	America's Shrine to Music Museum	museum
South Dakota	1880 Train	railroad
South Dakota	Custer State Park	scenic
South Dakota	Badlands National Park	scenic
Utah	Lagoon Amusement Park	amusement
Utah	Monument Valley Navajo Park	cultural
Utah	Temple Square	cultural
Utah	Golden Spike National Monument	historic
Utah	Arches National Park	scenic
Utah	Bryce Canyon National Park	scenic
Utah	Canyonlands National Park	scenic
Utah	Glen Canyon National Recreation	scenic
Utah	Zion National Park	scenic
Utah	Park City	ski
Washington	Space Needle	architecture
Washington	Seattle Art Museum	art
Washington	Deception Pass State Park	beach
Washington	Grand Coulee Dam	education
Washington	Pioneer Square Historic District	neighborhood
Washington	Point Defiance Park	park
Washington	Cascades National Park	scenic
Washington	Mount Rainier National Park	scenic
Washington	Olympic National Park	scenic
Washington	San Juan Islands	scenic

"We would like to divide our time between two places, one for pleasure (weather), and one to be close to family. We're also planning a 35th anniversary trip to Italy, and we'll go in 12 to 18 months."

~Karl W. Ruyle, 61,
Retired from the U.S. Gov't

South America

Easter Island	history
Machu Picchu	history
Lake Titicaca	lake
Statue of Christ the Redeemer	monument
Amazon River	river
Los Glaciers National Park	scenic
Angel Falls	waterfalls
Iguacu Falls	waterfalls
Galapagos Islands	wildlife

Asia

Bagan	archaeology
Millennium Tower	architecture
Petronas Towers	architecture
Raffles Hotel	architecture
Batu Caves	cave
Meiji Shrine	cultural
Angkor Temple	history
Royal Grand Palace	history
Sensoji Temple	history
Banaue Rice Terraces	history
Forbidden City	history
Great Wall of China	history
Hue Imperial Palace	history
Prambanan Temples	history
Royal Barges National Museum	museum
Mount Fuji	scenic
Phang Nga Bay	scenic
Three Gorges of the Yangtze River	scenic
Victoria Peak	scenic

South Pacific

AMP Tower Centrepoint	architecture
Sydney Opera House	architecture
National Gallery of Australia	art
Museum of New Zealand Te Papa	museum
Aoraki Mount Cook	scenic
Fiordland National Park	scenic
Kakadu National Park	scenic
Tongariro National Park	scenic
Uluru-Kata Tjuta National Park	scenic
Great Barrier Reef	scenic

Southern Africa

Great Zimbabwe Ruins	archaeology
Robben Island	museum
Cape Point	scenic
Serengeti National Park	scenic
Table Mountain	scenic
Kruger National Park	scenic
Mount Kenya National Park	scenic
Kalahari Desert	scenic
Victoria Falls	waterfalls
Kilimanjaro National Park	wildlife
Maasai Mara Game Reserve	wildlife
Moremi Wildlife Reserve	wildlife
Etosha National Park	wildlife

Northern Africa

Abu Simbel	archaeology
Carthage	archaeology
Hassan Tower	archaeology
Hatshepsut's Temple	archaeology
Karnak Temple	archaeology
Place of the Dead	archaeology
Pyramids and Sphinx	archaeology
Valley of the Kings	archaeology
Medina of Fez	history
Medina of Tunis	history
Egyptian Antiquities Museum	museum

Caribbean

Pink Beach	beach
Seven Mile Beach	beach
Sainte-Anne Beach	beach
Trunk Bay	beach
Turtle Beach at Buck Island	beach
Anse La Roche	beach
Grace Bay	beach
Old Havana	history
Morne Trois Pitons National Park	scenic
Dunn's River Falls	scenic

Central America

Teotihuacan	archaeology
Tikal	archaeology
Palengue	archaeology
Panama Canal	history
Monte Alban	history
National Museum of Anthropology	museum
Arenal Volcano	scenic
Chichen Itza	scenic
Copper Canyon	scenic
White Mountain	scenic
Monteverde Cloud Forest	scenic

Canada

CN Tower	architecture
National Gallery of Canada	art
Butchart Gardens	botanical
Old Quebec	history
Algonquin Provincial Park	scenic
Banff National Park	scenic
Columbia Ice Fields	scenic
Jasper National Park	scenic
Kluane National Park and Reserve	scenic
Niagara Falls	scenic
Loch Lomond	ski
Mont Saint-Anne	ski
Red Mountain	ski

Middle East

Aleppo	archaeology
Troy	archaeology
Ephesus	archaeology
Palmyra	archaeology
Petra	archaeology
Blue Mosque	architecture
Hagia Sophia	architecture
Kathmandu Durbar Square	architecture
Topkapi Palace	architecture
Palace of the Winds	architecture
Ellora Temple Caves	cave
Western Wall	cultural
Masada	history
Old City of Sana'a	history
Temple Mount	history
Dead Sea	scenic
Kaziranga National Park	scenic

Eastern Europe

Delphi	archaeology
Buda Castle Palace	architecture
Budapest Central Synagogue	architecture
Charles Bridge	architecture
St. Alexander Nevski Cathedral	architecture
Fisherman's Bastion	architecture
Knossos	architecture
Bran Castle	castle
Kutna Hora	castle
Prague Castle	castle
Wawel Royal Castle	castle
Postojna Cave	cave
Rila Monastery	cultural
St. Basil's Cathedral	cultural
Acropolis	history
Auschwitz-Birkenau	history
Kremlin	history
National Archaeological Museum of Athens	museum
State Hermitage Museum	museum
Tatras National Park	scenic

Western Europe

Disneyland	amusement
Giant Ferris Wheel	amusement
Legoland	amusement
Pompeii	archaeology
Roman Aqueduct at Segovia	archaeology
Cologne Cathedral	architecture
Notre Dame Cathedral	architecture
Seville Cathedral	architecture
Sistine Chapel and Vatican Museums	architecture
St. Peter's Basilica	architecture
Alhambra	architecture
Louvre	art
D-Day Beaches	battlefield
Flanders Fields	battlefield
English Garden	botanical
Tivoli Gardens	botanical
Castle of St. George	castle
Heidelberg Castle	castle
Chenonceau Castle	castle
Chillon Castle	castle
Drottningholm Palace	castle
Neuschwanstein Castle	castle
Cave of Lascaux	cave
Caves of Drach	cave
Brandenburg Gate	history
Bryggen	history
Colosseum	history
Suomenlinna Sea Fortress	history
Hofburg Palace	history

Versailles	history
Pantheon	history
Eiffel Tower	monument
Guggenheim Museum Bilbao	museum
Prado Museum	museum
Museum of National Antiquities	museum
Hardanger Fjord	scenic
Jet d'Eau	scenic
Jungfrau	scenic
Leaning Tower of Pisa	scenic
Matterhorn	scenic
Grindelwald	ski
Innsbruck	ski
Nordseter	ski

United Kingdom

Blackpool Pleasure Beach	amusement
Roman Baths and Pump Room	archaeology
National Gallery	art
Edinburgh Castle	castle
Caernarfon Castle	castle
Blarney Castle	castle
Oxford University	education
Trinity College Dublin	education
Big Ben and Parliament	history
Stonehenge	history
Buckingham Palace	history
Giants Causeway	history
Glendalough	history
Hadrian's Wall	history
Warwick Castle	history
Westminster Abbey	history
Tower of London	museum
British Museum	museum
Cliffs of Moher	scenic
Cotswolds-Golden Valley	scenic
Snowdonia National Park	scenic

"I would like to become a famous quilter and quilt teacher. Perhaps even own a partnership in a quilt store at age 65."

~Anonymous Librarian

Amusement

Lagoon Amusement Park	Utah
Paramount's Kings Island	Ohio
Seaworld	Ohio
Six Flags Great America	Illinois
Adventureland	Iowa
Valleyfair	Minnesota
Atlantic City Boardwalk	New Jersey
Paramount's Kings Dominion	Virginia
Seaworld	Texas
Six Flags Over Texas	Texas
Six Flags Over Georgia	Georgia
Dollywood	Tennessee
Busch Gardens	Florida
Disney World	Florida
Seaworld Adventure Park	Florida
Universal Orlando	Florida
Six Flags	Missouri
Disneyland	California
Knotts Berry Farm	California
SeaWorld	California
Disneyland	Western Europe
Giant Ferris Wheel	Western Europe
Legoland	Western Europe
Blackpool Pleasure Beach	United Kingdom

"My goal is to spend one long weekend in Boston in 2009, New York City in 2010, and Miami Beach in 2011."

~Andrew Massaro, Financial Planner, Edelman Financial Services

Aquariums

Great Lakes Aquarium	Minnesota
National Aquarium	Maryland
South Carolina Aquarium	South Carolina
Mystic Aquarium	Connecticut

Archaeology

Ocmulgee National Monument	Georgia
Knife River Indian Villages National Site	North Dakota
Bagan	Asia
Great Zimbabwe Ruins	Southern Africa
Abu Simbel	Northern Africa
Carthage	Northern Africa
Hassan Tower	Northern Africa
Hatshepsut's Temple	Northern Africa
Karnak Temple	Northern Africa
Place of the Dead	Northern Africa
Pyramids and Sphinx	Northern Africa
Valley of the Kings	Northern Africa
Palengue	Central America
Teotihuacan	Central America
Tikal	Central America
Aleppo	Middle East

Ephesus	Middle East
Palmyra	Middle East
Petra	Middle East
Troy	Middle East
Delphi	Eastern Europe
Pompeii	Western Europe
Roman Aqueduct at Segovia	Western Europe
Roman Baths and Pump Room	United Kingdom

Architecture

Corn Palace	South Dakota
Empire State Building	New York
Rockefeller Center	New York
Sears Tower	Illinois
Chateau de Mores Historic Site	North Dakota
Washington National Cathedral	District of Columbia
Space Needle	Washington
Millennium Tower	Asia
Petronas Towers	Asia
Raffles Hotel	Asia
AMP Tower Centrepoint	South Pacific
Sydney Opera House	South Pacific
CN Tower	Canada
Buda Castle Palace	Eastern Europe
Budapest Central Synagogue	Eastern Europe
Charles Bridge	Eastern Europe
Fisherman's Bastion	Eastern Europe
Knossos	Eastern Europe
St. Alexander Nevski Cathedral	Eastern Europe
Alhambra	Western Europe
Cologne Cathedral	Western Europe
Notre Dame Cathedral	Western Europe
Seville Cathedral	Western Europe
Sistine Chapel and Vatican Museums	Western Europe
St. Peter's Basilica	Western Europe
Hagia Sophia	Middle East
Palace of the Winds	Middle East
Topkapi Palace	Middle East
Blue Mosque	Middle East
Kathmandu Durbar Square	Middle East

Art

Philadelphia Museum of Art	Pennsylvania
Cleveland Museum of Art	Ohio
Toledo Museum of Art	Ohio
Metropolitan Museum of Art	New York
Museum of Modern Art	New York
Art Institute of Chicago	Illinois
Eiteljorg Museum	Indiana
Indianapolis Museum of Art	Indiana
Des Moines Art Center	Iowa
Walker Art Center	Minnesota

Joslyn Art Museum	Nebraska
Redlin Art Center	South Dakota
Russell Museum	Montana
Bradford Brinton Memorial Western Art	Wyoming
Denver Art Museum	Colorado
Corcoran Gallery of Art	District of Columbia
National Gallery of Art	District of Columbia
Baltimore Museum of Art	Maryland
Sewell Biggs Museum of American Art	Delaware
Kimbell Art Museum	Texas
Seattle Art Museum	Washington
Gibbes Museum of Art	South Carolina
Honolulu Academy of Arts	Hawaii
Hillstead Museum	Connecticut
Wadsworth Atheneum	Connecticut
Museum of Fine Art	Massachusetts
Museum of Art	Rhode Island
Mobile Museum of Art	Alabama
Norton Art Gallery	Louisiana
Mississippi Museum of Art	Mississippi
Portland Museum of Art	Maine
Currier Gallery of Art	New Hampshire
Bennington Museum	Vermont
Spencer Museum of Art	Kansas
Nelson-Atkins Museum of Art	Missouri
Philbrook Museum of Art	Oklahoma
National Gallery of Australia	South Pacific
National Gallery of Canada	Canada
Louvre	Western Europe
National Gallery	United Kingdom

Battlefields

Little Bighorn Battlefield National Monument	Montana
Antietam National Battlefield	Maryland
Chickamauga & Chattanooga Military Park	Georgia
Kings Mountain National Military Park	South Carolina
Shiloh National Military Park	Tennessee
Vicksburg National Military Park	Mississippi
D-Day Beaches	Western Europe
Flanders Fields	Western Europe

Beaches

East Hampton Beach	New York
Rehoboth Beach	Delaware
Padre Island	Texas
Deception Pass State Park	Washington
Cumberland Island	Georgia
Bald Head Island	North Carolina
Kiawah Island	South Carolina
Hulopoe Beach	Hawaii
Wailea Beach	Hawaii

Coast Guard Beach	Massachusetts
Jasper Beach	Maine
Fort Desoto Park	Florida
St. George Island State Park	Florida
Anse La Roche	Caribbean
Grace Bay	Caribbean
Pink Beach	Caribbean
Seven Mile Beach	Caribbean
Sainte-Anne Beach	Caribbean
Trunk Bay	Caribbean
Turtle Beach at Buck Island	Caribbean

Botanical

Longwood Gardens	Pennsylvania
Rainforest	Ohio
International Peach Gardens	North Dakota
Maymont	Virginia
Ogebay Park	West Virginia
Callaway Gardens	Georgia
Middleton Place	South Carolina
Magnolia Plantation	South Carolina
Brookgreen Gardens	South Carolina
Bernheim Arboretum and Research Forest	Kentucky
Mitchell Park Horticultural Conservatory	Wisconsin
Bellingrath Gardens & Home	Alabama
Jungle Gardens	Louisiana
Rip Van Winkle Gardens on Jefferson Island	Louisiana
Cypress Gardens	Florida
Missouri Botanical Garden	Missouri
Crystal Bridge at Myriad Botanical Gardens	Oklahoma
Desert Botanical Garden	Arizona
Butchart Gardens	Canada
Minnesota Landscape Arboretum	Minnesota
Idaho Botanical Garden	Idaho
English Garden	Western Europe
Tivoli Gardens	Western Europe

Castles

Biltmore Estate	North Carolina
Gillette Castle State Park	Connecticut
Breakers	Rhode Island
Chateau-Sur-Mer	Rhode Island
Elms	Rhode Island
Wilson Castle	Vermont
Hearst Castle	California
Bran Castle	Eastern Europe
Kutna Hora	Eastern Europe
Prague Castle	Eastern Europe
Wawel Royal Castle	Eastern Europe
Castle of St. George	Western Europe
Chenonceau Castle	Western Europe

Chillon Castle	Western Europe
Drottningholm Palace	Western Europe
Heidelberg Castle	Western Europe
Neuschwanstein Castle	Western Europe
Blarney Castle	United Kingdom
Caernarfon Castle	United Kingdom
Edinburgh Castle	United Kingdom

Caves

Wyandotte Caves	Indiana
Mystery Cave	Minnesota
Jewel Cave National Monument	South Dakota
Lewis and Clark Caverns State Park	Montana
Luray Caverns	Virginia
Lost World Caverns	West Virginia
Smoke Hole Caverns	West Virginia
Mammoth Cave National Park	Kentucky
Blanchard Springs Caverns	Arkansas
Meramec Caverns	Missouri
Onondaga Cave State Park	Missouri
Lehman Caves	Nevada
Batu Caves	Asia
Ellora Temple Caves	Middle East
Postojna Cave	Eastern Europe
Cave of Lascaux	Western Europe
Caves of Drach	Western Europe
Carlsbad Caverns National Park	New Mexico

"I would like to send my mother on a trip to see Europe in six years."

~Anonymous, 29, Attorney

Cemeteries

Arlington National Cemetery	Virginia
Andersonville Historical Site	Georgia

Churches

Cathedral of St. Helena	Montana

Cultural

Monument Valley Navajo Park	Utah
Temple Square	Utah
Mesa Verde National Park	Colorado
Oconaluftee Indian Village	North Carolina
Polynesian Cultural Center	Hawaii
Mashantucket Pequot Museum	Connecticut
Alaska Native Heritage Center	Alaska
Canyon De Chelly National Monument	Arizona
Casa Grande Ruins National Monument	Arizona
Montezuma Castle National Monument	Arizona

Monument Valley Navajo Tribal Park	Arizona
Walnut Canyon National Monument	Arizona
Aztec Ruins National Monument	New Mexico
Bandelier National Monument	New Mexico
Española Pueblos	New Mexico
Taos Plaza	New Mexico
Ozark Folk Center	Arkansas
Meiji Shrine	Asia
Western Wall	Middle East
Rila Monastery	Eastern Europe
St. Basil's Cathedral	Eastern Europe
Longfellow-Evangeline State Historic Site	Louisiana

Drives

Beartooth Scenic Highway	Montana
Blue Ridge Parkway	Virginia
Historic Columbia River Highway	Oregon
Blue Ridge Parkway	North Carolina
Natchez Trace Parkway	Mississippi
Alaska Highway	Alaska
Avenue of the Giants	California
Highway One	California
Napa Valley	California
Lincoln Highway	Nevada

Educational

New York Stock Exchange	New York
United Nations	New York
West Point	New York
Soudan Iron Mine	Minnesota
Air Force Academy	Colorado
Liberty Science Center	New Jersey
U.S. Naval Academy	Maryland
Grand Coulee Dam	Washington
Project Oceanology & Lighthouse Program	Connecticut
Yale	Connecticut
Huntington Library	California
Stanford University	California
Fleischmann Planetarium	Nevada
Harvard University & Museums	Massachusetts
Oxford University	United Kingdom
Trinity College Dublin	United Kingdom

"Travel the national parks at a very slow pace — now."

~Dick Drake, 56, Software Engineer

Entertainment

Oregon Shakespeare Festival	Oregon
Pendleton Roundup	Oregon
Alabama Shakespeare Festival	Alabama
Las Vegas	Nevada

Farm

Shepherd of the Hills Homestead	Missouri

For Kids

Children's Museum of Indianapolis	Indiana
Lincoln Children's Museum	Nebraska
Curious Kids' Museum	Michigan
Circus World Museum	Wisconsin
Lynn Meadows Discover Center	Mississippi
Jasmine Moran Children's Museum	Oklahoma

History

Golden Spike National Monument	Utah
Gettysburg National Military Park	Pennsylvania
Independence National Historical Park	Pennsylvania
Valley Forge National Historical Park	Pennsylvania
Perry's Victory and Peace Memorial	Ohio
Sauder Village	Ohio
Cahokia Mounds State Historic Site	Illinois
Lincoln's New Salem Historic Site	Illinois
Lincoln Boyhood National Memorial	Indiana
Spring Mill State Park	Indiana
Herbert Hoover National Historic Site	Iowa
Arthur Bowring Sandhills Ranch State Park	Nebraska
Scotts Bluff National Monument	Nebraska
Fort Abraham Lincoln State Park	North Dakota
Fort Union Trading Post National Historic Site	North Dakota
Nez Perce National Historical Park	Idaho
Edison National Historic Site	New Jersey
Morristown National Historical Park	New Jersey
Capitol	District of Columbia
Library of Congress	District of Columbia
White House	District of Columbia
Fort McHenry National Monument	Maryland
Carter's Grove	Virginia
Colonial Williamsburg	Virginia
Jamestown Settlement	Virginia
Monticello	Virginia
Mount Vernon	Virginia
Yorktown Victory Center	Virginia
Nemours Mansion and Gardens	Delaware
Harper's Ferry National Historical Park	West Virginia
Alamo	Texas
Lyndon B. Johnson National Historical Park	Texas
Little White House State Historic Site	Georgia
Martin Luther King Jr. National Historical Site	Georgia
Fort Sumter National Monument	South Carolina
East Battery, Charleston	South Carolina
Pu'uhonua O Honaunau National Park	Hawaii

USS Arizona Memorial	Hawaii
Cumberland Gap National Historical Park	Kentucky
Locust Grove Historic Home	Kentucky
My Old Kentucky Home State Park	Kentucky
Shaker Village of Pleasant Hill	Kentucky
Belle Meade Plantation	Tennessee
Hermitage	Tennessee
National Civil Rights Museum	Tennessee
Freedom Trail	Massachusetts
Touro Synagogue National Historic Site	Rhode Island
Ave Maria Grotto	Alabama
Klondike Gold Rush Historic Park	Alaska
Sitka National Historic Site	Alaska
Arkansas Post National Memorial	Arkansas
Boot Hill	Kansas
Eisenhower Center	Kansas
Fort Scott National Historic Site	Kansas
State Capital	Kansas
Mark Twain Boyhood Home	Missouri
Fort Sill Military Reservation	Oklahoma
Oklahoma City National Memorial	Oklahoma
Tombstone	Arizona
Santa Fe Plaza	New Mexico
Mormon Station State Historic Park	Nevada
Gunston Hall Plantation	Virginia
Easter Island	South America
Machu Picchu	South America
Angkor Temple	Asia
Banaue Rice Terraces	Asia
Forbidden City	Asia
Great Wall of China	Asia
Hue Imperial Palace	Asia
Prambanan Temples	Asia
Royal Grand Palace	Asia
Sensoji Temple	Asia
Medina of Fez	Northern Africa
Medina of Tunis	Northern Africa
Old Havana	Caribbean
Monte Alban	Central America
Panama Canal	Central America
Old Quebec	Canada
Masada	Middle East
Old City of Sana'a	Middle East
Temple Mount	Middle East
Acropolis	Eastern Europe
Auschwitz-Birkenau	Eastern Europe
Kremlin	Eastern Europe
Brandenburg Gate	Western Europe
Bryggen	Western Europe
Colosseum	Western Europe
Hofburg Palace	Western Europe
Pantheon	Western Europe
Suomenlinna Sea Fortress	Western Europe
Versailles	Western Europe
Big Ben and Parliament	United Kingdom
Buckingham Palace	United Kingdom

"I would like season tickets to the Kennedy Center."

~Marilyn Voight, 57, Special Ed Teacher

Giants Causeway	United Kingdom
Glendalough	United Kingdom
Hadrian's Wall	United Kingdom
Stonehenge	United Kingdom
Warwick Castle	United Kingdom
Westminster Abbey	United Kingdom

Industry

Hershey's Chocolate World	Pennsylvania
Forest History Center	Minnesota
Homestake Gold Mine	South Dakota
Crystal Gold Mine	Idaho

Lakes

Coeur D'Alene Lake	Idaho
Lake Tahoe	California
Lake Tahoe	Nevada
Lake Titicaca	South America

Monuments

Status of Liberty and Ellis Island	New York
Crazy Horse Memorial	South Dakota
Mount Rushmore National Memorial	South Dakota
Lincoln Memorial	District of Columbia
Thomas Jefferson Memorial	District of Columbia
Vietnam Veterans Memorial	District of Columbia
Washington Monument	District of Columbia
Gateway Arch	Missouri
Statue of Christ the Redeemer	South America
Eiffel Tower	Western Europe

Museums

Carnegie Cultural Complex	Pennsylvania
Johnstown Flood Museum	Pennsylvania
Landis Valley Museum	Pennsylvania
Rock and Roll Hall of Fame	Ohio
Adler Planetarium & Astronomy Museum	Illinois
Field Museum	Illinois
Museum of Science and Industry	Illinois
Humboldt County Historical Museum	Iowa
Pella Historical Village Museum	Iowa
Bily Clock Museum	Iowa
Living History Farm	Iowa
Museum of Nebraska History	Nebraska
Museum of the Fur Trade	Nebraska
Plainsman Museum	Nebraska

Stuhr Museum of the Prairie Pioneer	Nebraska
University of Nebraska Museum	Nebraska
Dakota Dinosaur Museum	North Dakota
North Dakota Heritage Center	North Dakota
America's Shrine to Music Museum	South Dakota
Bonneville Museum	Idaho
Discovery Center of Idaho	Idaho
Montana Historical Society Museum	Montana
Museum of the Rockies	Montana
Buffalo Bill Historical Center	Wyoming
Cheyenne Frontier Days Old West Museum	Wyoming
Nelson Museum of the West	Wyoming
New Jersey State Museum	New Jersey
Old Barracks Museum	New Jersey
Holocaust Memorial Museum	District of Columbia
National Air and Space Museum	District of Columbia
Smithsonian Institution	District of Columbia
Historic St. Mary's City	Maryland
Museum of the Confederacy	Virginia
Brandywine River Museum	Delaware
Hagley Museum	Delaware
Winterthur Museum Garden and Library	Delaware
Sixth Floor	Texas
Space Center	Texas
Oregon Museum of Science and Industry	Oregon
Discovery Place	North Carolina
Bishop Museum and Planetarium	Hawaii
Kentucky Horse Park	Kentucky
National Corvette Museum	Kentucky
American Museum of Science and Industry	Tennessee
Country Music Hall of Fame	Tennessee
Gilmore Classic Car Club Museum	Michigan
Kalamazoo Aviation History Museum	Michigan
Van Andel Museum Center of Grand Rapids	Michigan
Lumberjack Special & Camp Five Museum	Wisconsin
Wisconsin Maritime Museum	Wisconsin
Concord Museum	Massachusetts
Anniston Museum of Natural History	Alabama
Carver Museum	Alabama
U.S. Space & Rocket Center	Alabama
Mississippi Agriculture & Forestry Museum	Mississippi
Anchorage Museum of History	Alaska
Kennedy Space Center Complex	Florida
Mid-America Science Museum	Arkansas
Frontier Army Museum	Kansas
Kansas Space Center	Kansas
Kauffman Museum	Kansas
National Cowboy Hall of Fame	Oklahoma
Will Rogers Memorial Museum	Oklahoma
Heard Museum	Arizona
National Automobile Museum	Nevada
Cole Land Transportation Museum	Maine
Maine Maritime Museum	Maine
Royal Barges National Museum	Asia
Museum of New Zealand Te Papa	South Pacific
Robben Island	Southern Africa

"I want to travel to the Catholic Shrines of Europe in five years."

~Anonymous, 33, Finance for U.S. Gov't

Egyptian Antiquities Museum	Northern Africa
National Museum of Anthropology	Central America
National Archaeological Museum of Athens	Eastern Europe
State Hermitage Museum	Eastern Europe
Guggenheim Museum Bilbao	Western Europe
Museum of National Antiquities	Western Europe
Prado Museum	Western Europe
British Museum	United Kingdom
Tower of London	United Kingdom

Music

Kennedy Center	District of Columbia
Wolf Trap Farm for the Performing Arts	Virginia
Opryland	Tennessee
Preservation Hall	Louisiana
Branson	Missouri

Parks

Central Park	New York
Lincoln Park	Illinois
Point Defiance Park	Washington
Golden Gate Park	California

Rafting

Hells Canyon National Recreation Area	Idaho

Railroads

Boone and Scenic Valley Railroad	Iowa
1880 Train	South Dakota
Durango and Silverton Narrow Gauge Railroad	Colorado
B&O Railroad Museum	Maryland
Cass Scenic Railroad	West Virginia
Hawk's Nest Canyon Tramway	West Virginia
Tweetsie Railroad	North Carolina
National Railroad Museum	Wisconsin
Boothbay Railway Village	Maine
White Pass	Alaska
White River Scenic Railroad	Arkansas
Cumbres Scenic Railroad	New Mexico

Rivers

Amazon River	South America
Nile River	Middle East
Yangtze River	Asia

"After retiring at 55, I'll create cross-stitch designs, and for kicks I'd like to be able to sell them for more than they cost to create."

~Anonymous, Gov't Worker (Info Tech)

Scenic

Arches National Park	Utah
Bryce Canyon National Park	Utah
Canyonlands National Park	Utah
Glen Canyon National Recreation	Utah
Zion National Park	Utah
Cuyahoga Valley National Rec. Area	Ohio
Adirondack Park	New York
Indiana Dunes National Lakeshore	Indiana
Ledges	Iowa
North Shore Drive	Minnesota
Lewis and Clark State Park	North Dakota
Theodore Roosevelt National Park	North Dakota
Badlands National Park	South Dakota
Custer State Park	South Dakota
Boise National Forest	Idaho
Craters of the Moon National Monument	Idaho
Gates of the Mountains Recreation Area	Montana
Glacier National Park	Montana
Devils Tower National Monument	Wyoming
Grand Teton National Park	Wyoming
Yellowstone National Park	Wyoming
Black Canyon of the Gunnison National Park	Colorado
Great Sand Dunes National Monument	Colorado
Pikes Peak	Colorado
Rocky Mountain National Park	Colorado
Assateague Island National Seashore	Maryland
Great Falls Tavern and Museum	Maryland
Shenandoah National Park	Virginia
Fort Delaware State Park	Delaware
Blackwater Falls State Park	West Virginia
Monongahela National Forest	West Virginia
New River Gorge National River	West Virginia
Big Bend National Park	Texas
Crater Lake National Park	Oregon
Silver Falls State Park	Oregon
Wallowa Lake State Park	Oregon
Washington Park	Oregon
Cascades National Park	Washington
Mount Rainier National Park	Washington
Olympic National Park	Washington
San Juan Islands	Washington
Okefenokee Swamp Park	Georgia
Stone Mountain	Georgia
Cape Hatteras National Seashore	North Carolina
Grandfather Mountain	North Carolina
Great Smoky Mountains National Park	North Carolina
Hilton Head Island	South Carolina
Haleakala National Park	Hawaii
Hawaii Volcanoes National Park	Hawaii
Waimea Canyon State Park	Hawaii
John James Audubon State Park	Kentucky
Great Smoky Mountains National Park	Tennessee

Isle Royale National Park	Michigan
Mackinac Island & Fort	Michigan
Pictured Rocks National Lakeshore	Michigan
Apostle Islands National Lakeshore	Wisconsin
Devil's Lake State Park	Wisconsin
St. Croix National Scenic Riverway	Wisconsin
Cape Cod National Seashore	Massachusetts
Block Island	Rhode Island
Norman Bird Sanctuary	Rhode Island
Jean Lafitte Historical Park & Preserve	Louisiana
DeSoto National Forest	Mississippi
Florewood River Plantation State Park	Mississippi
Gulf Islands National Seashore	Mississippi
Acadia National Park	Maine
Monhegan Island	Maine
Vinalhaven Island	Maine
Crawford Notch State Park	New Hampshire
Franconia Notch	New Hampshire
Lake Winnipesaukee	New Hampshire
White Mountain National Forest	New Hampshire
Green Mountains National Forest	Vermont
Lake Champlain Islands	Vermont
President Calvin Coolidge State Historic Site	Vermont
Denali National Park	Alaska
Glacier Bay National Park	Alaska
Kenai Fjords National Park	Alaska
Mendenhall Glacier	Alaska
Everglades National Park	Florida
Buffalo National River	Arkansas
Hot Springs National Park	Arkansas
Mammoth Spring State Park	Arkansas
Petit Jean State Park	Arkansas
Chickasaw National Recreation Area	Oklahoma
Wichita Mountains National Wildlife Refuge	Oklahoma
Grand Canyon National Park	Arizona
Petrified Forest National Park	Arizona
Capulin Volcano National Monument	New Mexico
Catalina Island	California
Sequoia and Kings Canyon National Park	California
Yosemite National Park	California
Great Basin National Park	Nevada
Lake Mead National Recreation Area	Nevada
Los Glaciers National Park	South America
Mount Fuji	Asia
Phang Nga Bay	Asia
Three Gorges of the Yangtze River	Asia
Victoria Peak	Asia
Aoraki Mount Cook	South Pacific
Fiordland National Park	South Pacific
Kakadu National Park	South Pacific
Tongariro National Park	South Pacific
Uluru-Kata Tjuta National Park	South Pacific
Cape Point	Southern Africa
Kalahari Desert	Southern Africa
Kruger National Park	Southern Africa
Mount Kenya National Park	Southern Africa
Serengeti National Park	Southern Africa

"Play in my own band. Close to doing it (one year?)"

~Anonymous, 44, Economics Professor

Table Mountain	Southern Africa
Dunn's River Falls	Caribbean
Morne Trois Pitons National Park	Caribbean
Arenal Volcano	Central America
Chichen Itza	Central America
Copper Canyon	Central America
Monteverde Cloud Forest	Central America
White Mountain	Central America
Algonquin Provincial Park	Canada
Banff National Park	Canada
Columbia Ice Fields	Canada
Jasper National Park	Canada
Kluane National Park and Reserve	Canada
Niagara Falls	Canada
Dead Sea	Middle East
Kaziranga National Park	Middle East
Tatras National Park	Eastern Europe
Hardanger Fjord	Western Europe
Jet d'Eau	Western Europe
Jungfrau	Western Europe
Leaning Tower of Pisa	Western Europe
Matterhorn	Western Europe
Cliffs of Moher	United Kingdom
Cotswolds-Golden Valley	United Kingdom
Snowdonia National Park	United Kingdom
Great Barrier Reef	South Pacific

"I wanted to attend acupuncture school to expand my work as a therapist and to live in England — so I enrolled, was accepted and will leave on October, 2001."

~John Archambeault, 37, Social Worker/ Psychotherapist

Shopping

Magnificent Mile	Illinois
Rodeo Drive	California
5th Avenue	New York
Mall of America	Minnesota

Skiing

Camelback Ski Resort	Pennsylvania
Park City	Utah
Holiday Valley	New York
Sun Valley	Idaho
Jackson Hole	Wyoming
Aspen	Colorado
Mount Hood	Oregon
Sugarloaf	Maine
Loon Mountain	New Hampshire
Killington	Vermont
Squaw Valley	California
Cloudcroft	New Mexico
Loch Lomond	Canada
Mont Saint-Anne	Canada
Red Mountain	Canada
Grindelwald	Western Europe
Innsbruck	Western Europe
Nordseter	Western Europe

Sports

Churchill Downs and Derby Museum	Kentucky
Pro Football Hall of Fame	Ohio
National Baseball Hall of Fame	New York
College Football Hall of Fame	Indiana
Indianapolis Motor Speedway	Indiana

Towns/Villages/Neighborhoods/Homes

Graceland	Tennessee
Harriet Beecher Stowe Center	Connecticut
Mark Twain House	Connecticut
Rosecliff	Rhode Island
Arlington Antebellum Home & Gardens	Alabama
Nottoway Planation	Louisiana
Beauvoir	Mississippi
Natchez Pilgrimage	Mississippi
Billings Farm	Vermont
Hildene	Vermont
Greenwich Village	New York
Times Square	New York
San Antonio River Walk	Texas
Pioneer Square Historic District	Washington
French Quarter	Louisiana
Chinatown	California
Jamestown	Rhode Island
St. Augustine	Florida
Virginia City	Nevada
Conner Prairie	Indiana
Amana Colonies	Iowa
Harold Warp Pioneer Village	Nebraska
Virginia City	Montana
Trail Town	Wyoming
Wyoming Territorial Park	Wyoming
South Park City Museum	Colorado
Cape May	New Jersey
Waterloo Village	New Jersey
Wheaton Village	New Jersey
Delaware Agricultural Museum and Village	Delaware
Odessa	Delaware
Old Salem	North Carolina
Fayette Township	Michigan
Henry Ford Museum & Greenfield Village	Michigan
Old World Wisconsin	Wisconsin
Stonefield State Historic Site	Wisconsin
Mystic Seaport	Connecticut
Deerfield	Massachusetts
Old Sturbridge Village	Massachusetts
Plymouth Planation	Massachusetts
House of Seven Gables Historic Site	Massachusetts
Narragansett Pier	Rhode Island
Old Alabama Town	Alabama

"In my 50s, I would like to be a frequent visitor to international flea markets, collecting treasures and learning about different cultures."

~Anonymous, 28
Teacher

Mobile's History Districts	Alabama
Laurel Valley Village	Louisiana
Kennebunkport	Maine
Canterbury Shaker Village	New Hampshire
Weirs Beach	New Hampshire
Robert Frost Farm	New Hampshire
Saint-Gaudens National Historic Site	New Hampshire
Shelburne Museum	Vermont
Woodstock	Vermont
Eureka Springs	Arkansas
Old Cow Town Museum	Kansas
Chimayo	New Mexico

"Over the next 10 years, I want to visit all 50 states and every continent. (I have 10 states and 3 continents to go.)"

~Kevin Lander, 37
U.S. Gov't

Waterfalls

Niagara Falls	New York
Angel Falls	South America
Iguacu Falls	South America
Victoria Falls	Southern Africa

Wildlife

Galapagos Islands	South America
Etosha National Park	Southern Africa
Kilimanjaro National Park	Southern Africa
Maasai Mara Game Reserve	Southern Africa
Moremi Wildlife Reserve	Southern Africa

Zoos

Bronx Zoo	New York
Minnesota Zoo	Minnesota
Sullys Hill National Game Preserve	North Dakota
Cape May County Park and Zoo	New Jersey
National Zoo	District of Columbia
Baltimore Zoo	Maryland
Oglebay's Good Zoo	West Virginia
Oregon Zoo	Oregon
Detroit Zoological Park	Michigan
Audubon Zoo	Louisiana
Sedgwick County Zoo	Kansas
Oklahoma City Zoo	Oklahoma
San Diego Zoo	California

The lists that appear on these pages are, of course, nowhere near complete. Consider them just as a starting point for your adventures, and send me your additions for inclusion in future editions.

STOP!

Have you completed these goal worksheets?

Yes? Read on!

No? Return to page 44!

The chapter you've just completed is meant to be *interactive*: You're not supposed to merely read these lists — you're supposed to act on them!

CHAPTER 3

How to Achieve Your Goals

CHAPTER 3

How to Achieve Your Goals

Now, your goals are in place. You want to buy a beach home in 10 years, take the family on a trip in three years, drive a convertible in five years, celebrate your parents' 50th wedding anniversary in 12 years, pay for a hospital wing in 15 years.

Whatever your goals, let's create a plan to help you achieve them.[42]

By definition, goals are about the future, not the present. We know what that trip to Turkey costs today, but we don't know what it will cost by the time you get there. Therefore, we must make some assumptions about the future.

For each of your goals, answer these questions as best you can:

1. How much money would you need to implement this goal TODAY?

> Put this answer in terms of the money you'll need for the goal's first (or only) year. Some goals, like a trip to Turkey, are a one-time event. Others, such as paying for college, are incurred over several years, and require several cash infusions. Still others (most notably retirement) require monthly or annual streams of income. Thus, don't state here the full cost, but only the first year's expense. And state the cost as though you were paying it TODAY.

[42] And let's not move on until you've completed this part, please. I would have liked to put the rest of the book under lock and key until you have completed Part I, but Dave Conti, my editor at HarperCollins, didn't go for that idea.

For example, if your goal is to buy a $40,000 car, you don't need the full $40,000 right away. All you need is enough cash for the down payment, tax, title and insurance — and, of course, the first year's monthly payments. This is a lot less than $40,000.

2. How many times will you need this money?

This is where you tackle the total expenses. That "trip of a life-time" is a one-time expense. But you'll need college tuition four times (for each year of college), and retirement will require a cash infusion for each year you expect to live.

It's possible, and even likely, that the cash you'll need in Year Two differs from the cash you'll need in Year One. In our car example, you'll pay for the down payment and sales taxes only once, and thus ownership of the car might require much less cash in Year Two and beyond. By itemizing the implementation of your goal in this manner, you can create assumptions that are more realistic and attainable.

3. When are you going to implement or achieve the goal?

If it's a multi-year goal, focus on the soonest you will begin implementing it.

4. What's the current value of any investments that you are setting aside for this goal?

Don't assume that you will be able to achieve your goal merely because you have assets. Unless you earmark certain assets toward a specific goal, it's quite possible, even likely, that you'll end up spending that money on something else.

5. How much money will you get from outside sources that you will be able to apply toward this goal?

While you're at it, name the sources.

6. How much money are you saving monthly toward this goal?

Be sure to consider all sources that you can realistically count on to help you achieve your goal. If you're planning for retirement, factor in any money that your employer is putting into your retirement account on your behalf (since that money is [or will be] yours, even though "you" aren't saving it). But if you're focusing on a trip to Turkey, you'd best ignore your retirement plan, since those assets should not be used for such a goal.

7. What's the inflation rate going to be between now and when you need the money?

The further away your goal, the greater the impact of inflation. Be sure to answer this question in terms of the expenses you'll incur, not merely on what you think overall inflation will be. For example, according to Ibbotson Associates, inflation in the U.S. has averaged 3.2% from 1986 to 2000, but it averaged 7.0% from 1971 to 1985. And we all know that education and health care costs in the past decade have exceeded average inflation rates, while prices for consumer electronics have fallen. So project future inflation rates with care.

8. What tax rate will you be paying between now and then?

Unless you're planning on a significant increase or decrease in income, a good way to start is to look at last year's tax return. Divide the money you paid in taxes last year by last year's income; the answer is your effective tax rate.

For example, say you earned $65,000 last year and paid $17,300 to federal and state income taxes. That means your effective tax rate is 27%.

9. **What average annual rate of return will you earn on your savings and investments between now and the attainment of your goal?**

I've set this as your last assumption for two reasons. First, you have the least control over it. After all, you can control how much you save every month, and how much you'll spend implementing your goal. You can even control inflation and tax rates, to a degree anyway. For example, by keeping your old car, the cost of a new one is irrelevant. Likewise, by modifying your income you might be able to keep yourself within certain tax brackets.

But you cannot exercise any control whatsoever over the rate of return you'll earn on your investments.

Second, as you'll soon see, this assumption (the rate of return) has the greatest impact on your plan. Indeed, it will determine by itself whether your plan will succeed or fail. It also will determine for you how you should invest your money.

Feeling Queasy?

By now, you're feeling uncomfortable about this process, because (let's admit it) you really aren't sure about the answers to any of those questions.

That's okay. That's why your answers are called *assumptions*. So, when dealing with assumptions, it's important that you acknowledge how the process works. It goes like this:

1. For each element of your goal that requires it, make an assumption.

"Financial planning will enable me to travel the USA — a dream I have had a long, long, time."

~Pat Gallagher, 64, Public Health Nurse

2. Realize that all your assumptions are probably wrong.

3. Further realize that not only are all your assumptions probably wrong, you don't even know if each is wrong just a little bit or whether each is extremely, embarrassingly wrong.

4. Don't worry about #3, because as you get closer to your goal, the correct answer to #1 will become clearer. You may discover that what you said earlier is wrong, but you'll also discover that this fact doesn't matter much (at least, not as much as it matters that you update your assumption).[43]

5. And as #4 begins to prove true, you'll bc able to update the answers you gave in #1.

6. Repeat this process until each of your assumptions become fact.

[43] Too often, people get hung up on the fact that their prior assumptions have proven wrong. Instead of just changing the assumption so that it's now more accurate, they wallow in their misery over having been wrong in the past. Remember: Achieving goals is all about the future. The past is largely irrelevant and completely unchangeable. So, move on!

Steve learns that airfare to Turkey today is $1,400. He assumes the cost will grow 4% per year and that he'll make the journey in five years. In an effort to predict what airfare will cost at the time he expects to begin his trip, he has just made two assumptions!

He also uses this prediction, in conjunction with other assumptions, to try to determine how much money he needs to save so that he can afford to buy his ticket.

Periodically, over the next several years, he checks with the airlines to see if his assumption about the future price of airfare is correct. Based on what he discovers, along with a review of his investments, he changes his savings strategy as needed — enabling him to home in ever closer to his goal.

How to Build Your Plan

Now that you've got your goals and assumptions in place, let's find out how much your goal will cost by the time you plan to achieve it.

It's easy to do this: Just increase your goal's current cost by the rate of inflation, for as many years as it will be before you achieve the goal. It's that simple.

Well, okay, maybe an example will help: Steve has determined that his trip to Turkey will cost $10,000. He plans to go in five years, and he assumes that costs will increase 4% per year between now and then.

So, we have to convert the "present value" of Steve's trip into a "future value."[44] It's easy. The formula is:

$$FV = \$10{,}000 \times 1.04 \times 1.04 \times 1.04 \times 1.04 \times 1.04 = \$12{,}167$$

[44] These terms are abbreviated as PV and FV. Sorry that I had to introduce jargon. But, considering that we are on page 100 and it's the first use of jargon, that ain't bad.

Notice that the inflation rate of 4% is expressed as 1.04 and that we are multiplying it five times because we have five years to reach Steve's goal. This math shows us that, assuming a 4% inflation rate and a current cost of $10,000, Steve's trip will cost $12,167 in five years.

> Equations are more important to me, because politics is for the present, but an equation is something for eternity.
>
> ~Albert Einstein

Although the formula is simple, it's rather cumbersome (imagine plotting a goal (such as retirement) that you won't reach for 40 years!). And since you're likely to hit the wrong key on your calculator at some point, it's also highly annoying. Besides, you probably hate math.

For all these reasons, I strongly recommend that you ignore the formula and forget the math,[45] and use a compounding calculator or spreadsheet program instead. Better yet, hire a financial advisor to do it for you![46]

If you try to determine Steve's future cost of travel without compounding, you'd merely multiply 4% of $10,000 ($400) by 5 years, and add that result ($2,000) to the current cost. Result: $12,000. Thus, you'd estimate too low.[47]

It's also worth noting that, in this example, we are compounding annually, not monthly. I mention this because the frequency of compounding directly impacts the speed with which money grows.[48]

[45] Hooray!
[46] If I advise against using the formula, why did I bother showing it to you? Because all the planners on my staff said I had to. They love that stuff.
[47] This might not seem like a big deal — $12,000 vs. $12,167 — but we're talking about a small-dollar, short-term goal. The impact of failing to compound on a bigger, longer-term goal — like college or retirement — is huge.
[48] For more on compounding, see Chapter 13 of *The Truth About Money*.

Next: Subtract What You'll Get From Outside Sources

Now that you know the amount of money you need, we must determine where that money will come from. Ideally, you'll get others to pay for it.[49] So, let's consider the outside sources that in many cases will be sufficient to achieve your goal. These sources include:

- Pensions
- Social Security
- Trusts
- Alimony
- Grants/scholarships
- Gifts/inheritances

That last bullet is mostly a joke. Far more people are anticipating inheritances than will actually receive them. Researchers for the Federal Reserve Bank in Cleveland found Baby Boomers won't inherit nearly as much as they're expecting.[50]

The study cited five reasons for this:

1. **Inheritances are unevenly distributed. Most Americans don't have wealthy parents, and your parents can't give you what they don't have.**
2. **Much of the wealth enjoyed by elders is annuitized. This means that when they die, the money is gone. (Pensions and Social Security income are good examples, for these payments often end when the retiree dies.)**
3. **People are living longer than ever, in case you haven't noticed, and they increasingly are spending all their money during their extended lifetimes. This not only means you might wait longer than you expect, it means there might not be much left for you!**
4. **Many elders are spending their money on themselves, rather than squirreling it away for their spoiled children and grandchildren to enjoy.**
5. **Your elders have lots of heirs. In *The Truth About Money*, I described how a grandfather's millions netted each grandchild only $33,668. Thus, even if you are an heir, it's unlikely that you can effectively predict how much you'll get (unless you've specifically been told).**

   And if you do get an inheritance, don't think you're going to cash that check immediately after the funeral, either. Depending on the deceased's estate plan (or lack thereof), probate could delay your inheritance for years. And if trusts are involved, there could be strings attached you can't even imagine.

Bottom line: Most people — probably including you — would do best to ignore the possibility of reaching your goals via gifts or inheritances.

[49] Remember, I said, "ideally"!

[50] And they expect a lot — estimates range from $14 trillion to $136 trillion, according to the study.

The point is that you need to make assumptions about the amount and frequency of income or money that you'll get from outside sources.

Once you've estimated the amounts you reasonably can expect to get from outside sources, subtract that amount from the amount you need (as determined in Step 2). What's left is the shortfall.

Let's return to our example to see how this works. In Step 2, we found that Steve's goal will cost $12,167. When he considers outside sources, he quickly realizes that no one is going to chip in on his trip. So:

Amount Needed	$12,167
– Money from Outside Sources:	– 0
Shortfall	$12,167

Looks like Steve hasn't made any progress. Oh well. That just means that achieving his goal is all up to him.[51] That takes us to Step 4, our final step.

> If A is success in life, then A equals X plus Y plus Z. Work is X; Y is play; and Z is keeping your mouth shut.
>
> ~Albert Einstein

[51] Just as achieving your goal is likely all (or mostly all) up to you.

The Final Step: Use Your Income or Investments to Eliminate Any Shortfall

There are four quick and simple parts to this step. First, we'll examine your current savings balances to determine their Future Value. Then, we'll examine the amount you're saving monthly to determine the FV of that money. Third, we'll combine the two. And fourth, we'll see whether that total is enough for you to reach your goal. So . . . one part at a time:

> Do not worry about your difficulties in Mathematics. I can assure you mine are still greater.
>
> ~Albert Einstein

Part One

> Increase the value of your current investments by your expected annual rate of return for the number of years your money will remain invested. The answer will be the FV of your current investments.

Here's what Steve discovered:

Current value of investments	$750
Annual rate of return	5%[52]
Years to goal	5
Future Value of Current Investments	$ 957

Part Two

> Review the amount you're saving monthly[53] and compound it by your assumed rate of return and the number of years to your goal.

[52] Use whatever rate of return you like. A 5% return might seem low, but remember that we're working with a short-term goal. If the goal was more distant, such as retirement, an 8% or 10% return might be justified.
[53] You are saving monthly, aren't you?

Here's what Steve discovered:

Amount of monthly savings	$100	
Monthly rate of return	0.42%	(5% ÷ 12 months)
Months to goal	60	(5 yrs × 12 months)
Future Value of Monthly Savings[54]	$6,801	

Part Three

Add together the FV of your current investments with the FV of your monthly savings. This will show you how much money you'll have by your deadline.

Here's what Steve discovered:

	Future value of current investments	$957
+	Future value of monthly savings	$6,801
	Total Future Value of Assets	$7,758

Part Four

Subtract the amount you will have saved (the Total Future Value of Assets, above) with the amount required to achieve the goal (this was the first assumption you made). Determine if you'll have enough.

Here's what Steve discovered:

	Total future cost of goal	$12,167
–	Total future value of assets	$7,758
	Net Surplus or (Shortfall)	($4,409)

Steve's math shows that, based on his assumptions, he'll be $4,409 short of his goal.[55]

[54] Notice that, for this calculation, I converted into months the rate of return and time to fund the goal. Since Steve is saving monthly, it seems appropriate to compound the returns monthly as well. But this is not required. This also explains why you need a financial calculator or spreadsheet program; doing the calculations without these totals would be difficult.
[55] Houston, we have a problem.

People don't know that the software and Internet sites they're using are often seriously flawed. When we evaluated 10 Roth IRA Conversion software programs, we got nine different answers. When Keith Maurer, a pioneer in the life insurance business, studied six online insurance calculators, he reached a similar conclusion. His study, published in *Investment Advisor*, and ours both found that different online calculators produce significantly different results even when you input the same data. So, think twice about using financial software and Internet calculators.

In fact, SmartCalc's Web site (one of the 10 we tested) noticed this problem, rhetorically asking, "Why can't we [the makers of Roth conversion software] all agree?" It adds, "If you've tried a few of the Roth IRA calculators . . . you've probably noticed a disquieting fact: You can run the same numbers on five different calculators and get five different answers. Obviously, somebody has some explaining to do."

Indeed they do.

This is why software and the Web do not threaten financial planners. Someday, computers might do the job, but that day is far off (although I'm helping the process along, as a consultant to dot-coms that are working on this).

One problem for the programmers: Financial planning is more art than science. Every person's cultural, social, family, economic, emotional and historical circumstances are different — and the rules and goals often change, with no mathematical precision or predictability.

That's why consumers who rely on software actually could do themselves more harm than good. It's also why many people who try to handle their finances using nothing but computers eventually turn to financial advisors for help — to fix the problems they've created for themselves.

To solve the problem, Steve needs to change at least one of his assumptions. <u>And this is where people often destroy the validity of their plans.</u> After all, if Steve wants to solve his problem most easily, all he has to do is change the rate of return he'll earn on his investments. By assuming a 40% annual return, he'll convert that $4,409 shortfall into a $10,323 surplus! He not only solves his problem, he could take his trip *twice*![56]

Unfortunately, this is exactly what many people do when playing with financial planning calculators or spreadsheets — whether their own or others'. I hope you see the error: It is ridiculous for Steve to assume that he will earn a 40% annual return. Yet, this is what people often do: They create a plan that has little or no chance of success.

Indeed, most of your assumptions are about things over which you have no control: future inflation rates, tax rates, and investment rates of return. When making assumptions, most people select reasonable fig-

[56] Houston, we have liftoff!

I'll never forget the day my friend Charlie told me he'd decided to retire. "Already gave notice to my boss," he told me, chest bursting with pride and excitement.

Charlie, 47 years old, went on to explain that he'd used a mutual fund company's online calculator, which showed that his current savings and investments were enough to sustain his lifestyle; his paycheck was no longer necessary. "No reason to keep working!" he exclaimed. His last day would be December 31, a few months away.

I asked Charlie if I could look at his calculator's printout. He brought it to my office the following week. It was several pages, covering such topics as life insurance, net worth, income and expenses and so forth. I noticed that the tax assumptions were blank.

"Charlie," I said, "This report says your retirement income will be $60,000."

"Right," he replied.

"Is that gross or net?" I asked.

"What do you mean?" he responded.

"I mean, do you want to earn $60,000 and then pay taxes, so that you live on about $40,000–$45,000, or do you want to be able to spend $60,000 after you've paid income taxes?"

"I want sixty grand net," he replied. "Why?"

"Because," I reluctantly told him, "these calculations show that your income will be $60,000 – but they do not show that you are paying any income taxes. According to this, you are in a "zero" tax bracket!"

Charlie looked like he'd been punched in the stomach. "Oh, no," he groaned. "When I was using the program, I clicked through the tax section and intended to return to that part later. But I forgot!"

The program did not warn Charlie that he assumed a 0% tax bracket, and it efficiently reported to him that, based on that assumption, he could retire today. If Charlie adjusted his plan to include taxes, his income would be as much as one-third less than he had thought – definitely not enough to retire on. Later that afternoon, Charlie told his boss he needed to see him right away.

So much for relying solely on software.

ures. But when the plan fails, they change those figures — often beyond prudence.

Don't make that mistake. Instead of changing the elements of your plan that you can't control, focus on the parts you *can* control. By looking at your list of assumptions, you'll quickly see that there are only three assumptions that you truly control:

1. The cost of your goal
2. The amount you save toward it
3. The date you will achieve it

If you reduce the cost, you reduce the amount of money you need to save. If you increase your monthly savings, you'll have more money. And if you delay your goal, you give your savings more time to grow. In each case, you make your target more attainable. Therefore, if your plan shows that you are short of your goal, these are the only three assumptions you should consider changing.

"Be a Peace Corps volunteer; go on an archaeological dig in Egypt, Mexico, Peru or Africa; and go on a safari in Africa when I am 55–60 years of age."

~A. Shawn Jones Clarke, 45, Massage Therapist

If Steve flies coach instead of first-class, he makes the trip more affordable. If he increases his savings from $100 to $142 per month, he'll achieve his goal of going to Turkey in five years. Or, instead of increasing his savings, his current plan of saving $100/month will enable him to take the trip in six and a half years.

And, of course, depending on what's most important to him, he might modify all three assumptions – cutting some of the costs, saving a little more and delaying his goal a little longer.

If you insist on changing your assumptions about future inflation rates, tax rates, and investment rates of return, please be very careful, and make sure your figures are realistic.

Should You Rely on Income or Assets to Achieve Your Goal?

Steve's got a new problem that we ought to talk about. Say he's decided to cancel his subscription to cable TV, freeing up the $42 a month he needs to reach his target. At the end of five years, he's got the $12,167 he needs to take the trip.

See the problem?[57]

When Steve returns from Europe, he'll be broke. This dilemma is a common one for goal-setters, especially when considering retirement goals: Do you live off your income, or do you invade principal?

Ideally, you'll be able live off the income produced by your savings and investments, but this isn't always practical or realistic — or even necessary. To see if Steve can do this with his trip to Turkey, we must determine how much income his by-now-accumulated money can produce:

	Total future value of assets	$12,167
×	annual rate of return	10%
	Total investment income	$1,267

Well, it was a nice idea, but obviously, it won't work. Even if Steve can earn 10% per year from his investments, he can't get to Turkey and back on $1,267. Thus, he has no choice but to spend some or all of his principal.

Because his trip is a one-time event, spending down the principal is not a problem. In fact, it's a given. But what if the goal under discussion is retirement?

Say you're about to retire. If your assets are able to generate enough income to meet your needs, you have no problem. But what if your income is not enough? Such a scenario (which is quite common) forces you to decide whether to spend some of your principal to make up the difference.

Would you be willing to do so?

[57]No, the problem is not that he'll miss HBO.

If you spend some of your principal, you'll get all the income you need. But that means you'll have less principal next year, which means your account will produce less income than it did before, which means you'll have to dig deeper into your principal, which means your income in the third year will be that much further reduced, meaning you'll invade the principal even more, which means . . .

And so goes the downward spiral. It won't be long, you figure, before you have no principal left. That means no income at all. And now you know what it means to suffer from Bag Lady Syndrome.

You see, it's almost as if retirees observe an 11th Commandment: THOU SHALT NOT SPEND PRINCIPAL. People fear running out of money, and they'll do anything to avoid this problem — even if it means radical reductions in lifestyle and refusal to spend money they truly could afford to spend.

One of my retired clients told me she wanted to increase her income, which was about $7,000 a month. She wanted to boost that figure by $1,000.

"Would that be okay?" she nervously asked. "Well," I told her, "according to our calculations, we can send you an extra $9,000 a month. How about if I increase your monthly check by, say, just $3,000?"

She refused. And although her kids will be grateful, she won't be around to hear their words of praise.

Well, let me ask you: If you run out of money, so what?

I mean, why is running out of money *bad*?

You think it's bad because, if you're broke, you'll have to move in with your kids.[58] But that's not a realistic concern. Why? Because the amount of money middle-class retirees spend and the amount of money they can afford to spend are so far apart that most could afford to dramatically increase their spending and still never be anywhere close to running out of money. Instead, the only thing that many retirees are ensuring is that they are going to die without spending much of their money. And that is absolutely pointless.

[58] I agree: That would be bad.

So, I want all you retirees who are reading this[59] to know that it is perfectly fine to spend your principal. Just make sure you don't spend it so quickly that you go broke too fast. Ahhhhhhh . . . now we're getting to the real point, aren't we? Yes, you agree that it's okay to spend principal, provided you don't spend it too fast.

In other words, you are willing to go to Turkey, *provided that upon your return, you'll be able to take yet another trip.*

My message is this: Don't fear spending principal. Traditionally, retirees don't like to spend money. Many of them are Depression Babies and lived through World War II. They remember the oil embargo of the '70s, and they know how hard it is to save money. Consequently, they are loath to spend the money they've got. And as a result, they die with lots of money unspent. It all seems rather pointless to me. Fortunately, as the survey results described on page 115 suggest, attitudes among retirees are improving. But too many still cling to the old ways.[60]

Take a look at the lifestyle of a retiree you know, and answer these questions:

- When is the last time they bought a new car?
- Or even just a TV — one that has a remote control, let alone a satellite dish?
- Do they even own a CD or DVD player?
- Have they ever taken a flight using a one-way ticket?[61]
- Why do they insist on reading menus right to left? Tell 'em to order the shrimp cocktail, for crying out loud — the heck with what it costs!

My point is that retired people are often so focused on maintaining a living they sometimes forget to have a life.

If you don't want to spend your money on things that you consider irresponsible, flagrant or selfish — like a first-class airline ticket — then spend your money on your family and on your community. In the process,

[59] Yes, I'm talking to both of you.

[60] For more on how to properly handle your assets in retirement — such as giving your money to your kids while you're still around to enjoy watching them spend it — refer to Rules 30, 55 and 56 in *The New Rules of Money*.

[61] I mean, it's not like they've got to get back to work by Monday. Why don't they just "stay on vacation" until they're ready to come home?

you'll enrich your spirit — and that is truly the achievement of genuine wealth, for it's wealth of the heart.

As I relate in *The New Rules of Money*,[62] nothing beats watching your children spend the money you've given them on houses and bicycles and cars and college, or helping your church or local hospital meet their desperately needed goals. So, either spend your money on yourself, or on others, but spend the money. After all, there is a big difference between being wealthy and being materialistic. Just because you might not like the latter doesn't mean you must avoid being the former.

So, repeat after me: *It's okay to spend principal.*

You're Not Convinced

When going about the process of creating a retirement plan (something we'll delve into in a moment), a key assumption is your life expectancy. This, in fact, is perhaps the primary reason you don't spend even more money than you already do.

> ***"When I'm 65, I will white-water raft for two weeks down the Colorado River."***
>
> **~Anonymous, 40, Marketing Director**

That's because you're already well-versed in all the statistics.[63] You know that life expectancies have never been greater, and that they are continuing to lengthen. You know that advances in medicine and biotechnology are enabling your generation to live longer than any generation before you.

This is why you don't want to spend your money. You're not worried about the future; you're just being pragmatic. You figure that if you're going to live to 95 — let alone 115 — you need to conserve your money so that it's available to you later, even if (or especially if) "later" really means "much later."

But I want you to realize that your new extended life span is likely to cause you to live your life in a completely different way than you expect.

[62] I'm about to tell you what it says in Rules 30, 55 and 56. See? Now you don't have to go buy it.
[63] Partly because I recite so many of them in Chapter 1 of *The Truth About Money*. Hint hint.

You see, you expect to live your life the way your grandparents lived theirs: They grew up, went to school, went to work, retired, then died. Theirs was a linear lifeline. They completed one part of their life before beginning the next.

But that's not how life will be in the future. In fact, it's probably not even that way for you now. Instead of going to school, working, then retiring, it's more likely that you are among the generation that goes to school, works, returns to school, works, retires, returns to school, retires again, returns again to work, and so on — in a cyclical rather than straight-line fashion.

> Every man dies.
> Not every man lives.
>
> ~Tim Robbins

This notion, expounded upon by Ken Dychtwald in his many excellent books on aging, reflects the fact that the old model simply doesn't work with today's life expectancies. Think back to the early 20th century, when people were hardly expected to reach age 65. Everything was compressed: They stopped their education in their early teens, married in their late teens,[64] started having children by 20, and worked until death. If there was a retirement (being still a primarily agricultural society, retirement was enjoyed by the relatively few industrial workers), it occurred only during the few final years of life.

> Basically, I no longer work for anything but the sensation I have while working.
>
> ~Alberto Giacometti (sculptor)

Today, it's unreasonable to think you will attend school for 25 years, work until 65 and then spend 45 years in retirement. If nothing else, you'll become bored to tears!

For these reasons, you instead will spend 20 to 40 years in your career — then quit to enter a completely new field. In between, you'll return to school to obtain new skills and knowledge, and you'll likely take an extended break in between — a "mini-retirement" of sorts that might last anywhere from a few months to several years. You'll then pick up where you left off. In fact, you are likely to engage in several of these practices

[64] A woman was an "old maid" if she was unmarried at age 21.

simultaneously: You'll go to school at night and take periodic sabbaticals from work.

This is already common. Police officers, fire fighters, military personnel, teachers and government employees can become eligible for pensions before they are 50. Most enter new careers after an extended vacation.

People like Marv Welt. Profiled by *Modern Maturity* magazine, he's been teaching inner-city kids for the past seven years. He's 75 years old.

Harold Allen retired in his 50s from the Philadelphia Water Department, then went to work helping prison inmates prepare for the workplace after their release.

Anne Eaton, a credit manager, enrolled in Georgia State University at age 69 and earned a master's degree in sociology with a specialty in gerontology.

"I recently retired at the age of 55. I would now like to explore my (untapped) creative side by taking different classes, develop my talent to its fullest potential and enjoy the '2nd' half of my life discovering me. I start classes this fall."

~Bea Sullivan, 55, Worked in school system for 24 years as Resource Assistant

And in the end it's not the years in your life that count. It's the life in your years.

~Abraham Lincoln

THIS OLD FELLOW IS ONE HUNDRED TODAY
WHAT'S THE SECRET?
WHEN YOU REACH EIGHTY YOU HAVE TO CLEAN UP YOUR ACT
7.12
PARKER

By permission of Johnny Hart and Creators Syndicate, Inc.

Zelda Lipman holds a master's degree in educational psychology and worked 20 years as a pre-med advisor at the University of Miami. At age 74, she's taking courses in Shakespeare that are offered by her former employer, as well as those taught at Yale and Duke University. She also studies computers and finance.

Of all Americans who say they will work after retirement, 68% say they won't be doing it for the money, according to a survey by Rutgers University. A separate study by Cornell University agrees: Most retirees work to keep active; not because they need the money (see below).

And the National Center for Education Statistics says the percentage of adults 65 and older who participate in learning activities has doubled since 1991, while participation rates for those 55 to 64 has jumped from 23% in 1991 to 37% in 1999. This is confirmed by a study by Peter D. Hart Research Associates, which found that 37% of older adults say that continuing education is a "very important part" of their retirement plans.

The only things more important than education, say a majority of retirees, are travel (cited by 57% as the most important part of their retirement plans) and volunteerism/community service, cited by 50% of those surveyed.

WHY THEY WORK

To keep active	89%
Have free time	73%
Maintain social contacts	68%
Desire additional income	63%
Not ready to retire	58%
Maintain professional contacts	56%
Need additional income	41%
Health insurance	10%

Walter Pincus graduated from Georgetown University's Law School in 2001 at age 68 after a journalism career at *The Washington Post.*

Jennie Mae Tucker retired from banking and now engages in field research expeditions for Earthwatch. At age 77, she's been doing this for nearly 20 years.

Mary Fasano got a Harvard degree at age 89.

Lillian Brown taught at one university for 10 years, quit, and joined another. She then taught for another 10 years and retired. Then she joined a third university and has been there for 20 years. In the meantime, she's taken time off to travel and write her books. And she's retired half a dozen times. *She's a serial retirist.*

And she's not alone.

Here are some organizations you or your elders might want to investigate:	
AARP	822-484-3410 www.aarp.org
American Society on Aging	415-974-9600 www.asageing.com
National Council on the Aging	202-4789-1200 www.n4a.org
OASIS	314-862-2933 www.oasisnet.org
Senior Surfers	800-577-0669 www.seniorsurfers.org

Face it. Your life can be — and likely will be — much more like Lillian's and the others I've described than like your own great-grandparents. Like Lillian, you'll work a bit, stop for a while, then work some more.

But this type of life is nothing at all like what you're used to. How do you structure a life like that?

Through goal setting.

Just make the decision that you're going to work for a certain amount of time, to accumulate a certain amount of money. That's a goal. When you've achieved it, you'll be on to the next goal.

This notion is not so far-fetched. Lots of folks have been doing this for decades. They spend each winter in Vail as ski instructors and each summer in San Diego as lifeguards. And they repeat the cycle each year. People like this used to be called beach bums. Today, more and more people are beginning to realize this can be a full and complete life.

Remember: It's a Process, Not a Product

Because your life will undergo frequent changes, and because your assumptions require constant updating, financial planning is a lifelong process, not a report you shove onto a shelf and ignore.

This means you need to revise your plan periodically. (As mentioned, we know your plan's assumptions are wrong. Therefore, they require periodic revision.) You should revise your plan if:

- one to three years have passed since you last updated it
- there have been any changes in your:
  - goals
  - health
  - marital status
  - occupation or employment
  - income
  - expenses
- there has been a birth or death in the family.

A Case Study

Enough talking Turkey.[65] Despite my suggestion that you plot a strategy that will enable you to bungee-jump off a bridge in Sri Lanka, retirement likely remains your #1 financial planning goal. From a teaching perspective, it's also the most comprehensive, so let's examine the following case study to finish our exploration of the financial planning process.

Here are the facts of this case:

- Mike and Janet are married. He is 49, she is 50.
- They both work, earning a combined income of $95,000 per year.

[65] Sorry, I couldn't resist.

- They have three kids, all of whom are expected to go to college:
  - Jill, 17
  - Harry, 15
  - Susan, 12
- At retirement, Janet will receive a pension.
- They both will receive Social Security.
- They have $375,000 in savings and investments, including IRAs and retirement accounts at work.[66]
- They save $1,200 a month.[67]

Here are their retirement goals:

- They want to retire at age 60.
- They want to have $90,000 in income in each year of their retirement (in today's dollars).

Here are their key assumptions:

- 4% annual inflation.
- They will pay for weddings for each daughter,[68] with an expected PV of $20,000 each.[69]
- They will send each child to college, at a PV of $60,000 per child.
- They will live to age 95.

[66] But the value of their home and future salary increases are excluded. The first is irrelevant, because they have to live somewhere, and the second is unknown. By omitting both, we create a couple of "safety-net" features that will help if some of our other assumptions prove to be too optimistic.

[67] Does that sound like a lot? It's not. They're saving about $800 per month merely by contributing 10% of their pay to their 401(k) plans; they are saving just $400 per month additionally. This is not unrealistic.

[68] Hey you moms and dads of baby girls! Betcha forgot to plan for this expense, huh!

[69] *Brides* magazine pegs the average national cost at about $15,000; *Washingtonian* puts it closer to $30,000.

The calculations show the following:

If their current investments and future savings earn:	They need to save this additional amount each month until retirement:
6%	**$3,900**
8%	**$2,379**
10%	**$907**
12%	**$21**

Do you believe Mike and Janet can increase their monthly savings by nearly four grand per month?

No, of course not.

Do you believe they can save an extra twenty bucks per month?

Sure.

Then there you have it. If their investments earn only 6% per year, they will fail to achieve their goal. At 12%, they easily succeed.

This leads to the critical question: Is it possible for them to earn a guaranteed return of 12% per year?

No.

Is it at least possible?

Yes.

Is 12% a reasonable target?

Hmmmmmmmmmmm.

> There are people who have money and people who are rich.
>
> ~Coco Gabrielle Chanel

Ah, now we begin to see the challenge: 6% is realistic, but it fails to meet our goal, while 12% achieves the goal, but is far from certain.

So let's examine this from a different perspective. If Mike and Janet increase their savings, delay their retirement, or accept a lower income in retirement, they can accept a lower rate of return. And the lower the return they need, the more likely they'll achieve it. Therefore, their portfolio should be designed to earn somewhere between 8% and 10% per year.[70]

Now, consider this question: Are 20% annual returns available in the marketplace?

Sure.

Are such returns a sure thing?

No, of course not.

Indeed, striving for a 20% annual return entails very high risk. And since Mike and Janet are likely to achieve their goal with a 10% or 12% return, there's no reason for them to seek 20% returns. The only way to obtain higher returns is to take higher risks.

Wall Street phrases it this way: The greater the return, the greater the risk. Thus, it's critical that you take only as much risk as necessary for you to achieve your goal. It's the difference between *investing* and *speculating*. Remember that your plan is based on your goals, not on your market predictions. That's a good thing, too, because you're in control of your goals, but you're not in control of the market. So if you don't need to chase higher returns, there's no reason to do so.

This leads to the final, and perhaps most important, question on this subject. Let's say your plan says you need to earn a 10% return. You look at your year-end statement and see that you earned 14%. But you turn on the news and hear that the stock market averaged 22% for the year.

---

[70] Remember, this is just a case study, and for our purposes here, somewhat oversimplified. But you get the point.

Here's the question:

Are you happy or unhappy?

If you are unhappy, there's a word for you: Greedy.

Greed causes many people to fail financially. Instead of looking at the road in front of you, you stare at the activity on the shoulders — and then WHAM! You smack into the car in front of you.

It doesn't matter what's going on in the investment world around you; all that matters is whether or not you are making progress toward your goals. Indeed, as I revealed in *Ordinary People, Extraordinary Wealth,*[71] wealthy Americans do not gauge their success by the performance of some stock market index, but by the success of their own portfolio.

> A lot of people become pessimists from financing optimists.
>
> ~CT Jones

So, choose your goals, set a date for achieving them, write them down, and stay focused on them. And staying focused means, in part, not letting anything divert your attention from your goals.

Oops, You Forgot Something

So far, so good. You've selected your goals and carefully considered all the elements that go into them. You've made reasonable assumptions for everything from inflation and tax rates to the anticipated costs you'll incur to implement your goal.

[71] At bookst . . . oh, never mind.

You've also performed a variety of "what-if" scenarios to see how different assumptions generate different results.[72] After all this, you're comfortable that you've built an effective financial plan, one that reasonably can be expected to achieve your goals.

There's only one problem: You've ignored something that is highly likely to ruin your well-conceived plan.

The Omission That Could Ruin Your Plan — And a Whole Lot More

There's a story about a town in the Midwest that was suffering from a drought. The farmers' crops were facing ruin, yet no rain was in sight. So, the town's preacher announced that the upcoming Sunday's service would be devoted to a prayer for rain. The preacher's strong belief became infectious, and the townspeople grew excited as they happily anticipated the rain that would surely follow the preacher's sermon. Word quickly spread, and that Sunday morning, people from all over the county packed the little church's pews.

The preacher looked upon his congregation, whose faces were full of eagerness. Their clothes were neatly pressed, their hair done, their shoes shined. They believed in the preacher's ability to speak to the Lord, and they had faith that their prayers would be answered.

But the preacher never offered his prayer. Instead, he told the congregation to go home. "You do not truly believe it will rain," he said to the astonished gathering.

"Why do you say that?" someone asked.

"Because," the preacher replied, "no one has brought an umbrella."

[72] Taken to their (rather silly) extreme, "what-if" scenarios morph into something called Monte Carlo simulations. Some advisors use software to generate tens of thousands of scenarios in a pointless effort to determine with mathematical precision the likelihood that a given goal will be reached. What do I think of stochastic theory (Monte Carlo's scientific name) and advisors' efforts to rely on it when producing a financial plan? Well, let's put it this way: Most advisors playing with Monte Carlo simulations don't know that the idea was first promoted in the *Harvard Business Review* in 1964, and rejected as ineffective in 1972. It's such a silly idea that I'm addressing the whole thing in a *footnote*.

Did You Include an Umbrella in Your Financial Plan?

In addition to all the assumptions we've covered, your plan features one we haven't mentioned.

That assumption? That you are — and will remain — healthy.

As a result, you have neglected to consider the possibility that you will die prematurely, become disabled, or, in your elder years, require long-term care. By failing to consider these possibilities, your financial plan — by default — assumes that you will not experience them.

That is wishful thinking. Before today's 25-year-olds reach age 65, one in three will suffer a disability that lasts 30 days or longer, according to the Guardian Life Insurance Company of America, and one in four will die. And more than half of those who make it to age 65 will require long-term care, according to Americans for Long-Term Care Security.

"I want to sail the Caribbean by Jan. 2, 2012."

~Pat Day,
Financial Planner,
Edelman Financial Services

Your plan must take these scenarios into consideration.

- Assume you were to incur a disability tomorrow, from illness or injury, and that the disability prevents you from being able to continue working. Build a financial plan around that scenario, one that enables you to continue receiving the income you'll need to support yourself comfortably. Develop a similar plan for your spouse or partner.

- Assume you were to die tomorrow, and build a plan that protects your spouse and children from financial ruin as a result of losing the income you provide. If you or other family members are financially dependent on your spouse or partner, or other family member, do a similar projection for them as well.

- Assume you live into your elder years, and that you will require long-term care at some point. Build a realistic plan that enables you to provide yourself and your spouse with the level of care you'd each need and prefer.

This is, admittedly, less fun than planning a trip to Turkey. But it is no less crucial. Usually, the most cost-effective way to solve these scenarios is through insurance, and because I wrote extensively about how to buy life, disability and long-term care insurance in *The Truth About Money,* I won't repeat that information here.

Without question, the September 11 Attack on America has brought new attention to the need for adequate insurance protection. It's one of the many virtues that have arisen from the tragedy.

But I do want to elaborate on long-term care, because the entire context of this book is based on the premise that you are going to live a long time — long enough to enjoy that cyclical life span we discussed earlier. And the longer you live, the more likely you will incur the need for long-term care.

In fact, according to the Health Insurance Association of America, 72% of all Americans either have already faced the problem of long-term care costs or eventually will. This presents a special problem for consumers who rely on financial planning software or Internet sites, because those tools ignore LTC costs.

"I want elective cosmetic surgery that would include, but not be limited to, Lasic Eye; liposuction — tummy, hair transplant and do something about those jowls."

~Richard Quammen, 52, Accountant (Controller)

But financial planners don't make this mistake, and neither should you — which is why I'm talking about it here. In fact, according to a study by the American Council of Life Insurers:

- 85% of financial planners counsel their clients about the risk of incurring long-term care costs.
- 92% of planners say the risk applies equally to men and women.
- 80% say the risk applies equally to married couples and singles.

- 75% say the risk applies equally to people earning $30,000 a year or $150,000 a year.
- 75% say the risk applies as equally to your parents as to you.

But consumers do not share this concern. When ACLI surveyed consumers about long-term care costs, they found that:

- 50% of consumers have given little or no thought to the issue.
- 40% said they'd never even heard of it.
- 6% said they'd taken "some" action on it.
- Only 4% said they had actually solved the problem.

The current cost of care averages $45,000 annually, according to ACLI. The average daily cost of caregiving is $50 for adult daycare and $121 for care provided in nursing homes as shown in Figure 3-1. Thus, it is clear that long-term care has great potential to ruin your financial plan.[73]

I have never been in a situation where having money made it worse.

~Clinton Jones

[73] And it will get worse, not better. ACLI projects that the cost of care will increase to $190,000 by 2030.

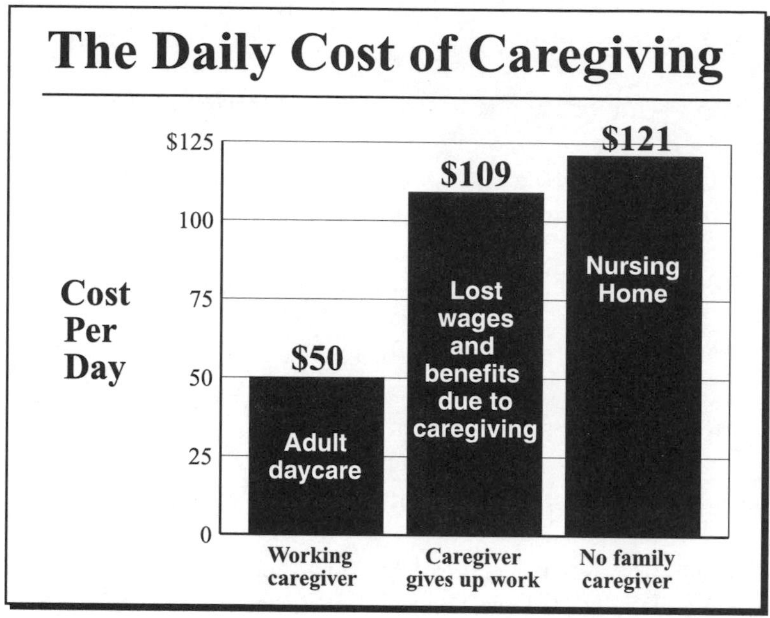

Figure 3-1

And you are much more likely to face this risk than you probably realize. Marriott Corporation, which has 154,000 employees, found that even though the average age of their employees is only 35, 15% already have elder care responsibilities.

Think you can avoid those costs by having a family member care for you? That's even worse: Family caregivers give up $659,139 in lost lifetime wages, pension benefits and Social Security earnings, according to the National Alliance of Caregivers.

"My goal is to be able to purchase a new designer handbag for every season of the year by age 35."

~Emma Burton, 29, Attorney

And the National Center for Women and Aging found that, of caregivers surveyed:

- 16% quit their jobs to care for a relative.
- 13% retired early.
- 22% took unpaid leave.
- 20% cut work to a part-time schedule.
- 64% used vacation or sick leave to provide care to a family member.
- 67% left work during the day to provide care.
- 69% arrived at work late or left work early.
- 29% gave up a promotion.
- 25% refused a job transfer.

If you think that's bad, it's nothing compared to the ultimate cost of care-giving. According to the *Journal of the American Medical Association*, 40% of care-giving spouses suffer from depression, and the University of Pittsburgh Center for Social and Urban Research found that, compared to others their age, those who begin to provide care for their husband or wife are 63% more likely to die within four years. Indeed, long-term care is the silent destroyer of financial plans.

You've ignored LTC partly because you aren't envisioning a future filled with health care problems, and partly because you've assumed that someone else would pay for it. According to a study by US Bancorp Piper Jaffray:

- 34% of those surveyed think their health insurance will pay for long-term care expenses.
- 30% think Medicare will cover the costs.
- 14% think Social Security will pay.

But the reality is that health insurance does not pay for long-term care. Neither does Social Security or Medicare. What does pay is Medicaid, the federal health insurance plan for the truly poor.[74]

> ***"I want to live in the south of Spain in my 70s."***
>
> **~Anonymous, 50, Antique Dealer**

Believe me, you don't want to qualify for Medicaid. Not only does it mean that you have little or no money, HHS's Center for Medicaid and Medicare Services (formerly called the Health Care Financing Administration) reported that 30% of patients in Medicaid facilities are malnourished. The Commonwealth Fund reports that more than half of all nursing homes do not have sufficient staff to provide quality care. Indeed, instead of relying on the government to determine the level of care you'll receive, you'll probably be much happier providing for your own care.

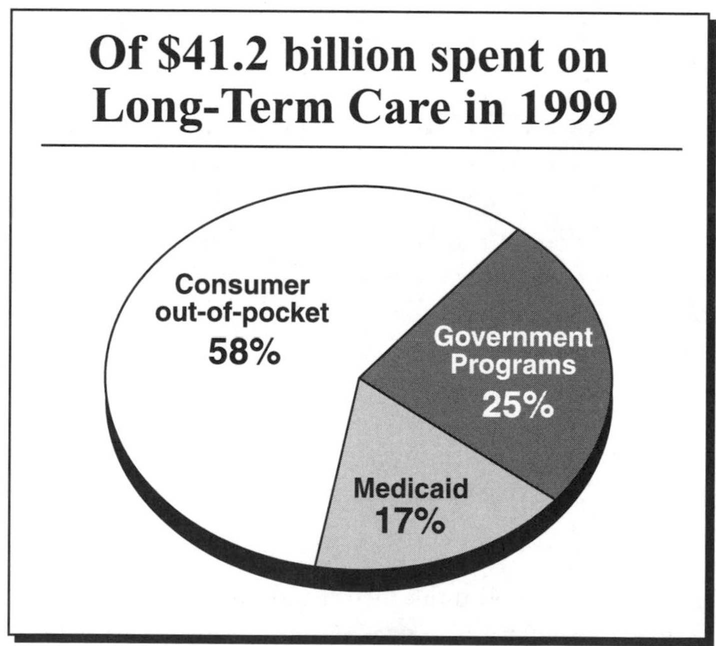

Figure 3-2

[74] For more information on Medicaid qualification rules, including a discussion of countable, noncountable and inaccessible assets, refer to Chapter 72 of *The Truth About Money*.

Say you or your spouse requires long-term care. Are you able to write a check for $4,000 to pay for this month's care? Remember, that would be four grand in addition to your regular monthly expenses — mortgage, auto, food and so on. Can you write that check today? Will you be able to write another one next month, and the month after that? How long could you keep it up?[75]

It's no surprise that ACLI's research found that 58% of consumers say they are not able to pay for the costs of long-term care. That's why "granny dumping" is increasing.[76]

For most people — likely meaning you — the best solution is to (a) own long-term care insurance and (b) don't delay getting it. Take a look at Figure 3-3. It shows the proportion of the U.S. population that can afford

Who Can Afford Long-Term Care Insurance?

Age Group	Portion Who Can Afford Cost	Average Cost of Coverage	Average Cost to Age 85	Average Years of Coverage
35-39	73%	$ 507	$ 24,336	48
40-44	71	605	26,015	43
45-49	81	734	27,892	38
50-54	72	905	29,865	33
55-59	63	1,204	33,712	28
60-64	47	1,709	39,307	23
65-69	31	2,432	43,776	18
70-74	10	3,610	46,930	13
75+	9	5,274	52,740	10

Figure 3-3

[75] Remember PV and FV? Today's cost is just the present value of the expense. Think what the FV might be when you're older and more likely to incur the cost.

[76] An extreme act of abandoning elderly, usually senile, patients, often in hospital emergency rooms, sometimes in bus or subway stations or other public areas such as parks. Those abandoned have no identification and are uncommunicative, and no one files a "missing person" report with authorities. They become wards of the state, confined to government-supported institutions for the remainder of their lives.

long-term care insurance based on different age groups, and the cost of coverage for those ages. Focus on columns three and four and you'll see a clear message: The younger you are when you buy LTC insurance, the cheaper it is — both now and over your entire lifetime.

For example, people in their late 40s will pay about $700 per year and have coverage for 35-40 years, assuming they live into their 80s. More than 80% of all Americans can afford this expense, according to ACLI research. In other words, the cost of long-term care should not be a national crisis.

But it is a crisis — because people are not buying this critically needed protection when they should. Instead, too many people wait until they are much older, seeking coverage only after they have developed some medical condition. Ironically, the very reason they suddenly are interested in pursuing coverage is the reason they cannot obtain it.

Even if you can qualify for a policy, waiting until you are 75 to buy it means you'll spend more than $5,000 per year for the coverage. By then, only 9% of those over 75 can afford the cost. Even if you can afford it, you'll spend in five years nearly double the amount that the 40-something spent, and you'll have coverage for only five years instead of 35-40 years! Clearly, waiting to get LTC insurance makes no sense.

If you are in your late 40s or early 50s (or older), buy long-term care insurance. NOW. Not only is it cheaper (both now and in the long run) but you'll never be healthier, or more able to qualify for the coverage.

My formula for success is rise early, work late and strike oil.

~J.P. Getty

Will you incur the need for long-term care? Some people have a "won't happen to me" mentality. Well, those people are in la-la land, because, according to ACLI:

- By 2030, the over-65 population will double.
- By 2030, the over-85 population will be the fastest growing segment of our population.
- By 2030, half of all women who reach 65 will reach 85; half of all men will live to 82.
- Those age 65 who will require long-term care at some point:
  - For women: One in two
  - For men: One in three[77]
- The nursing home population will double, to more than five million residents, over the next 20 years.

Long-term care is definitely a women's issue. According to the Center for Aging Research & Education:

- **75% of all nursing home residents are women,**
- **67% of elderly home health care recipients are women, and**
- **73% of family caregivers are women.**

[77] Why will fewer men over 65 need long-term care than women? Because their wives will be their caregivers. And recall what happens to caregivers from page 127.

Should You Self-Insure?

Fine. You're convinced that you (or your spouse) will require long-term care in the future. Why not just save for this expense, and pay for the costs out of your own pocket if and when those costs are incurred? After all, isn't that why you're engaging in financial planning anyway — to create wealth?

> ***"Go to a golf school within the next five years and learn how to lower my handicap."***
>
> **~Matthew Pope, 54, Operations Mgr.**

You raise a valid point.[78] So, let's test the theory. Let's say you're 45 years old. As Figure 3-4 shows, the cost of care is projected to be more than $1.2 million. To pay for that, you'd have to save $4,732 per year. But you could buy a policy that costs only $734 per year.

It's even more dramatic for 60-year-olds: A person that age would need to save $16,738 per year instead of spending just $1,709 per year for a policy. Buying a policy is a much more prudent approach, despite the fact that you might not need the insurance.[79, 80, 81, 82, 83]

Even if you already have sufficient assets or income to cover LTC costs, using your own resources is an inefficient use of capital. Even if you can afford to, spending your money on care means you will not use that money for your family or community.

---

[78] Okay, I raised it. But I knew you wanted to.

[79] You know I'm right, because you own auto insurance even though you know you won't need it.

[80] And don't try to claim that you own auto insurance only because you're required to do so — your coverage exceeds government requirements, doesn't it? So there.

[81] Ditto for homeowner's coverage: Yes, your mortgage lender requires you to maintain coverage, but you own more than they require — even though you know your house will never burn down.

[82] But, you say, it's possible that that fire or highway collision could occur today, and that's why you need that insurance today. But you won't incur long-term care costs until you are in your 60s, 70s or 80s (if at all) — and those ages are decades away, giving you plenty of time to save for the potential expense. Sorry, but this argument fails too. Consider: According to Americans for Long-Term Care Security, 40% of all long-term care patients are between the ages of 18 and 64. After all, it's not just old people who are involved in auto accidents.

[83] Face it: You need to buy long-term care insurance, if not right now, then much sooner than you thought.

Remember: A properly built financial plan is one that plans for the worst and hopes for the best, not the other way around.[84] If your entire financial plan is limited to the notion of going to Turkey, retiring at age 45, building that log cabin and living happily ever after, it's likely that your plan will fail. But if your plan includes contingencies that leave you prepared for the worst, then you will indeed execute a successful plan.

Is your policy premium tax-deductible?

The answer is: Supposedly, but don't count on it.

In 1997, Congress made long-term care premiums tax-deductible, provided the policy meets certain criteria. Lots of policies don't. But even if yours does meet the criteria (your agent or advisor can tell you), you can deduct the premium only if your total medical expenses exceed 7½% of your adjusted gross income. It's unlikely that you'll incur such high medical expenses, and that means you won't be able to claim the tax deduction – even if your policy qualifies for the deduction!

Therefore, ignore the tax issue and instead focus on buying the best policy for your needs. If it turns out that a tax-qualified policy is best for you, and if it does actually entitle you to a tax deduction, consider that a nice extra benefit. But don't go shopping for it.

Should You Self-Insure Instead?

If you are age:	The cost of care to age 85 will be:	You'll need to save annually:	Or buy a policy that costs annually:
45	$1,223,615	$4,732	$734
60	$588,580	$16,738	$1,709

Figure 3-4

[84] Plans for the best and hopes for the worst? Wait, that doesn't sound right . . . but you know what I mean.

Should You Try to Buy a Policy Without the Aid of an Advisor?

Long-term care policies are among the most complex insurance contracts that exist — much more so than life insurance policies. With life coverage, there's not much debate: You die, they pay. No one argues about whether or not you've met the definition of "death."[85]

But long-term care is different. Do you meet the qualifications for receiving benefits, as stipulated in the contract? Who decides? Which expenses are eligible? Will these costs be paid directly by the carrier, or must you pay the expense first and be reimbursed later, after submitting a claim form?

Most importantly, are you buying the benefits you think you are buying? One carrier's contract says the insurance company will pay:

> "100% of your cost up to 60% of your daily benefit."

That means this particular contract would pay no more than $90 per day — even though you bought $150/day coverage. This is why people who buy a policy based on price usually regret it. The more likely it is that a company will pay a claim, the more they will charge you for the coverage. If you buy a low-priced policy, don't count on getting benefits as quickly, as much or as long as others might get them.

> Trust everyone.
> But cut the cards.
>
> ~unknown

The problem is that you're not skilled at reading insurance contracts. Professional advisors are. Therefore, I recommend that you rely on the guidance of an advisor to help you choose the policy — and the carrier — that's best for you.

[85] "I dunno, Martha. Maybe he's only just a little bit dead!"

Do Your Parents Own an LTC Policy?

You should hope so, because if they run out of money due to long-term care, you'll begin to pay their bills — not because you have to (legally, you don't), but because you want to help protect their quality of life.

Many adult children buy policies for their parents, based on the sound reasoning that it's much cheaper to spend a couple of thousand dollars per year on policies instead of several thousand dollars per month on the cost of care itself.

What If You Don't Qualify for a Policy?

Don't assume that. Many people, fearing they'll be declined coverage, don't even bother submitting an application. Often, they worry that an existing medical condition renders them unable to obtain coverage. After all, in many cases, these folks have had their life insurance applications denied. Still, their fears often are misplaced.

One example: Heart conditions. It is common for life insurance carriers to reject applications for people with a history of heart disease, because the carriers are afraid the person might die from a heart attack. But some long-term care underwriters are less concerned by this. The obvious reason: LTC insurers don't care if you die. What they fear are conditions such as osteoporosis, rheumatoid arthritis and Parkinson's disease. Indeed, LTC carriers are worried that you might *live,* for your death would absolve them of financial liability.

So, don't assume that you or your parents are uninsurable. There's no downside to submitting an application, and who knows — you (or your parents) just might get approved.

You can buy a policy for your parents, but they will have to sign the application (so forget about obtaining the policy without their knowledge). Once the policy is in force, the company doesn't care who pays the premiums.

Have You Talked With Your Parents and Children About Long-Term Care?

My research for *Ordinary People, Extraordinary Wealth*[86] found that one of the secrets of wealthy people is that they talk with their families about money. Truly, this is something few people do. As evidence, consider the results of this study by the National Council on the Aging:

- Only 28% of parents have talked about long-term care with their kids.
- 93% of parents say they do not want their children to take care of them if it means the children have to use college savings that are set aside for the grandchildren.
    - But 50% of adult children say they would do this in order to help their parents, even if such action jeopardized their own kids' ability to attend college.
    - Furthermore, another 12% say they already have done so.
- 90% of parents say they don't want their adult children to sacrifice their jobs.
    - But 69% of adult children say they would do so. And of those who have already provided financial assistance, 57% say they used money they had set aside for their retirement, gotten a second job or raided a college savings fund.

If you won't buy long-term care insurance *for* yourself, buy it *on* yourself for the sake of your children and grandchildren. Because, whether you like it or not, they will take care of you — even to their own detriment.[87]

A combination of studies released in 2001, by LifePlans and the National Alliance for Caregiving and by MetLife, confirms this. The research included analysis of data accumulated from the 1980s and 1990s, as well as surveys of more than a thousand caregivers across the United States.

---

[86] On sale now!
[87] Proving that you've done a great job raising them.

The researchers found that family caregivers were 50% more likely to hold jobs if the recipients of care had long-term care insurance. Furthermore, among college-educated caregivers who care for relatives, 85% of the caregivers were able to keep working when the relative receiving care had LTC coverage, but only 45% of the caregivers were able to keep working when the relative lacked coverage.

If you're the elder, you need to get long-term care insurance so your children don't have to give up their careers or run out of money in their efforts to provide care for you.

And if you're the junior, you need to make sure your parents have coverage so you don't lose your career or go broke paying for their care.

Indeed, long-term care is a family-wide, intergenerational issue. Have that conversation today with your parents and with your kids. If you don't do it now in the comfort of your living room, you'll do it later in the stressful environment of a hospital waiting room.

And although this discussion has emphasized long-term care, you need to apply it equally to life insurance and disability insurance. Remember: Plan for the worst.

PART II

Choosing Investments for Your Financial Plan? Let a Baker Show You How to Do It

Part II

Choosing Investments for Your Financial Plan? Let a Baker Show You How to Do It

By now, your goals are in place — an exotic vacation, a mountaintop retreat, coaching underprivileged youth, showing grandchildren where their ancestors were born, you tell me! — and you've determined how much money you're going to need to achieve them. All you have to do now is figure out where to stash all that cash until you're ready to spend it.

If you're like many people, the idea of investing probably either bores or intimidates you. Stick with me, though, because your effort will pay off. Besides, you've got to learn how to invest your money, because I don't know any other way for you to get the money you'll need to reach your goals.[88]

Unfortunately, lots of people skipped right past the first part of the book. They aren't reading this section, either. Instead, they jumped ahead to the section on ingredients. As a result, they start buying investments (the ingredients) without first developing a strategy (creating a recipe) to implement the financial plan they created. That's as silly as getting into a cab without first knowing where you want to go. So, glad you're sticking with my itinerary here.

[88] Actually, I do. But Dave Conti — remember him from footnote 42? — deleted my chapters on The Secret Formula of Lottery Winners and Marrying Rich.

Therefore, in this part, you will learn:

1. How to have your cake and eat it, too (meaning, how to spend money without going broke)

2. How many slices you'll want to have in your cake, how much of each slice to have and what flavors you want them to be

3. How to choose the ingredients for each slice of your cake

Here's where I introduce my cake analogy, as warned in the book's opening pages. Hope you find it helpful in understanding the process, and that it's not too annoying.

As you'll see, there are five cakes you can choose to bake. These five represent the well-established universe of cake baking, uh, investment management. Everyone who bakes, er, invests, falls into one of these five — whether they realize it or not. They are:

1. Pound Cake

2. Marble Cake

3. Today's Special

4. Cupcakes, not Cake

5. Ric's Recipe[89]

[89] Gee, can you guess which one I endorse?

CHAPTER 4

Pound Cake, the One-Investment Portfolio

CHAPTER 4

Pound Cake, the One-Investment Portfolio

A pound cake features one (typically boring) flavor. It's like a portfolio that contains just one (low-risk, hence boring) investment. Let's see how this applies to goals.

In our case study of Mike and Janet (from page 117), we postulated that if they were able to achieve their goals with a 6% return, then that should have been their target. That's because we learned that we should take only as much risk as needed to achieve our goals.

To better understand this point, let's consider another case study, Holly, 28. She wants to buy a $200,000 house in two years. She has saved $18,000 to date and adds $300 each month. Where should she invest her money for the next two years?

My advice: bank CDs.

Here's why. To buy a $200,000 house, Holly will need about $25,000 for the down payment, closing costs, moving expenses and such. She already has more than half that figure, and at the rate of $300 per month, she'll accumulate another $7,200 over the next two years *even if she earns no interest at all.* But if she attempts to accumulate much more than $25,000 in two years, she might place the money into investments that actually lose money.[90]

[90] Imagine if she had bought stocks in March 2000, just before the market began declining.

A Bird in Hand

Without taking any investment risks at all, Holly will be able to buy her home in two years. Thus, she would be foolish to invest in anything riskier than the safest of investments.

> If you want a guarantee, buy a toaster.
>
> ~Clint Eastwood

If your situation is similar to Holly's — if you can achieve your financial goals via a risk-free return — then you should seek investments that provide those returns. Never take unnecessary risks.

In other words, you'd be baking a cake that contains just one dull, boring, but very safe ingredient. And you'd end up with a pound cake. One flavor, uninspiring, very predictable. There's not even any icing. But one thing is certain: It won't cause a tummy ache.

But if you will not achieve your goals by earning a risk-free return — if pound cake will not satisfy your appetite — then limiting yourself to a cake of one simple flavor is not appropriate for you.

The ingredient for our pound cake? Cash – and by that, I mean not just the dollar bills in your hand, but also "cash equivalents." Cash equivalents are U.S. Treasury Bills, bank CDs, money market funds, money market accounts,[91] and checking and savings accounts. Each of these are considered "same as cash," because your money remains very safe and available just about any time you want it – just like the cash in your hand – with the added benefit that you earn interest.

Now, that makes sense, doesn't it? Tell me, then, why so many households are eating pound cake? According to Forrester Research, 18% of U.S. households who have at least $50,000 have *all* their money in the bank — refusing even to contribute to a 401(k).

[91] Money market funds are offered by mutual fund companies; money market accounts are offered by banks.

Clearly, these millions of Americans are not excited about the opportunity to create wealth. Instead, they are afraid they might lose the money they already have. Is it possible you share their fear?

Figure 4-1 shows why you might feel that way. The chart depicts an investment, and it sure ain't vanilla. And, no, it's not an EKG readout, either[92] — it's the performance of the S&P 500 Stock Index on a monthly basis since 1926. Come to think of it, that *does* look like an EKG readout.[93]

So let me ask you what this chart seems to be confirming. In your opinion, is the stock market risky?

Yes.

Is it volatile?

Yes.

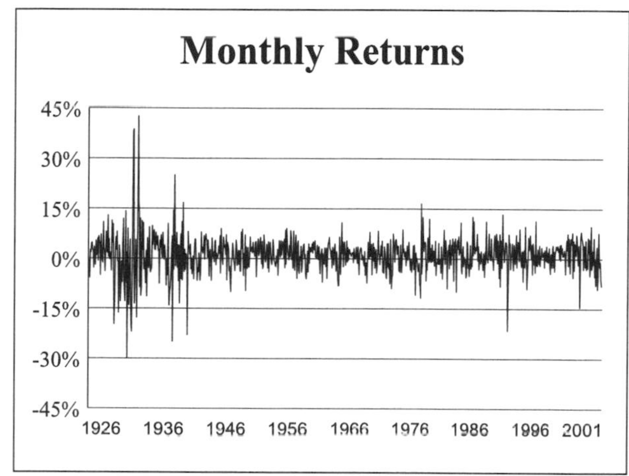

Figure 4-1

Is it unpredictable?

Yes.

Is it unstable?

Yes, already!

> ***"My goal is to travel more, especially to southeast Asia, Australia, South Pacific Islands and Egypt. I also want to go to the Winter Olympics within the next 5–10 years."***
>
> **~Lois Alexander, 69, Retired Microbiologist**

[92] Wise guy.

[93] After all, the stock market has been known to cause heart attacks.

That chart explains why you feel this way. And certainly, the performance of the stock market in 2000 and 2001 confirms your fear about investing in the stock market: You can lose a lot of money in stocks in short period.

But let's put this into historical context. Take a look at Figure 4-2.

How Often Did the Dow Decline?
1900–1999

Extent of Decline	Number of Declines	Average Duration	Such Declines Occurred About Once Every
5%–9%	328	40 days	4 months
10%–14%	108	3⅓ months	12 months
15%–19%	51	7 months	2 years
20% or more	29	1 year	3 years

Figure 4-2

Since 1900, the stock market has experienced more than 300 declines of 5% or more, lasting 40 days on average. These declines occur, in fact, an average of three times every year, and a third of them get worse.

Skip to the bottom of the chart and you'll see that, in the last 100 years, there were 29 declines of 20% or more. They lasted an average of one year and occurred, on average, every three years.

That's why you need not be concerned about how the stock market performed in 2000 and 2001. Like all the others, this most recent decline was historically normal: It began about three years after the previous 20% decline (August 1998) and lasted about as long as such declines typically last. Thus, instead of feeling insecure about that decline, you should have felt relieved that the market was operating normally.

Indeed, if you want to see something *really* scary, take a look at Figure 4-3. Say you had invested $100,000 into a one-year bank CD in 1980, using that year's $15,000 in interest income to pay your bills. Each year, your interest income would have fluctuated due to changing interest rates. In 2001, you'd have earned only $6,800 in interest. But due to inflation, you would need $26,110 to buy what $15,000 bought 21 years earlier. Now, *that's* scary.

Recognize that if you bake yourself a pound cake, one that's made of nothing but "risk-free" investments such as bank CDs, the only risk you're free of is the risk that you might lose principal.[94] Indeed, "risk-free" ingredients, ah, investments, do nothing to protect you from inflation risk or tax risk, but both of those risks can be as devastating as the loss of principal.[95] This is scary indeed.

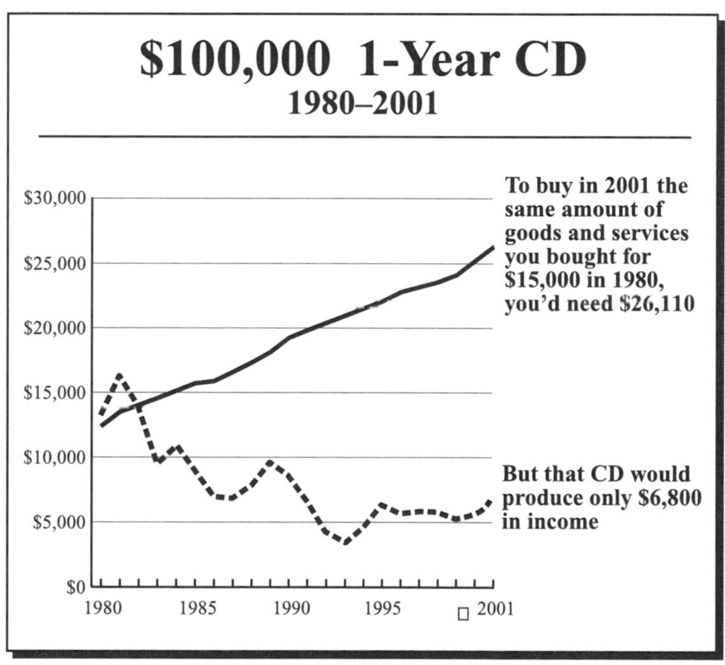

Figure 4-3

[94] This is called "default risk" and is covered in greater detail in — you guessed it — *The Truth About Money*.

[95] In fact, even more so, because taxes and inflation are a sure thing, while default risk isn't.

So, instead of scaring yourself about what you perceive to be the risks of baking exotic cakes, er, investing in the stock market, let's just change the way you view the risk. Look at Figure 4-4 below.

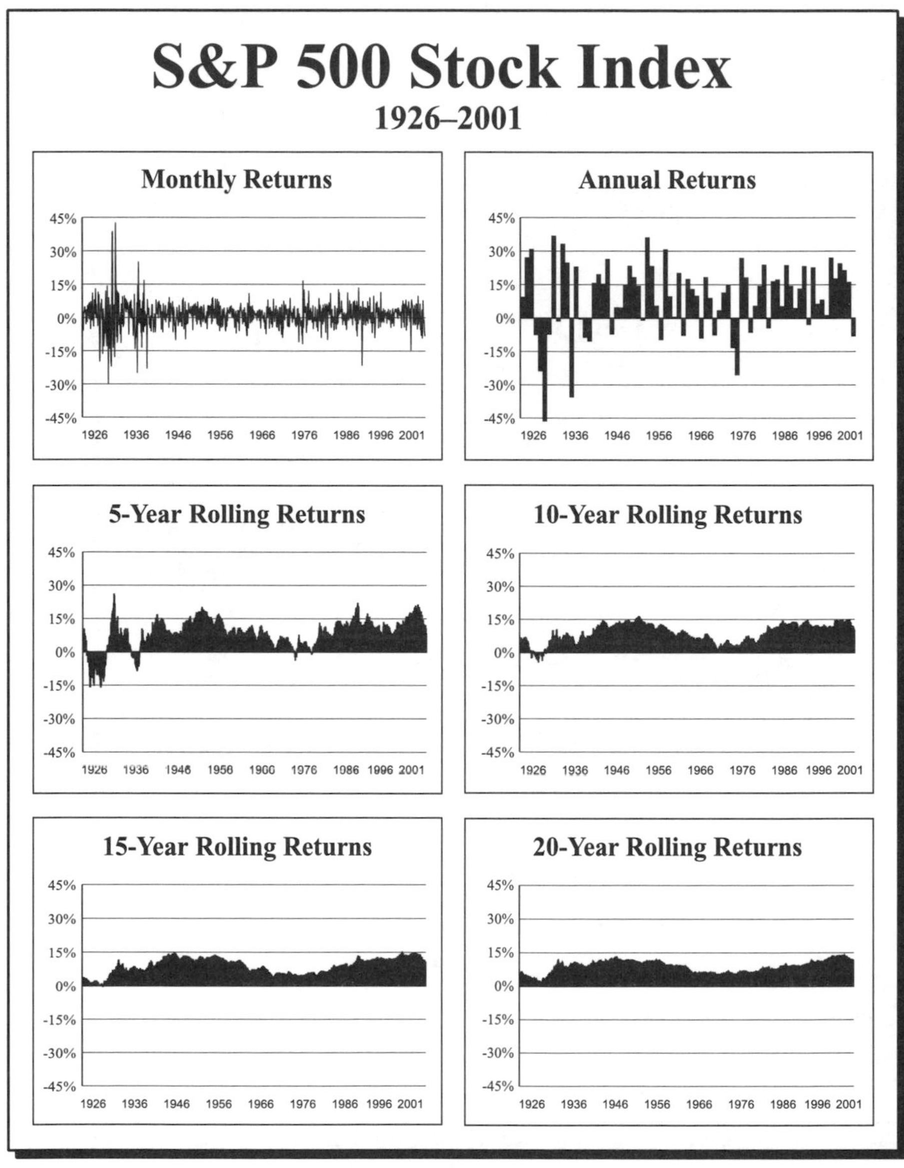

Figure 4-4

Clearly, investing in the stock market for 30 days will yield unpredictable results. But investing for 20 years is much more reliable. By changing your perspective, you can change the question from "Will stocks make money?" to "How much money will stocks make?"

"Actually catch a squirrel by end of next summer."

~Dojar, 9,
Ric and Jean's weimarancr

Still, the fact remains that stock prices occasionally fall. It's called a "bear market" when they fall 20% or more. Guess what happens after every bear market? We experience a "bull market." And every bull market is followed by a bear market, which is followed by a bull market, which is followed by a bear market, and so on.

As Figure 4-5 on the following page shows, bull markets have historically lasted longer and risen higher, while bear markets, in comparison, have been shorter-lived and haven't fallen much. This should strike you as an excellent environment in which to grow wealth.

"I have been a teacher for over 25 years and have always wished I could provide a fully stocked library for my students. I'll do it in 10 years (when I retire)."

~Bettejane Weiss, 54,
Vice Principal

People who keep all their money in risk-free investments when other ingredients are more appropriate either don't understand the risks they're facing due to taxes and inflation, or they don't understand the true nature of the stock market, or both.

But often, they begin to get the message, and that's when they slowly become willing to leave safety behind in favor of the opportunity for higher returns. That's when they say, "Okay, I get it. Stocks are okay for some of my money."

And that's when they start thinking about marble cakes.

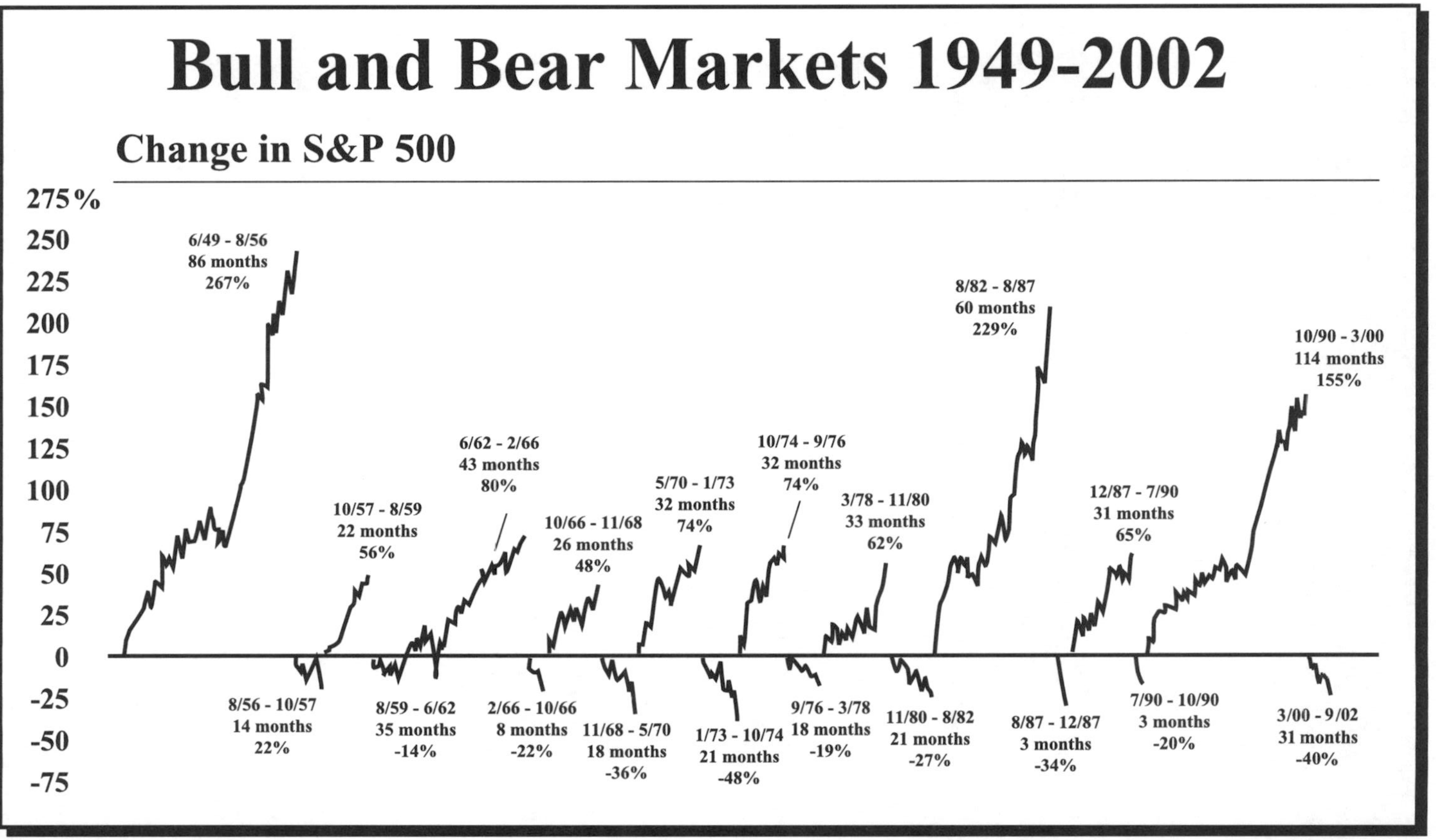
Bull and Bear Markets 1949-2002
Change in S&P 500
275%
250
225
200
175
150
125
100
75
50
25
0
-25
-50
-75
6/49 - 8/56
86 months
267%
8/56 - 10/57
14 months
22%
10/57 - 8/59
22 months
56%
8/59 - 6/62
35 months
-14%
6/62 - 2/66
43 months
80%
2/66 - 10/66
8 months
-22%
10/66 - 11/68
26 months
48%
11/68 - 5/70
18 months
-36%
5/70 - 1/73
32 months
74%
1/73 - 10/74
21 months
-48%
10/74 - 9/76
32 months
74%
9/76 - 3/78
18 months
-19%
3/78 - 11/80
33 months
62%
11/80 - 8/82
21 months
-27%
8/82 - 8/87
60 months
229%
8/87 - 12/87
3 months
-34%
12/87 - 7/90
31 months
65%
7/90 - 10/90
3 months
-20%
10/90 - 3/00
114 months
155%
3/00 - 9/02
31 months
-40%

Figure 4-5

CHAPTER 5

Moving Beyond One-Flavor Cakes

CHAPTER 5

Moving Beyond One-Flavor Cakes

Marble cakes have two flavors, vanilla (cash, cash equivalents and bonds) and chocolate (stocks). Thus, parts of these cakes are very low in risk while other parts are very high-risk, but marble cakes have no other ingredients whose risks are in-between.

Marble Cake	
Cash & Bonds (vanilla)	**Stocks (chocolate)**
Savings Account	Style
Checking Account	Size
Money Market Fund	Domain
T-Bills	
CDs	
Savings Bonds	
U.S. Agencies	
Municipal Bonds	
Corporate Bonds	
Fixed Annuities	
Life Insurance Cash Value	

Figure 5-1

On page xiii, I asked you two questions. Return to that page now to remind yourself of your answers, because next, you'll see how those answers compare with the information I'm about to share with you.

At this point, a little investment background is in order: Broadly speaking, all investments fall into two categories: equities (assets you own) and debt (assets you lend).[96] Therefore, if you are unwilling to invest in stocks (the equity category, as stocks represent ownership), you are, by default, investing in bonds or cash (the debt category, as bonds and cash represent loans to companies or governments).

With that background in mind, let's look at your answer to the question on page xiii, "What percentage of your money would you be willing to place into stocks?"

> When choosing between two evils, I always like to try the one I've never tried before.
>
> ~Mae West

If you said you are willing to invest 100% of your money into stocks,[97] and if you had done this from 1926 to 2000, you would have earned an average annual return of 13.3%, according to Ibbotson Associates. If you instead had placed 100% of your money into bonds, you would have earned an average annual return of 5.4%.

Therefore, if you mixed these two ingredients to produce a marble cake — investing in some combination of bonds and stocks — your cake's average annual return would have been somewhere between 5.4% and 13.3%, as shown in Figure 5-2.

This leads us to the second question (from page xiii). In it, you predicted an average annual return for your cake (investment portfolio). Was your prediction reasonably close to the historical performance of the stock and bond markets of the past century, considering how you said you were willing to invest?

I often discover a huge difference between what people expect from their investments and what such investments have historically produced. Often, people expect their investments to earn 10% per year, despite the fact that they refuse to invest any money at all into stocks. And I've encountered even more people who believe their investments will earn 20% per year

[96] Real estate, as an owned asset, is part of the equities category. Bonds and cash equivalents are part of the debt category. For more on this, read Part I of *The Truth About Money*.
[97] And it's hard to think of anything more aggressive than placing 100% of your money into the stock market.

simply because that's what their investments earned for a couple of years in the late 1990s. Indeed, Sanford Bernstein & Company found in July 2000 that consumers surveyed said they expected their portfolios to grow 15% to 26% per year for the next 10 years.

Is it reasonable for a person to predict that his portfolio will grow 15% per year even though he's placing only half of his assets into stocks? I don't think so.

What Portion of Your Money Are You Willing to Place into Stocks?

1926–2000

If you had placed this portion of your assets into stocks:	Your portfolio's average annual return would have been:
0%	5.4%
10%	6.2%
20%	7.0%
30%	7.8%
40%	8.6%
50%	9.4%
60%	10.1%
70%	10.9%
80%	11.7%
90%	12.5%
100%	13.3%

Figure 5-2

Too often, people fail to realize that the stock market's performance from 1982 to 1999 was unprecedented. The 17.9% average annual return enjoyed by the S&P 500 Stock Index in those 18 years, as reported by Ibbotson Associates, was substantially above the S&P 500's 75-year average of 13.3%.

"I would like to offer career counseling services to high school students and teenagers who otherwise do not have opportunities for this service. In 2003."

~Anonymous, 62, Education Administrator

You need to understand that there is a direct correlation between the amount of money you place into stocks and the rate of return you will earn, just as a baker understands that the success of his cake lies not just in the ingredients he uses, but in the proportion of each.

But is the difference between 0% in stocks and 100% in stocks all that big a difference? Does it really matter whether you invest 40% vs. 60% in stocks?

Let's look at the results. A person who invested $100 in bonds from 1926 to 1999 would have ended the century with $4,649, based on the aforementioned 5.4% annual return.

Meanwhile, the person who invested $100 into stocks for that same period, at 13.3%, would have had $909,459.

So, yes, it does make a huge difference.

But this example makes one (very big) assumption: That after you identify the portion of your money that you're willing to place into stocks, you stick with that decision for 75 years. Many readers will challenge this notion as unrealistic. What they'd rather do, they'll say, is periodically shift between stocks and bonds. They want to choose . . . Today's Special.

"My goal is to live for a month in a thatched Irish cottage overlooking the sea."

~Joe Gilmore, Financial Planner,
Edelman Financial Services

Chapter 6

The Dangers of Eating Today's Special

CHAPTER 6

The Dangers of Eating Today's Special

Unlike risk-free investments — which produce a steady, consistent rate of return — stock returns are highly volatile. Sometimes, stock prices are rising, and other times they are falling. Therefore, wouldn't it make sense to own stocks only when stock prices are rising?

If you had done that from 1926 to 1999 — if you had owned stocks only in those years when stock prices rose — your $100 would have grown to $16,482,782 by 1999. You would have switched from one to the other 34 times in those 75 years, owning bonds in 26 years and stocks during the other 49.

What we're talking about, of course, is the notion of switching between vanilla and chocolate. But how do you know when to do that?

Owning the Best Each Year
1926–2000

Stocks Beat Bonds		Bonds Beat Stocks
1926	1967	1929
1927	1968	1930
1928	1971	1931
1933	1972	1932
1935	1975	1934
1936	1976	1937
1938	1978	1939
1942	1979	1940
1943	1980	1941
1944	1983	1946
1945	1985	1953
1947	1986	1957
1948	1987	1960
1949	1988	1962
1950	1989	1966
1951	1991	1969
1952	1992	1970
1954	1994	1973
1955	1995	1974
1956	1996	1977
1958	1997	1981
1959	1998	1982
1961	1999	1984
1963		1990
1964		1993
1965		2000

Figure 6-1

Nobody knows — but a lot of people try. They follow the "experts" by simply tuning in to some financial television network each morning and doing whatever the people on TV tell them to do. And they read magazines and follow the advice plastered on those monthly covers. And they subscribe to investment-tips newsletters and dutifully obey the commands issued.

Business Week published one of the financial press's most memorable magazine covers on August 13, 1979. The nation was still reeling from the worst post-WWII recession ever, inflation was at an all-time high, we

At a dinner party not long ago, I met a gentleman who was in town visiting friends. "Where are you from?" I asked.

"I live in Portland, Oregon," he replied. "Moved there just a few months ago. Was in San Francisco before that."

"Were you born in San Francisco?" I asked.

"No, I was raised in the Midwest," he answered. "I've moved around a bit."

"Is that right?" I said. "Where have you lived?"

"Well," he began, "back in 1990, I lived in Bremerton, Washington. Then in 1991, I moved to Provo, Utah. A year later, I moved to Sioux Falls, South Dakota. In 1993 — lemme see now — yes, in 1993, I lived in Rochester, Minnesota. After that, I went to Raleigh/Durham, North Carolina."

By now, I was staring at him, and I didn't realize that my mouth was open.

"In 1995 I transferred myself to Gainesville, Florida," he continued. "Then, after nearly a year, I moved again, this time to Madison, Wisconsin. I went to Nashua, New Hampshire, in 1997, and on to Boulder in 1998. Then, San Francisco and now, Portland."

"Wow! You moved every year in the past decade," I remarked. "Why have you moved so often?"

"I read *Money* magazine," he said, apparently surprised at the question.

I didn't see the connection. "So . . . ?" I said, leading him to elaborate.

"Every year, *Money* releases its study of the best place to live in America," he said with pride. "So, every year, I move to the town that *Money* says is the #1 town in America."

"That's really interesting," I said. "Most people just use *Money* magazine to decide what mutual fund to pick."

"Oh, I would never buy a mutual fund simply because the current issue of some magazine says it's the best fund!" he exclaimed. "That would be stupid!"

were still suffering from the oil embargo, American hostages were still in Iran, and stock prices had been stagnant for more than six years.

Acknowledging all this, *Business Week*'s cover story was called "The Death of Equities," and talked about bonds, oil and gold.

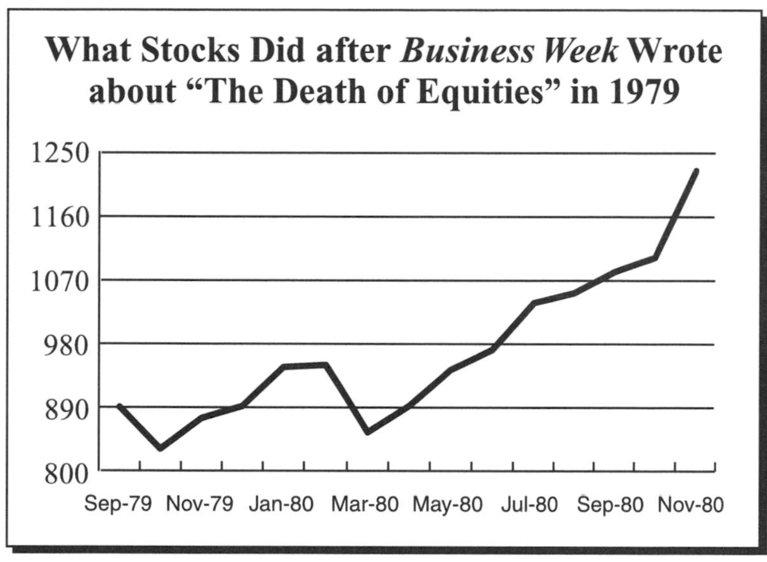

Figure 6-2

"By age 70, I want to buy a beach home with access to the bay and ocean with property so we can entertain the grand-children and great-grandchildren. The goal is to establish a family legacy of fun, sun and sand — keyed to memory of grandpa and grandma."

~Richard Kasyjanski, 51, Reinsurance Manager

As if on cue, the stock market soon began its recovery, leading to a historic two-decade bull market during which the Dow Jones Industrial Average skyrocketed from 887 to a high of 11,750, a 1,225% increase. Over the same 22 years, meanwhile, gold prices (then near an all-time high of more than $800/ounce) have fallen to less than $300/ounce.

How about *Forbes*? Its April 27, 1992, issue fretted over "The Crazy Things People Say to Rationalize Stock Prices," prices *Forbes* believed were ridiculously high. Well, maybe people weren't so crazy after all: When the story was published, the Dow was at 3389. Figure 6-3 shows what happened next.

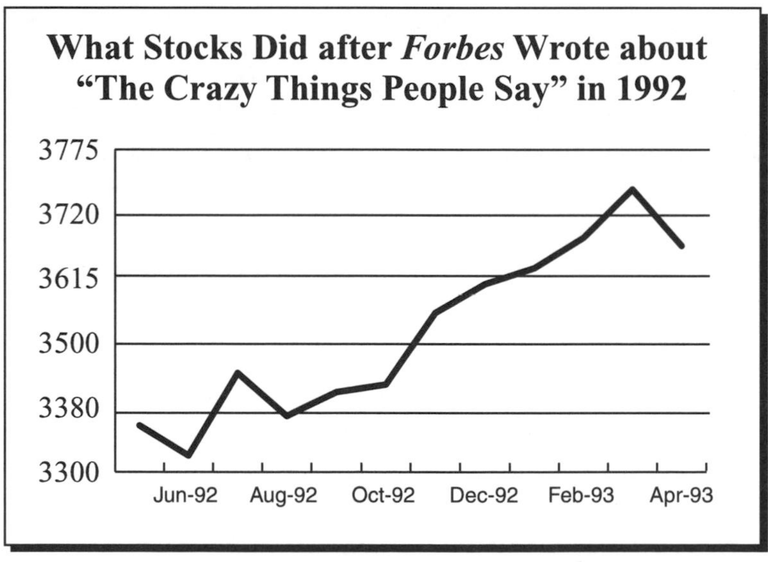

Figure 6-3

U.S. News and World Report warned, "Investor Beware!" on March 11, 1996. I'm not sure what we were supposed to be waring,[98] because the Dow was still only at 5587.

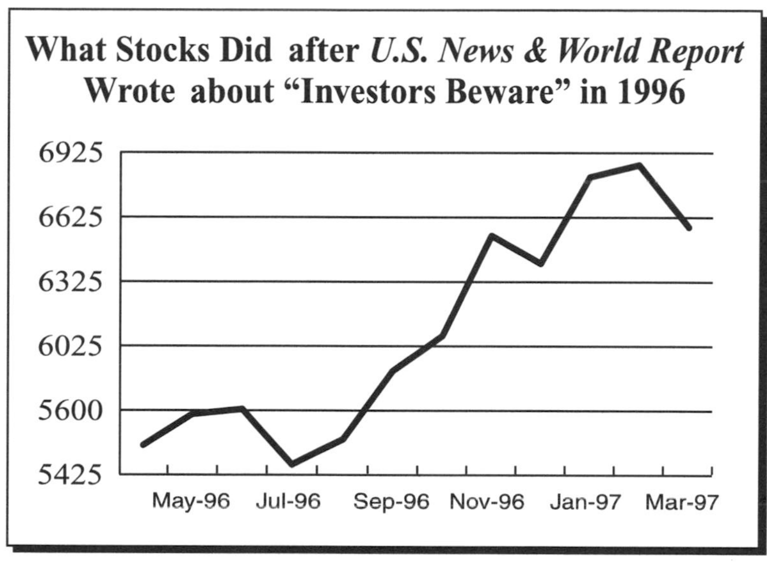

Figure 6-4

> ***"I would like to start a rock band. I've been playing the guitar since age 14, but rarely played with other musicians. I've always wanted to be in a band, and still, at age 34, plan to, probably in 5 years."***
>
> **~Noel S. Leavitt, 34, Engineer**

[98] Is that a word?

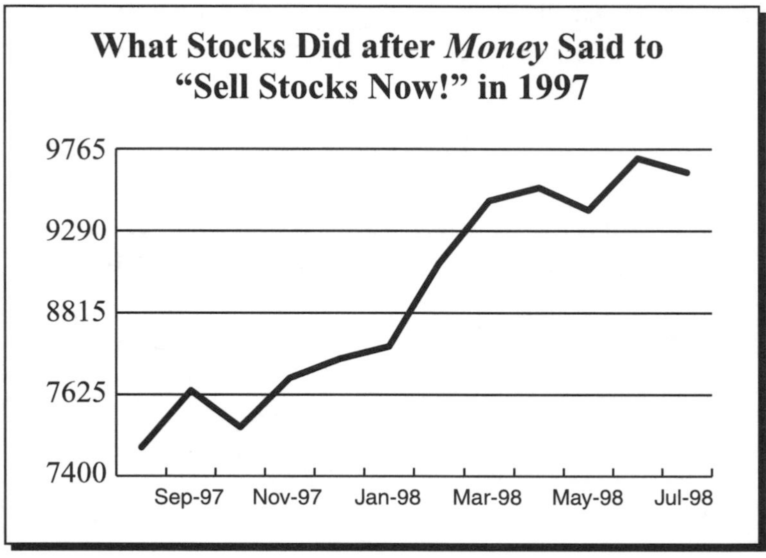

Figure 6-5

In August 1997, *Money* magazine urged its readers to "SELL STOCK NOW!" Bad idea: The Dow, then at 7622, gained 50% within the next three years.

> *"Above all else, by 62, I would like to own beachfront property (preferably the Gulf Coast) and have the luxury to live there with my husband and write a series of Mississippi novels (I want to be the next William Faulkner)."*
>
> **~Anonymous, 53, SVP - Sales and Marketing**

That prestigious pub *The Economist* wrote about "America's Bubble Economy" in April 1998. Instead of bursting, the Dow kept growing.

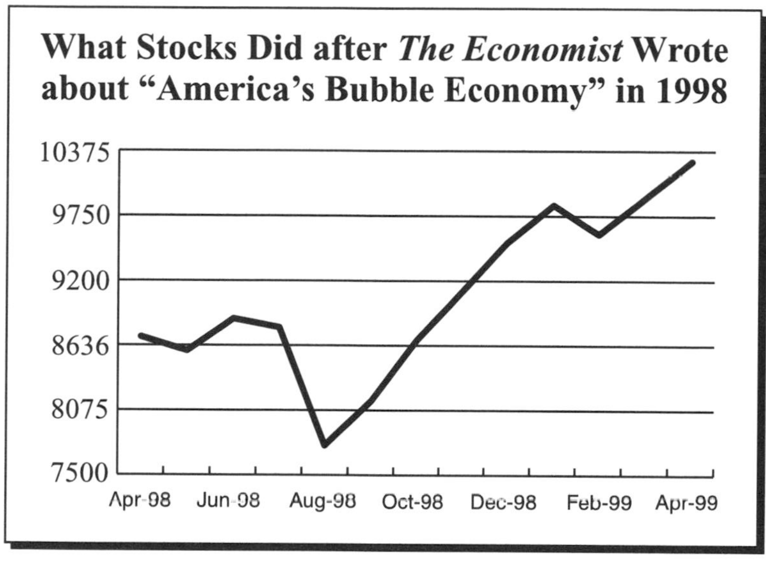

Figure 6-6

A wise man puts aside
10% of the money he gets
– and 90% of the advice.

~Harry Karns

Fortune magazine displayed angst on its September 1998 cover, "The Crash of '98," where it asked "Can the U.S. Economy Hold Up?" Apparently, it could, for in the next two years, the Dow added nearly 3,000 points to its then-8712 figure.

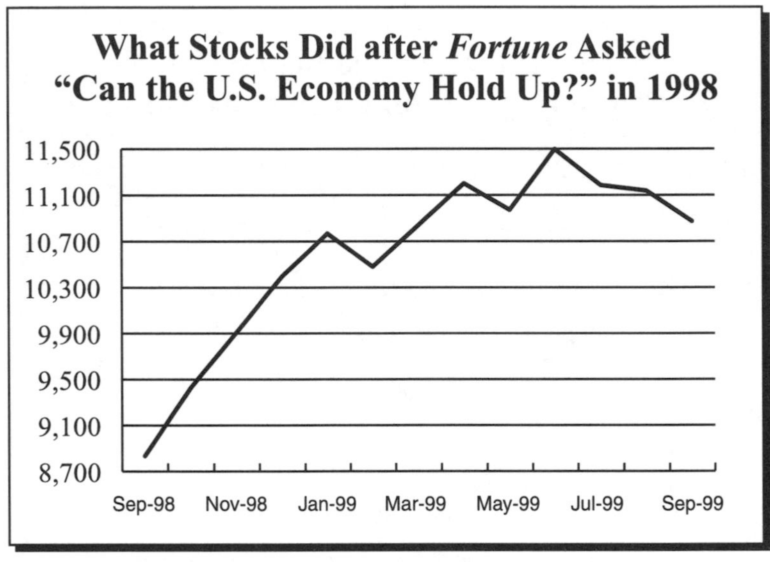

Figure 6-7

"We'll take an extended tour of China and visit its historical landmarks, to take our daughters back to the country where they were born. We'll do this in 2008 (when they'll be 12 and 9)."

~Mark Maines, 44, naval officer (soon to be high school teacher), and Renee D. Maines, 41

Not a single publication predicted that the tech stock meltdown would begin in March 2000. But exactly one year later, *after* the NASDAQ had already fallen 65% (its worst-ever 12-month loss), *Newsweek*'s March 26, 2001, issue found the courage to ask, "How scared should you be?"

Plenty, if you follow the advice of magazine covers.

It seems the media never get it right. The so-called (and typically self-proclaimed) experts simply can't predict the future. And worst of all, they are not subject to any accountability.

Have you ever seen an "expert" report on how his or her prior predictions did? Fat chance. Instead, bobbing head after bobbing head flash across the screen to tell you what to BUY NOW! Rarely does any stock promoter disclose on the air or in print whether they own the stock they're touting.

Are Analysts More Reliable Than the Pundits?

This is not mere conversation. I am talking about a genuine crisis for investors. That's because investors — those who follow the advice of their broker as well as those who conduct their own research — base their investment decisions (directly or indirectly) on the analysts' reports issued by Wall Street firms.

To state it briefly — something no one ever accuses me of doing — you should ignore stock market analysts, just as you should ignore the predictions you see, hear and read in the media.

With that said, you can now skip the next 10 pages, and go directly to Chapter Seven. But if you want to learn more, you may prefer to read the remainder of this chapter.

Every major Wall Street firm hires stock analysts. Their job is to investigate publicly traded companies and issue a recommendation to their firm's stockbrokers. The brokers then "dial for dollars," telling their clients (on the basis of the analyst's report) to buy, or sell.

But can you rely on the analysts' reports?

Apparently not. In the first three months of 2001, as shown in Figure 6-8, 12,339 stock rating reports were issued by Wall Street analysts, according to Zacks Investment Research, but only 87 of those reports contained sell recommendations — just 0.71% of the total. That seems bizarre when considering that the S&P 500 Stock Index *fell* 11.5% during that three-month period, according to Ibbotson Associates.

How could so many Wall Street professionals fail to issue sell signals in a period of overwhelmingly negative market performance? There are two major theories.

The Analysts

	# of Stocks They Rate	# of "Sell" Ratings
Prudential	727	21
Gerard Klauer	231	3
Raymond James	430	4
CS First Boston	1,328	12
Solomon Smith Barney	1,355	10
Merrill Lynch	1,918	13
Goldman Sachs	1,168	7
Morgan Stanley	1,239	5
UBS Warburg	1,095	4
Lehman Brothers	886	3
Bear Stearns	936	3
J.P. Morgan	1,026	2
	12,339	**87**

Figure 6-8

The first theory is based on the fact that analysts often own the very stocks on which they are issuing reports. If they tell investors to sell, they'll cause the price to fall — hurting their own investments. But if they tell investors to buy, the price will rise. Thus, analysts suffer from a huge *personal* conflict of interest.

How bad is it? Pretty bad, according to the U.S. Securities and Exchange Commission. Laura Unger, as acting chair of SEC, told Congress that more than 5% of the stock analysts it reviewed were personally selling shares of stocks while telling consumers to buy them. Another 28% bought shares of stock before the stocks were available to the public. Unger told Congress in July 2001 that the SEC enforcement division is investigating further to determine if analysts are involved in "an intentional manipulation or fraud."

Considering that the SEC's small review revealed improprieties one out of three times, it seems clear that there is a widespread – if not institutional – problem. It's scary, because so many consumers base their investment decisions on what analysts say.

The SEC's accusations are so damning that the industry isn't even bothering to challenge them. Thomas Bowman, president of the Association for Investment Management and Research, the trade group for analysts, told Congress in those same hearings, "We do not dispute that some firms pressure their analysts to issue favorable research on current or prospective investment banking clients."

As found through an investigation by *Institutional Investor* magazine, stock analysts at virtually every major brokerage firm are permitted to own stocks in the companies they rate. Even worse, they are permitted to buy stock in com-

Can Analysts Own Stock in the Companies They Rate?

	Can the analyst buy: Publicly traded stock?	Can the analyst buy: Stock not yet available to public?	If an analyst owns the stock he's rating, must he disclose the fact?
Merrill Lynch	yes	yes	no
CS First Boston	yes	yes	no
Goldman Sachs	yes	yes	no
Lehman Brothers	yes	yes	no
DB Alex. Brown	yes	yes	yes
J.P. Morgan	yes	yes	yes
Solomon Smith Barney	yes	yes	no

Figure 6-9

panies that are not yet available to the general public. By investing in pre-IPO[99] stocks, the analysts are highly motivated to endorse the IPO to consumers, so the stock will grow substantially on its first day of public trading. And worst of all, as shown in Figure 6-9, their employers do not require analysts to disclose their positions when issuing their recommendations.

Data from Investors.com seem to confirm that there is a conflict of interest. According to the Web site, when ana-

It can be pretty bad when a stock analyst issues a report about a stock he or she owns, because the analyst has a financial incentive to see the stock rise in value. Nothing could be worse than a potential conflict of interest.

Except for an actual conflict of interest.

Companies know that many investors will buy only the stocks that analysts tell them to buy. The problem is that there are lots more companies than analysts. In fact, according to IBES International and NASDAQ, nearly half of all publicly traded companies are ignored by stock analysts.

So, how can you get an analyst to report on your company? Simple: Pay him. And if you're going to pay him, you certainly want to get your money's worth — and that means you're going to get a favorable report.

But do you suppose that the analyst discloses that he has been paid to issue his report? All I can say is that I've never seen one that does.

[99] Initial Public Offering, when a company first sells its stock to the public.

In the face of widespread condemnation of analysts' behavior — and only days before appearing before Congressional hearings on the matter — the Securities Industry Association released in June 2001 new guidelines for securities firms and their analysts. These voluntary guidelines, issued in the hopes that Congress would not create any laws mandating changes in behavior, include the following provisions:

- **An analyst's pay should not be directly linked to any transactions.**
- **Analysts should not seek approval of their reports from the firm's underwriting division prior to releasing them.**
- **The underwriting divisions should not promise current or prospective clients that they will receive favorable ratings from the firm's analysts.**
- **Analysts should disclose any information that may affect their recommendations.**
- **Any personal trading by analysts should be consistent with their investment recommendations.**
- **If an analyst has a personal interest in any stock on which he or she is reporting, the report should disclose this fact.**

The SIA told Congress that many of its members, including the 14 largest brokerage firms that handle 95% of the underwriting in the U.S., have endorsed the guidelines. That seems to suggest that big improvements are under way.

lysts touted the stocks of companies that had paid their employers huge underwriting fees, investors who followed the analysts' advice lost an average of 53.3%. When listening to analysts whose firms had no relationship with the companies being analyzed, investors still lost — but they lost only 4.2%.

The second theory has been advanced by no less than Arthur Levitt, former chairman of the U.S. Securities and Exchange Commission. Mr. Levitt and others have noted that most analysts work for investment firms — firms that have both underwriting divisions and brokerage divisions. The former raises capital for corporate America, earning millions of dollars in fees for its services; the latter sells stocks and bonds to retail investors,[100] earning millions in commissions for executing those trades.

"I have always wanted to tour Africa and see wildlife in its natural state."

~Sally Signorelli, age withheld, Document Support for Debt Management Co.

[100] Read: Consumers.

Say Widget Inc. is planning to issue additional stock in an effort to raise the capital it needs to grow its business. Widget will take bids from various underwriters, awarding the business to the firm it thinks will raise the most capital at the least cost. But if an analyst at that firm issues a sell signal on Widget's stock, Widget will be miffed — and award the business to a competitor. This would cost the investment firm millions of dollars in lost profits and hurt their prestige.

There's supposed to be no contact between a firm's underwriting division and its brokerage division,[102] just as a newspaper's editorial staff isn't supposed to have contact with the advertising staff. Although you seldom hear that an advertiser has succeeded in slanting or even killing a news story, such unethical behavior has proven to be routine on Wall Street.

"By 60, I want to see the Aurora Borealis. By 50, I want to be fluent in Spanish and Italian. By 47, I want to learn to water color."

~Jean Edelman,
Office Mom,
Edelman Financial Services

Thus, this theory goes, the underwriting division exerts extreme pressure on its analysts to *never* issue a sell signal.[101] Clearly, analysts suffer from a huge *professional* conflict of interest.

Is it any wonder that people are upset over the advice they've been given by the major Wall Street firms?

Upset — and poorer. According to a study by Case Western Reserve University's Weatherhead School of Management, people who followed expert recommendations lost, on average in the following six months, 3.8% of their money. The study reports that recommended securities typically feature higher-than-average volatility and higher-than-average price-to-earnings ratios.

[101] That's why you see so many "hold" recommendations. Analysts who fear being fired for saying "sell" issue "hold" recommendations. "Hold," of course, is nonsensical; you either want to sell a stock you own or buy (more of) it — telling you to "hold" doesn't tell you anything. That's why "hold" has largely become regarded as a "polite" way of telling investors to sell.
[102] Analysts work for the brokerage division.

The regulators are not willing to wait for improvements. The NASD's regulatory arm, which writes the rules governing Wall Street's marketing activities, has proposed a rule that would require securities analysts who appear on television to reveal on-air whether they own shares in the stocks they are touting. They also would have to disclose if the firms they work for own 5% or more of the stock or if the firm has received any investment-banking fees from the company. The proposal also would require that potential conflicts of interest be featured more prominently in print media.

The SEC supports the NASD's action. It has noted that 13 of the 14 SIA members that endorsed the SIA's new guidelines said that they didn't need to make any changes to meet the new standards. The SEC considers the situation so dangerous for investors that it issued in June 2001 an "Investor Alert" to warn consumers about the risks of following analyst recommendations. Previous Investor Alerts warned against identity thieves, fraudulent telemarketers and perpetrators of a Nigerian "advance fee fraud." Looks like Wall Street analysts — and their firms — are in pretty bad company.

How bad is the situation? Pretty bad, according to *Fortune* magazine. It profiled the case of Mike Mayo, a "star analyst" who was fired from his job at Credit Suisse First Boston, one of Wall Street's biggest investment firms.

How big a star was Mayo? Well, *Institutional Investor* ranked him the nation's #1 regional banking analyst, whose picks produced a 52% annual return for the four years 1997–2000, and *Fortune* in July 2000 had named Mayo one of the nation's 15 best stock researchers. Mayo was most famous for issuing a buy recommendation on bank stocks in December 1994. Until that point, bank stocks had languished; after Mayo's call, the S&P bank index rose 254%.

Then came the spring of 1999.

Mayo made a new call: "In no uncertain terms," *Fortune* says he told a roomful of CSFB brokers, "sell bank stocks."

He was right again, for soon after, bank stocks began falling, often dramatically.[103] By December, the S&P bank index was down 21%, ending the year with its worst performance relative to the S&P 500 in 54 years.

Yet within a year, Mayo was fired, and *Fortune* makes it clear that he was fired because he dared to issue a sell signal. Wrote the magazine, "If, in fact, stocks are headed for disaster, you won't hear it from the analysts."

Still unconvinced that you should avoid analysts' recommendations? Then consider this: In August 2002, the North American Securities Administrators Association added "analyst research conflicts" to its list of "Top 10 Investment Scams." Need I say more?

[103] In a single day that August, for example, Bank One's stock fell 25%.

This information has probably convinced you that taking advice from the "experts" is not going to help you determine when to buy stocks and when to sell them. You'd be better off making your own decisions.

Right?

Well, to see if you'd be any good at that, consider the work done by Terrence O'Dean, a researcher in the field of behavioral finance at the University of California at Davis. He wrote a study published by the *Journal of Finance.*

In his work, O'Dean examined the trading records at a large discount brokerage firm. His study reviewed the accounts for 78,000 households from 1991 to 1996, in an effort to determine who makes more money, active traders or investors who buy and hold.[104]

The "experts" aren't even as good as flipping a coin.

Bianca Research measured the long-term ability of Wall Street analysts to accurately measure future interest rate directions. The researchers looked at the six-month prognostication abilities of the "experts" for every six-month period dating back to 1982.

The discovery: Analysts were able to correctly predict future interest rates a mere 28% of the time.

It's even worse than you think: Since interest rates can only do one of three things (rise, fall, or remain constant), a random pick should garner the correct answer 33% of the time. But the experts couldn't perform even that well.

Indeed, relying on "the experts" is worse than relying on chance. If you're watching the pundits on TV, it's time to change the channel.

O'Dean found that active traders underperformed the stock market by 10% per year. By contrast, average households underperformed by only 1% per year — an amount roughly equal to the fee investors typically pay to own mutual funds.

But why do active traders under perform? It wasn't because they picked bad stocks, the study found. No, what hurt them was the fact that their extensive buying and selling created substantial trading costs, and every time they sold for a profit, they lost as much as 50% of those profits to federal and state income taxes. In other words, the baker's problem was not bad ingredients; it was the fact that the baker kept switching ingredients.

[104] Since discount firms offer no advice and retain no analysts, the assumption is that those who invest via discount firms engage in their own research, and do not follow the advice of others.

At least one professional baker has fled the kitchen. The following is a statement by David Menashi, publisher of *Fundline,* the #1 market timing newsletter as rated by the *Hulbert Financial Digest* for the past 5-, 8- and 10-year periods:

> As far as I'm concerned, market timing is a thing of the past . . . the market has become too fragmented to be able to apply market timing successfully. . . . Therefore, as my parting shot I would urge you to believe that market timing has become a losing proposition . . . minimize the temptation to switch in and out. Stay fully invested through thick and thin.

Menashi wrote the above on July 1, 2000, as part of his announcement that he was terminating his 32-year-old newsletter.

It is impossible to effectively decide which flavor is going to be today's special, for the markets move too fast and are filled with too much noise from so-called experts.

You're not a "long-term investor" merely because you are someone who owns investments for a long period of time. You are a long-term investor only if you hold each of your investments for a long period of time.

Got it?

But is such market-timing a common practice, or am I raising an issue that simply is not a problem for most investors? Consider this: Stock funds hold $4.6 trillion in investor assets. In the 12-month period ending August 31, 2000, according to Forrester Research, 42% of those assets were moved. How can so many people claim to be "long-term investors" while moving nearly half of their investments within a one-year period?

The truth is simple. Despite their claims, most people are not long-term investors. Want more evidence? Look what happened as we entered 2001.

January 2, 2001 investors withdrew $13.1 billion from stock mutual funds. This was, according to *Mutual Funds* magazine, the largest one-day outflow of money in mutual fund history.[105]

[105] What caused the massive selling? Investors had a terrible time in 2000, and they wanted to sell their investments. But doing so would have forced them to incur capital gains taxes, so they waited until January 2 — the first trading day of the new year. By delaying their trades until 2001, investors were able to push their transactions into the new tax year.

January 3, 2001	the NASDAQ jumped 14.2%. It was that index's largest one-day gain ever.
January 4, 2001[106]	investors added $17.2 billion to their stock funds, the largest one-day inflow in mutual fund history.

It's time for me to come clean, and admit to you the truth about a dark secret of mine. It's this: I've been wrong all these years.

Okay. Fine. I admit it. For years I've been telling my radio and TV audiences — and my clients of course — that the buy-and-hold strategy always beats market timing. For years I've been saying that you're doomed to failure if you try to engage in "market timing," a strategy where you try to buy stocks before they rise and try to sell them before they fall. For nearly 20 years, I've said that buy-and-hold always beats market timing.

I'm wrong.

This fact was revealed to me by a study published in the February 2001 issue of *Financial Analyst Journal*. This study tests and compares — once and for all time — the results between the market timing and buy-and-hold strategies. The authors studied data from 1995 through 1999 to determine whether market timing was an effective strategy compared to the buy-and-hold strategy.

They analyzed a variety of monthly, quarterly and annual market timing strategies, producing more than one million possible market timing sequences with, as you'd expect, more than one million different outcomes. Each of these outcomes was compared to the buy-and-hold strategy for the same time period. Now, you know me — and you know my position has always been that the buy-and-hold strategy wins 100% of the time against market timers. Yet, to my shock and dismay, this massive, authoritative, and indisputable study of a million-plus investing scenarios concluded that the buy-and-hold strategy did not beat market timing 100% of the time. Imagine my shock. Imagine my shame.

Imagine my astonishment to discover that the buy-and-hold strategy beats market timing only 99.8% of the time.

It's true. The study's authors determined that market timing beat the buy-and-hold strategy in only 0.2% of the back-tested, real-data simulations. So while I've always said that market timers will never beat those who buy and hold, the truth is, out of 1,000 people who try market timing, two of them will succeed. Imagine my embarrassment.

[106] Yeah, you can feel it coming . . .

People are funny. They insist on selling low and buying high — and then they wonder why their investments don't make any money.

That's what frustrates people who seek out Today's Special. They go to the bakery and see on the top shelf pound cakes filled with fixed income investments. On the middle shelf are pound cakes filled with stocks, and on the bottom shelf are marble cakes containing both. But what's missing are cakes of any other flavors.

This is why shoppers who seek Today's Special fail in their market-timing efforts. Trying to guess which will taste best is a loser's game. This is because deciding whether or not to accept chocolate — I mean stocks — is too vague a question.

You see, even if you've decided that now's the time to pick chocolate, or stocks, you've still got to decide *which* stocks. Milk, dark, semi-sweet or bitter? Will you pick manufacturing stocks, or cyclicals? What about computer, airline, transportation, financial, agricultural, health care, utilities, defense, auto, and biotech stocks?

"I will run in a 1/2 marathon race (13 miles)."

~Kristine Duwar Chaze, Financial Planner, Edelman Financial Services

Two things are infinite: the universe and human stupidity; and I'm not sure about the universe.

~Albert Einstein

I am thoroughly confused when people tell me they track the prices of their investments every day, even though they have no intention of selling them. Do you do this?

WHY?????

If you plan to own your investments for five or 10 years or more, why do you look at the prices every day? You're not selling, so the current price is irrelevant. Thus, there's no point in checking.

Don't say that you check "just for fun" or "merely to stay abreast." The truth is this: Looking at the prices constantly (hourly or daily) or even frequently (once or more per week) could do you much harm. Why? Because you will not buy more if the price is up (because you've already invested all your money), but you might be tempted to sell if the price is down. Thus, by checking prices often, you could become a market timer. The best way to protect yourself from this disease is to not infect yourself with today's information.

You see, it's not a stock market, it's a market of stocks. And you've got to decide which stocks you want.

Real estate investors face the same question. Will they buy commercial properties, or residential ones? What about agricultural, industrial, retail, or resort properties? Have they considered other areas of the real estate world, including mortgage, construction and development companies?

> Never tell me the odds.
>
> ~Han Solo

When people begin to realize that markets are really composed of sub-markets, they begin to reject the notion of trying to pick Today's Special. They even forgo the whole idea of baking a cake. Instead, they bake cupcakes.

To put your odds of buy-and-hold success into perspective, consider these statistics, published by the Forum for Investor Advice:

Odds that you'll win the lottery: 1 in 4,000,000

Odds that you'll be dealt a royal flush: 1 in 650,000

Odds that Earth will be struck by a meteor during your lifetime: 1 in 9,000

Odds that you'll be robbed this year: 1 in 500

Odds that the airlines will lose your luggage: 1 in 186

Odds that you'll be audited by the IRS: 1 in 100

Odds that you'll get snake eyes when rolling the dice: 1 in 36

Odds that you'll go to Disney World this year: 1 in 10

Odds that the bottled water you buy contains tap water: 2 in 10

Odds that you'll eat out today: 5 in 10

Odds that an investment in stocks will make money in any given year: 7 in 10

That's right, over the past 100 years, the stock market has made money 70% of the time. The fact that it didn't in 2000 or 2001 is both uncommon and irrelevant to your long-term planning. Therefore, you should not let recent performance affect your long-term investment strategy.

Chapter 7

Is a Tray of Cupcakes Better Than a Cake?

CHAPTER 7

Is a Tray of Cupcakes Better Than a Cake?

Instead of owning a chocolate cake (stock) just some of the time (the market timer's method), many people always eat chocolate. They simply eat different kinds of chocolate. And they do this by baking cupcakes instead one large cake.[107]

In the world of investing, this is called "sector rotation." Rotators want to be in the sectors that are rising in value while avoiding the sectors that are falling. Sounds simple enough. The problem, though, is that there are a lot of sectors. There are even different levels of sectors.

For example, if your plan is to rotate among the various stock market sectors, and if you used the sectors identified by Ibbotson Associates, you'd have to choose among:

- Aggressive Growth
- Communications
- Emerging Markets
- Equity Income
- Financial
- Foreign
- Growth
- Growth & Income
- Health Care
- Natural Resources
- Precious Metals
- Real Estate
- Technology
- Utilities

[107] We'll explore this concept further in Chapter 12.

That's a big list. And it's not enough to pick the "winning" sectors — you've also got to pick them at the right time. After all, the guy who put all his money into tech stocks in 1996 was a genius, while the guy who did that in early 2000 was an idiot.

Figure 7-1 shows you the sector performance of the stock market for each year from 1984 to 2000. Do you see any patterns?

Neither do I. Instead, each year's rankings seem random.[108] Would you have been able to pick the best sectors each year? Would you have been able to avoid the worst?

And this assumes that you limited your switching efforts to the stock market. What if we go beyond stock sectors and expand into asset classes? Ibbotson gives you 185 to choose from:

Equity
- Domestic U.S. (26 categories)
- International (28)

Fixed Income
Domestic U.S.
- Corporate (17)
- Government (13)
- General (19)

International
- Corporate (10)
- Government (15)
- General (24)

Money Market (10)

Real Estate (9)

Other
- Exchange Rates (2)
- Hard Assets (1)
- Gold (2)
- Silver (3)
- Commodities (2)
- Hedges(1)
- Futures (1)
- Preferred stock (1)
- Art (1)

[108] Proving that "past performance is no indication of future results."

Sector Performance 1984–2000

	1984	1985	1986	1987	1988	1989	1990	1991	1992
Top Performer	Communication 24.0%	Foreign 46.6%	Foreign 47.0%	Precious Metal 38.3%	Communication 23.1%	Communication 46.7%	Health 14.7%	Health 65.2%	Financial 35.6%
2nd	Utility 21.8%	Health 41.0%	Precious Metal 35.6%	Natural Resources 14.3%	Financial 19.3%	Health 37.9%	Technology 0.7%	Financial 57.9%	Communication 14.7%
3rd	Real Estate 21.2%	Financial 39.3%	Utility 24.4%	Communication 9.8%	Equity-Income 18.3%	Emg Markets 31.6%	Utility -1.6%	Aggressive Growth 53.9%	Real Estate 13.9%
4th	Financial 15.8%	Real Estate 29.9%	Communication 22.0%	Foreign 8.5%	Foreign 17.2%	Utility 29.9%	Growth -4.5%	Technology 46.5%	Technology 12.8%
5th	Equity-Income 6.6%	Growth 29.4%	Real Estate 21.0%	Technology 4.1%	Utility 15.9%	Natural Resources 28.6%	Growth & Income -4.8%	Growth 37.5%	Aggressive Growth 10.5%
6th	Growth & Income 4.4%	Communication 29.1%	Emg Markets 20.6%	Growth 3.9%	Growth & Income 15.2%	Aggressive Growth 28.4%	Equity-Income -6.6%	Real Estate 32.9%	Utility 9.8%
7th	Growth -1.6%	Utility 29.1%	Equity-Income 17.3%	Growth & Income 2.1%	Growth 15.0%	Growth 27.4%	Aggressive Growth -9.1%	Communication 30.5%	Equity-Income 9.5%
8th	Foreign -2.4%	Aggressive Growth 28.0%	Growth & Income 16.5%	Health 0.6%	Aggressive Growth 14.8%	Precious Metal 26.0%	Natural Resources -9.7%	Growth & Income 29.2%	Growth 9.0%
9th	Health -2.8%	Growth & Income 27.4%	Health 16.3%	Emg Markets 0.2%	Real Estate 13.6%	Financial 24.3%	Emg Markets -10.4%	Equity-Income 26.5%	Growth & Income 8.4%
10th	Natural Resources -9.4%	Emg Markets 26.7%	Growth 15.2%	Equity-Income -1.3%	Health 11.9%	Growth & Income 23.8%	Foreign -10.8%	Utility 20.2%	Natural Resources 2.7%
11th	Technology -11.5%	Equity-Income 26.6%	Financial 13.9%	Aggressive Growth -2.6%	Emg Markets 10.5%	Equity-Income 22.5%	Communication -13.7%	Emg Markets 17.1%	Emg Markets 2.3%
12th	Aggressive Growth -11.7%	Technology 24.4%	Aggressive Growth 12.5%	Utility -8.7%	Natural Resources 6.7%	Foreign 21.8%	Real Estate -14.6%	Foreign 13.7%	Foreign -3.9%
13th	Emg Markets -11.8%	Natural Resources 15.4%	Natural Resources 11.6%	Financial -11.0%	Technology 4.0%	Technology 19.5%	Financial -15.9%	Natural Resources 4.7%	Health -5.0%
Bottom Performer	Precious Metal -29.2%	Precious Metal -6.8%	Technology 7.2%	Real Estate -12.2%	Precious Metal -17.2%	Real Estate 9.5%	Precious Metal -23.0%	Precious Metal -3.6%	Precious Metal -15.6%

	1993	1994	1995	1996	1997	1998	1999	2000
Top Performer	Precious Metal 80.3%	Technology 14.6%	Health 44.9%	Natural Resources 33.3%	Financial 46.8%	Technology 53.7%	Technology 143.8%	Health 56.11%
2nd	Emg Markets 69.2%	Health 1.9%	Technology 44.0%	Real Estate 31.5%	Communication 30.7%	Communication 47.5%	Communication 75.6%	Natural Resources 30.6%
3rd	Foreign 37.4%	Communication -0.8%	Financial 41.6%	Financial 29.0%	Growth & Income 27.7%	Growth 19.6%	Emg Markets 72.3%	Financial 28.01%
4th	Communication 30.5%	Growth & Income -1.0%	Aggressive Growth 37.0%	Technology 23.1%	Equity-Income 27.1%	Health 19.3%	Aggressive Growth 62.8%	Real Estate 26.77%
5th	Technology 24.4%	Real Estate -1.1%	Growth & Income 32.0%	Growth & Income 21.2%	Utility 25.6%	Utility 18.8%	Foreign 44.5%	Real Estate 8.85%
6th	Natural Resources 23.3%	Natural Resources -1.3%	Growth 31.5%	Growth 20.2%	Growth 25.1%	Growth & Income 17.6%	Natural Resources 30.1%	Equity Income 6.73%
7th	Aggressive Growth 20.6%	Foreign -1.6%	Equity-Income 29.8%	Equity-Income 18.9%	Real Estate 23.3%	Aggressive Growth 14.9%	Growth 28.9%	Growth and Income -0.88%
8th	Real Estate 18.4%	Growth -1.6%	Communication 28.2%	Emg Markets 14.2%	Health 20.7%	Equity-Income 11.7%	Health 18.0%	Growth -3.87%
9th	Utility 15.3%	Equity-Income -1.7%	Utility 27.1%	Aggressive Growth 13.8%	Aggressive Growth 17.2%	Foreign 9.5%	Utility 14.6%	Aggressive Growth -11.23%
10th	Financial 15.2%	Aggressive Growth -2.3%	Natural Resources 17.2%	Foreign 12.9%	Technology 10.5%	Financial 6.4%	Growth & Income 13.3%	Foreign -15.73%
11th	Equity-Income 13.9%	Financial -2.5%	Real Estate 15.1%	Health 12.4%	Foreign 6.4%	Precious Metal -12.0%	Precious Metal 6.5%	Prec Metals -16.72%
12th	Growth 12.3%	Utility -8.9%	Foreign 7.2%	Utility 10.6%	Natural Resources 2.1%	Real Estate -15.8%	Equity-Income 5.3%	Emg Markets -30.83%
13th	Growth & Income 11.3%	Emg Markets -10.0%	Precious Metal 5.3%	Precious Metal 10.0%	Emg Markets -3.3%	Natural Resources -25.2%	Financial -1.4%	Technology -31.76%
Bottom Performer	Health 2.8%	Precious Metal -13.1%	Emg Markets -3.9%	Communication 9.3%	Precious Metal -41.3%	Emg Markets -26.9%	Real Estate -3.6%	Communications -34.88%

Figure 7-1

With all these choices, it seems to make a huge difference when you buy and sell. According to *The Economist*, if in 1900 you had invested just *one dollar* into that year's best asset class, switching each year into what would become the next year's best asset class, you would have had, by 1999, thirteen quadrillion dollars. That's

$13,000,000,000,000,000

In contrast, Bill Gates, the world's richest man, has only[109]

$41,000,000,000

If the world's richest person has been unable to produce profits anywhere near the so-called mathematical potential, why do you think you'd be able to do it?

Oh, I'm sorry, I was being presumptuous. You don't think you can pick hot stocks, and you never try. You're right, of course. No one ever tries. Nobody ever invests money into some deal on the hopes that their small investment will turn into an overnight fortune. Certainly not you.

You, certainly, have never invested in tulips. You also can't imagine why anyone ever would.

Psst. Hey Buddy, Wanna Buy Some Tulip Bulbs?

I don't know if you're familiar with the "Tulip Craze." If you've never heard the story, you won't believe it's true. But it really happened.

The story dates back to 1559. Conrad Guestner brought the first tulip bulbs from Constantinople to Holland and Germany, and people fell in love with them. Soon the beautiful and rare tulip bulbs became a status symbol for the wealthy.

Although early buyers prized the lovely flower, it didn't take long for speculators to get involved. They discovered they could make money trading the bulbs, and by 1634, the rage for owning tulips had spread to the mid-

[109] As if!

dle classes of Dutch society; merchants and shopkeepers began competing for inventory in tulip bulbs.

How silly did it get? Well, near the height of tulip mania in 1635, a single bulb was traded for the following items:

- four tons of wheat
- eight tons of rye
- one bed
- four oxen
- eight pigs
- 12 sheep
- one suit of clothes
- two casks of wine
- four tons of beer
- two tons of butter
- 1,000 pounds of cheese and
- one silver drinking cup

The present day value of these items? Nearly $35,000!

"I want to sail the Mediterranean in my mid- to late 60s."

~William Watson, 50, News Service Owner

Can you imagine spending $35,000 for a *single* tulip bulb? This was happening in Holland in the mid-17th century. It was getting so bizarre that people were selling everything they owned — homes, livestock, everything — for the privilege of owning tulips, on the expectation that the bulbs would continue to grow in value. As a result, prices — in today's dollars — ranged from $17,000 all the way to $76,000. *For a single bulb.*

By 1636, tulip trading was added to the Amsterdam stock exchange, as well as to exchanges in Rotterdam, Haarlem, Levytown, Horne and other European forums. Popular interest shifted from hobbyists and collectors to speculators and gamblers. Tulip notaries and clerks were appointed to record transactions, and public laws and regulations were developed to control the tulip craze. In *The Ottoman Centuries: The Rise and Fall of the Turkish Empire,* author Lord Kinross writes that Sultan Ahmed III's reign became known as the Reign of the Tulip, and that the tulip became known as "the gold of Europe."

But in 1636, tulip prices weakened, as people began to liquidate their holdings. It began slowly, then gained momentum. Confidence was soon destroyed, and panic seized the market. Within six weeks, tulip prices crashed by 90%. There were widespread contract defaults, followed by liens against owners.

At first the Dutch government refused to interfere. Instead, it advised tulip holders to figure out for themselves some plan to stabilize prices and restore public confidence. The plans failed. Eventually, assembled deputies in Amsterdam declared null and void all contracts that were made prior to November 1636, the height of the mania. Buyers after that date were permitted to pay just 10% of the previously agreed price to settle their contracts. This left sellers with 90% losses.

But tulip prices continued to fall. Next, the provincial council in The Hague was asked to invent some measure to stabilize tulip prices and public credit. Those efforts failed. Tulip prices fell lower. In Amsterdam, judges refused to honor tulip contracts, regarding them as gambling activities. Thus, those who had invested huge sums to acquire tulip bulbs, on the hopes of selling them to others at even higher prices, suffered ruinous losses.

Tulip prices then plunged to less than the present equivalent of one dollar each. Imagine having bought a tulip for $76,000, only to discover that it was now worth less than a dollar! Commerce in Holland suffered a severe shock, and did not recover for many years.

Now, I know you are saying, "Come on! . . . Who could possibly have gotten caught up in that?"

I know how you feel. After all, we're talking tulips here — not food, shelter, clothing, or weapons for defense! We're talking TULIPS! What practical value could tulips have had in 1636? And what could cause people to lose such control of their senses???

"I will live in Scotland where my ancestors lived after I retire in 1½ years."

~Terry McAfee, 60, Chemist

As preposterous as this story sounds, be assured that it really did happen. And believe me when I tell you it could happen again.

No way, you say? Well, then, I have only two words for you:

Beanie Baby.

And if those two words don't put a chill in your spine, then try these:

Internet Stocks.

> **Below is an actual email I received in the summer of 2001:**
>
> I hope someone could get back to me. After buying your wonderful book, *Ordinary People, Extraordinary Wealth*, I have just a question. No where in your bookd [*sic*] mentioned anything about achieving instant wealth. Yes, I know, crazy, but somehow I thought that there were some tips to achieve this too! That is, aside from winning the lottery or going to Vegas and winning a jackpot! Is it only possible to achieve wealth through long term savings?
>
> Please respond as soon as possible.
>
> **I am not printing here my reply. I'll leave that to your imagination.**

You see, people flock to certain asset classes or sectors because, to be blunt, they want to get rich quick. Oh, they never state it that way, and they'd be insulted if you accused them of being greedy. For sure, they'd argue that they are just making informed, rational investment decisions that merely are taking advantage of opportunities in the marketplace.

Nonsense. These people are mad. People who paid $80 in 2000 for a single share of Cisco stock were as crazy as the guy who paid $76,000 in 1636 for one tulip bulb. All of them were delusional.

I have proof, too. Read *Extraordinary Popular Delusions*[110] *and the Madness of Crowds* by Charles Mackay, written in 1841. Also:

- *Manias, Panics and Crashes* by Charles P. Kindleberger
- *The Fortune Sellers: The Big Business of Buying and Selling Predictions* by William A. Sherden
- *Devil Take the Hindmost: A History of Financial Speculation* by Edward Chancellor
- *Money, Greed and Risk: Why Financial Crises and Crashes Happen* by Charles R. Morris

Indeed, you'll discover that the Tulip Craze was not an isolated event. It was followed by the South Seas Bubble of 1720. After stock in the South Seas company rose 1,000%, the market for the shares crashed, causing the stock to fall 84%.

Beware "Bubble Mania"

Event	Occurrence	Bubbled To	Decline After Bubble Burst
Tulip Craze	1634–36	5,900%	–93%
South Seas Bubble	1719–20	1,000%	–84%
Panic of 1893	1893	1,000%	–95%
Industrial Revolution	1921–29	497%	–87%
Silver Market	1979–82	710%	–88%
Japanese Stock	1965–89	3,270%	–63%
Internet Mania	1994–2001	4,000%	–83% so far

Figure 7-2

And don't think you're too smart to fall for something like this — because you're not as smart as Isaac Newton. On April 20, 1720, Newton sold his stake in the South Seas Company for a 100% profit. But when prices kept rising, he jumped back in, and lost the then-huge sum of $20,000. For the rest of his life, writes Charles P. Kindleberger in *Manias, Panics and Crashes*, Newton could never bear to hear the name South Sea. Said Newton, "I can calculate the motions of the heavenly bodies, but not the madness of people."

[110] See?

Year	Market Collapse	Country
1763	sugar	Amsterdam
1772	housing	Britain
1799	commodities	Hamburg
1819	commodities	England
1825	bonds, mines, cotton	England
1837	cotton, land	United States
1848	railways, wheat	Europe
1864	cotton	England, France and Italy
1873	railroad stocks, land	United States
1882	bank stocks	France
1890	silver and gold	United States
1893	land	Australia
1907	bank lending	Italy
1920	ships, commodities and inventories	Britain and United States

Figure 7-3

Time marches on, but history repeats itself. Panics and crashes have occurred repeatedly in the past 300 years, all over the world. See Figure 7-3 for examples provided by Kindleberger.

Although Figure 7-3 stops at 1920, that doesn't mean there haven't been financial crises since then. Quite the contrary:

- The Crash of '29 followed speculation in land and stock prices, and led to an 87% decline in the Dow Jones Industrial Average.
- Speculation in the foreign exchange markets led to a worldwide panic in the 1950s and 1960s; it didn't hit the U.S. until 1973 . . .
- . . . which was quickly followed by our worst recession since World War II. Although the cause is widely blamed on the oil embargo, let's not forget that the early 1970s saw speculation in everything from stocks and office buildings to oil tankers and Boeing 747s. Prices came tumbling down in 1974–1975.

- The dollar, U.S. farmland prices, oil, and Third World bank loans all crashed, sequentially, from 1979 to 82. The Hunt brothers tried to corner the silver market during this period, causing a crash in that market. Gold, too, hit its all-time high, which didn't last long.

For a more recent fright, consider the Japanese stock market, which has fallen 63% from its mid-1980s high — a decline from which the Japanese have not yet recovered.

And then of course, there's Internet Mania. It looks incredibly stupid now,[111] but at the height of the craze in 1998, people were paying absurd prices for technology and dot-com stocks. For example, in 1998:

- Amazon.com gained 1,066%
- eBay jumped 1,005%
- America Online rose 686%
- Yahoo! grew 684%
- Excite was up 280%
- Netscape increased 249%
- and E*Trade rose 203%

We all know what ultimately happened to these stocks.

I suppose that the people who bought these stocks, and others like them, can be forgiven for not learning the lesson of the South Seas company. After all, that crash occurred 300 years ago; the lesson we should have learned isn't found in 5th-grade history books.

By permission of Johnny Hart and Creators Syndicate, Inc.

[111] Actually, it looked stupid to us then — throughout the mania, my colleagues and I counseled our clients to avoid buying tech stocks. Some of our clients were annoyed in the late 1990s, but they were relieved (if not thrilled) by 2000.

A common measure of a stock's value is its "Price to Earnings Ratio," or P/E. The higher the P/E, the riskier the stock. Typically, the overall stock market's average P/E is 15 to 18. If that average falls lower, say to 12 or 13, investors consider stocks to be underpriced and therefore worth buying. If the average P/E reaches 21 or 22, investors consider the overall market to be overpriced. To put this in perspective, the stock market crashed in October 1987 when the average P/E reached 27.

Within this context, consider America Online's P/E in 1998. It was 453. And the other dot-coms? Many of them didn't even have a P/E because none of those companies had ever made a profit![112]

But investors bought these stocks anyway, and at ever higher prices — on the myth that someone else would come along and pay even more for them later.[113]

These folks weren't fazed by the fact that many of these companies were not making any money. As one Internet stock buyer, Dorine Essey, told *Forbes* magazine at the height of the mania, "I pay no attention to P/Es. They don't matter." Maybe not to her, and maybe not then. But I suspect they matter to her now.[114]

But what excuse do we have for forgetting about "The Nifty Fifty"? These were the glamour stocks of the early 1970s — companies like McDonald's, Xerox and Polaroid. After rising to incredible levels in the late 1960s and early 1970s, they collapsed in the 1974–78 recession. As recounted in *A Random Walk Down Wall Street*:

- McDonald's went from a high of $3.76 per share (split adjusted) in December 1972 to $2.40 in December 1980, a 36% loss over eight years.
- Xerox dropped from $49.74 per share to $19.95, a 60% loss.
- Polaroid fell from $63 a share to $12.50, an 80% loss.

This was only 30 years ago. There should be lots of people around today who remember what happened. Lots of people alive today also should

"I want to visit China in 2 years."

~Frank Gormas, 61, Retired, Telecommunications

[112] You can't divide a stock price by zero.
[113] This is called the "Greater Fools Theory." It's the basis for every mania.
[114] And if you think this Internet thing was limited to the nation's youth, who were raised on technology, think again: When Dorine was quoted by *Forbes*, she was 70 years old.

remember the electronics IPOs of the early 1960s; huge losses were sustained after those stocks enjoyed a quick run, too, as shown in Figure 7-4.

Or, when thinking of the Internet, did so many say, "This time, it's different!"?

Although Internet mania never made any sense, millions of people were happy to spend trillions of dollars to buy those stocks.

Manias occur periodically — history repeats itself — because people ignore the lessons of history. Too often, too many people think, "This time, it's different."

Even people who *know* it's a mania fall for it. They get in while the mania is in full force because they think they're smart enough to be able to get out before the mania ends.

By 1999, signs of a market top were everywhere. Literally. After seeing this ad on a telephone pole, I wrote in my newsletter *Inside Personal Finance* that the end of Internet Mania had to be near.

The sign reads, "INVESTORS . . . Powerful . . . but simple Stock Trading System 50–224% Returns Call xxx-xxxx."

That promotion violated more than a few SEC regulations, as well as the NASD Rules of Fair Practice. I particularly enjoy the fact that they promised exactly 224%. That sounds much more legitimate than 225%!

In my newsletter, I urged readers, when calling about the deal, to ask for the 224% return instead of the 50% return.

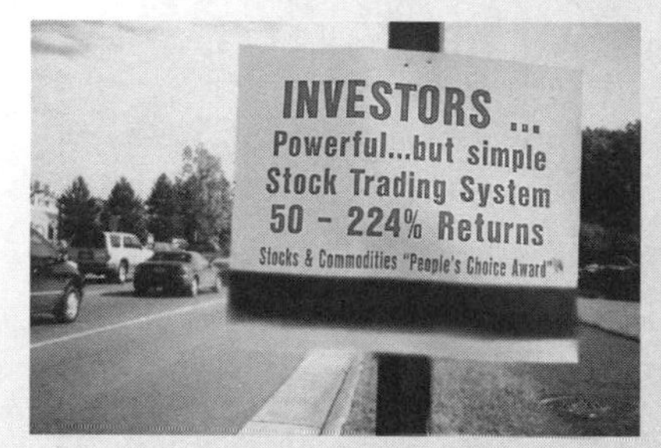

Stock	Became available to public	Initial Price	High in 1961	High in 1962
Hydro-Space Technology	July 19, 1960	3	7	1
Geophysics	December 8, 1960	14	58	9
Boonton Electronic	March 6, 1961	5½	24½	1

Figure 7-4

Earl Sparling is the author of *Mystery Men of Wall Street and the Great Crash*. Below is an edited version of the introduction to his book.

Giants of a new breed are in control today, different from the Vanderbilts and Morgans of the past. This is the story of the new kings, and also of the "greatest bull market in history," which they dominated.

These men operate in the stock market on a scale never dreamed of before. They speak casually of billions as the men of the old Wall Street spoke of millions. They have destroyed precedent and tradition. They have ushered in an era of major manipulation, of tidal movements in speculation, of pools and syndicates so enormous that the operating combinations of other days are dwarfed to toy proportions.

The automobile was spawning a new industry, a new race of giants, and the swiftest rise of fortunes the world had ever seen. The victors emerged with entirely new theories of industry and economy. . . . Wall Street and the bankers who once had ruled it had never seen that done before.

Defiant of tradition and precedent, operating on a scale never dreamed of in the past, these new men were helping to develop a stock market boom without example in Wall Street's history.

Gradually as prices went higher and higher the public flocked in, buying as never before. Millions who never touched stocks began speculating. There had been waves of public buying and other boom markets of course but never on such a scale . . . lawyers, grocers, physicians, waiters, clergymen and chorus singers were learning to acquire wealth without labor. From every lip dropped stories of fortunes gained in a week by this or that lucky stroke. Florists, jewelers, restaurateurs and tailors rejoiced in the collateral prosperity secured to them by the boom in stocks.

Sparling was not describing Internet Mania. He wrote the above in 1930, and was talking about the stock market of the 1920s and the Crash of '29.

History repeated itself — again — in the summer of 1962. Below are the abridged comments from *Life* magazine, written after the Dow Jones Industrial Average had dropped from an all-time high of 700 to about 550:

To the question, 'What has gone wrong in the stock market?' there can only be one real answer: The market came down because it had gone too high. It was such a vast bull market, rising so spectacularly, that anybody with eyes was bound to see it. Over the past eight years, millions of new investors jumped into the market . . . there were new companies with untried management, small earnings and dubious prospects — with nothing but a prayer and a catchy space age name — which were bid up as much as 400% within a few months . . . on the assumption that the prices would go still higher.

'The market was badly in need of a correction,' a market analyst said self-critically, 'the trouble was that we got away from any real study of security values and into a numbers game.'

Will we never learn?

We've already shown the folly of trying to pull that one off. But there's another folly that requires our attention: Too many people think some sectors simply are better than others — as if jumping from a vanilla cake to chocolate cake and back again can be an effective strategy.

So, let's see if such a strategy can work. We've already looked at stocks vs. bonds, so now we'll contrast the historical performances of:

- small cap stocks vs. large cap stocks[115]
- growth stocks vs. value stocks
- U.S. stocks vs. international stocks
- newly issued stocks vs. long-established stocks

Figure 7-5 compares the performance of small stocks with large stocks, from 1926 to 1999, as measured by the Small Company Stock Index and the S&P 500 Stock Index. Conventional wisdom says small stocks always beat large stocks, on the theory that it's easier for small companies to become big companies than it is for big companies to become even bigger ones.[116]

[115] Cap is short for "market capitalization," or the value of all the shares of a company. In July 2001, Microsoft's market cap was $361 billion, based on a $67 share price and the fact the company has issued about 5.4 billion shares.

[116] After all, it's easier to double one dollar than it is to double one billion dollars, and this makes sense since investors are focused on percentage increases rather than on increases in absolute values. Because small companies are more likely to go out of business than large ones, investors of small stocks say they get higher returns precisely because they are taking higher risks.

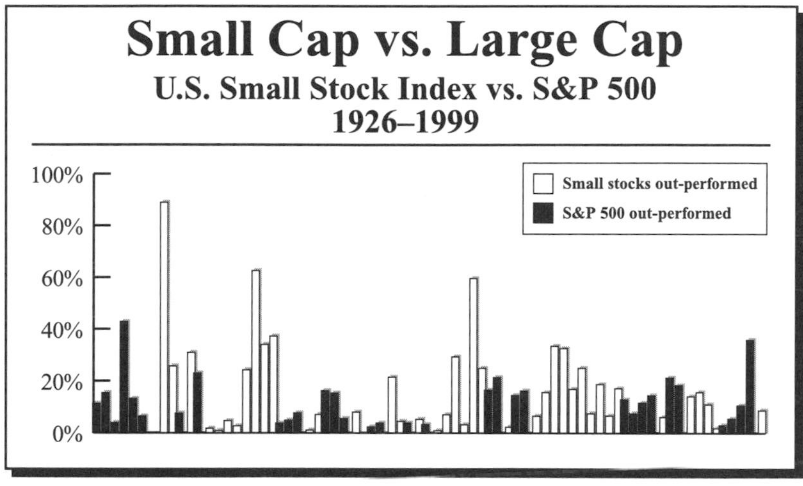

Figure 7-5

And Figure 7-5 shows this is not true: Not only do large cap stocks often beat small cap stocks, they do so unpredictably.

We see similar results when comparing the performance of growth stocks to value stocks from 1975 to 1998. Although growth stocks are supposed to make more money than value stocks, Figure 7-6 shows they ended up in a near dead heat. In fact, the S&P/BARRA 500 Growth Index beat the S&P/BARRA 500 Value Index 56% of the time over the 25 years ending 2000, while the S&P/BARRA 500 Value Index beat the S&P/ BARRA 500 Growth Index the remaining 44% of the time. One thing is certain: Growth beats value and vice versa.[117]

Growth vs. Value

1975–1998

	S&P Value Annualized	S&P Growth Annualized
1975–1979	**19.4%**	10.3%
1980–1982	14.3%	**15.3%**
1983–1988	**19.0%**	13.7%
1989–1991	12.9%	**23.7%**
1992–1993	**14.5%**	3.4%
1994–1998	19.9%	**27.9%**
Total Period	17.5%	16.3%

Figure 7-6

[117] My apologies to Yogi Berra.

"Own a home on the Chesapeake where I can park my new sailboat and one day take that boat to the Bahamas. In 10 years."

~Anonymous, 42, Landscape Contractor

Investors often struggle deciding whether to invest in U.S. stocks or international ones. Considering that only 24% of all publicly held stocks in the world are found in the United States, according to Federation Internationale des Bourses de Valeurs, investing in overseas companies certainly makes sense. But does doing so make more money?

Figure 7-7 compares the S&P 500 against the European, Australasia and Far Eastern Indexes for the period 1975 to 1999. Just like the prior charts, it shows random patterns and unpredictability.

So, okay, maybe it's a sucker's bet to choose between big and small stocks, or between foreign and domestic stocks. What about "getting in on the ground floor"? People love to play "if only" games.

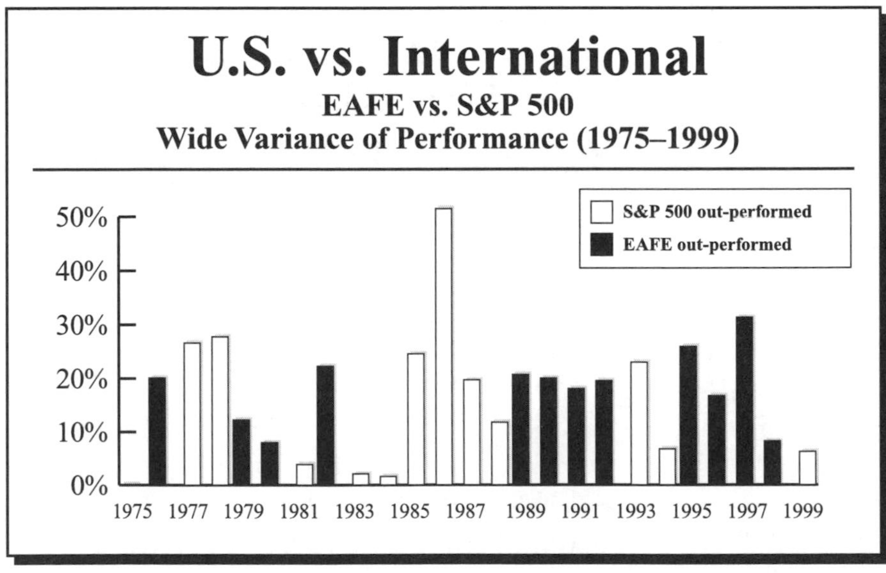

Figure 7-7

You know these games:

If only I bought IBM in the 1950s.

If only I bought McDonald's in the 1960s.

If only I bought Microsoft in the 1980s.

These *if onlys* entice people to buy into the "next" new thing. I'm referring, of course, to IPOs — Initial Public Offerings. That's what it's called when a company issues its stock to the public for the first time. You missed out on America Online, so you promise yourself you won't miss the next new thing. This is why IPOs garner lots of media attention, and why consumers clamor to buy shares.

> We have met the enemy, and he is us.
>
> ~Pogo

But are these investments profitable?

The University of Florida studied every IPO issued from 1970 to 1990. Its research found that, after six months, new issues were down an average of 1.1% from their opening price. But during the same period, the average price of other companies in the same industry were up 3.4%, or more than three times as much.

Similar results were found after five years: IPOs were up an average 5.1%, while their competitors' stocks were up an average of 11.8%.

Clearly, buying the stock of some hot new company is not nearly as profitable as many think. Just ask those who bought Internet stocks. *Business Week* compiled data on the performance of every dot-com's stock offering that occurred from January 1, 1997, to April 1, 2001. You'll see the results in Figure 7-8. According to the magazine, Wall Street launched 814 IPOs in that period. By April 1, 2001, only 367 of those companies were still in business. Of them, 316 (86%) were trading below their initial offering price, and 224 were down 75% or more. Investors have lost $2.5 trillion since NASDAQ hit its peak in 2000.

Who are the people getting hurt by this? Not the underwriters — they earn millions of dollars in fees every time they take a company public.

The Internet IPOs

	No. of IPOs	Avg. Return
Merrill Lynch	20	–82%
Robertson Stephens	38	–65%
CS First Boston	75	–41%
Goldman Sachs	47	–16%
Hummer Winblad	7	–91%
Internet Capital Group	6	–79%
idealab!	7	–84%
CMGI	7	–95%

Figure 7-8

Not the brokers — they earn millions of dollars in commissions every time they convince consumers to buy the shares. Not the company's founders — they walk away with millions (and in many cases, billions) of dollars raised by the IPO.[118] No, the people who get hurt — the ones who have lost $2.5 trillion so far — are the people buying now publicly available shares.

In March 2000, Merrill Lynch launched its own Internet mutual fund, called the Internet Strategies Fund. And why not? Investors were screaming for these hot stocks. Within a month, the firm's clients invested $1.1 billion, no doubt at the urging of Merrill's brokers. Bad timing: That same month, the NASDAQ reached its all-time high. A little more than one year later, the fund was down 77% and Merrill shut the fund down.

As Morningstar's Dan Culloton told *The Wall Street Journal*, "History shows that fund companies often introduce new funds at the worst possible times."

[118] After all, whose stock is it that you think Wall Street is selling to the public? When some guy starts a company, he owns 100% of the stock. When Wall Street launches an IPO, what they're selling to the public are the founder's shares. He's the seller and you're the buyer. And you think you're the smart one because you're clever enough to be buying this stuff? Think again.

Who were the buyers of those shares?

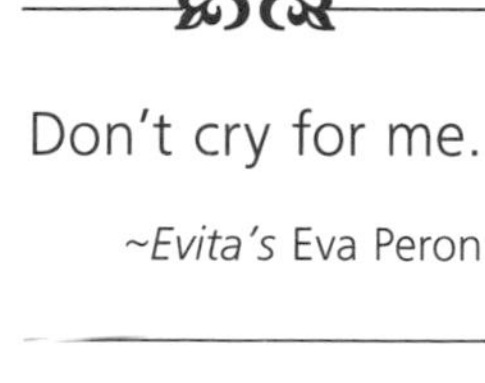

Don't cry for me.

~*Evita's* Eva Peron

- It wasn't Amazon.com founder Jeff Bezos. He's worth $1.7 billion, despite the fact that investors who bought Amazon's stock at its high have lost 87% of their investment as of June 2001.
- It wasn't Michael Saylor, founder of Microstrategy. He's worth $179 million, even though his stock is down 98%.[119]
- Don't cry for Priceline.com founder Jay Walker, either. Even though investors have lost 95% buying his stock, he's still worth $103 million. (He told *Newsweek* that the drop in his company's stock is "not the end of the world." Guess not.)
- TheStreet.com's founder, Jim Cramer, isn't among those wiped out by the stock's 95% plummet. His holdings are still worth $10.5 million.

All the above figures are from public filings and reflect only the value of each founder's company stake. Because they've all cashed in some of their stocks for millions, their net worths are certain to be higher than the figures you see here — usually much higher. So, no, the founders are not the ones to cry for. Instead, the losers are the retail customers who bought into their hype, paying ridiculously high prices to buy their shares or the shares of mutual funds that invested in them, like the one offered by Merrill Lynch. You should cry for the people who invested their retirement assets and regular savings. People who lost in a year money that had taken them perhaps a decade — perhaps a lifetime — to accumulate.

A criminal is a person with predatory instincts who has not sufficient capital to form a corporation.

~Howard Scott

[119] It fell 62% in a single day after the company reported it was making "accounting changes."

But was Merrill really at fault? Maybe Merrill was simply providing a product its customers wanted to buy. Doesn't much of the fault belong to the consumers who allowed themselves to become caught up in the fad — just like those who, centuries earlier, demanded tulip bulbs?[120]

Fads never last — vanilla remains the favorite flavor — and each fad's end comes without warning. Winning sectors are impossible to pick consistently because they always change. Trying to be in the market at the right time is a feat no one has been able to master. And this is why people who focus on cupcakes tend to succeed only at frustrating themselves.

So how should you bake your cake? Follow my recipe.

"My immediate goals are to continue restoring two antique cars and several home improvement projects. My longer term goals include finding some religious or humanitarian work, becoming computer literate, and perhaps finding another dog like the 1-in-a-million dog I had while growing up."

~Gordon Muir, 65, Retired,
Former Teacher and Corporate
Automotive Instructor

---

[120] You be the judge.

CHAPTER 8

Bake a Cake Using Ric's Recipe

CHAPTER 8

Bake a Cake Using Ric's Recipe

As a prelude to understanding how you should bake your cake (i.e., manage your money), consider this set of statistics: From 1971 to 1998, according to data from T. Rowe Price, you would have earned 13.7% per year if you had invested in the Wilshire 5000.[121] And if you had invested in international stocks, as represented by the EAFE Index, you would have earned the same 13.7% per year. Thus, in either case, $10,000 would have grown to $360,000.

> What we see depends mainly on what we look for.
>
> ~John Lubbock

But here's the interesting thing: If you had invested 70% of your money in the Wilshire and 30% into the EAFE, your return would have been 14.0%. That means your $10,000 would have been worth $390,000 — $30,000 more than if you had invested in one or the other.

That doesn't seem possible; after all, if each has an average of 13.7%, how can combining them produce 14.0%? It's simple: Although each produced an average of 13.7%, neither actually produced that amount in any given year — just as no family really has 2.3 children, even though that's the

[121] An index comprised of all U.S. stocks.

average. So, when combining their *actual* returns for each year, they were able to produce an average that was higher than either produced individually.

Understanding this is the key to understanding how money turns into wealth, so let me share with you an example I used in *The Truth About Money*. Two investors each have $25,000 to invest for 25 years. The first investor places his entire $25,000 into a bank CD earning 5%, and after 25 years, he has $84,659.

"Starting July 1, I'm going to live on a boat and travel the good old U.S.A. with my wife and dog."

~John Grimes, 58, Printer

The other investor splits his $25,000 into five piles of $5,000 each and invests like so:

Investment	Value after 25 years
$5,000 into lottery tickets	$ -0-
$5,000 stuffed under the mattress	$ 5,000
$5,000 into an ordinary savings account that earns 2% per year	$ 8,203
$5,000 into U.S. government-guaranteed bonds, earning 5% per year	$ 17,969
$5,000 into stocks, earning 12% per year	$ 85,000
$25,000	$115,135

The second investor has accumulated 36% more than the first investor.

And that's where our portfolio-modeling journey has taken us.

We've learned that:

- Those who bake pound cakes find that by using only one (albeit safe) ingredient, their money fails to grow enough to enable them to achieve financial success;

- Although marble cakes feature a second flavor, they still fail to win the blue ribbon. Similarly, investors get unsatisfactory results when they fail to maintain a proper balance between risk and reward;

- Cake eaters often discover that Today's Special is little more than day-old cake. Cakes considered "special" often are inedible, because they were cooked under a temperature set too high, or perhaps they were removed from the oven too soon. Investors get equally frustrating results when they put too much money into one investment, or when they sell investments too soon — something market timers often do in their futile effort to enjoy Today's Special; and

- Bakers who can't decide what to own play games bouncing among cupcakes, just as Sector Rotators jump out of one fad and into the next.

Thus, the recipe I'm about to show you evolved precisely because the other four recipes haven't worked. Or, stated more accurately, although each of the preceding four has positive attributes, each also has fatal flaws.

"Attend Wimbledon tennis match and take riverboat cruise within five to six years."

~Abraham Schwartz, 79, Retired

So, we're going to take the best from each recipe to develop a new, superior version:

- From the Pound Cake, we know it's important to go with ingredients that perform consistently, but we can't restrict ourselves to such ingredients because we'll end up with a cake so tasteless we won't want to eat it.

- From the Marble Cake, we recognize that adding an ingredient can help our cake rise to desired levels.

- From Today's Special, we learn the folly of picking what others are touting, merely because they are touting it.

- And by studying cupcakes, we know there are many flavors, and we'll get better results if we use all of them in every cake instead of only using some of them some of the time. We also learn that cakes don't necessarily rise faster by increasing the oven's temperature, and that moving our cake from oven to oven doesn't improve its flavor. We'll get better results by following our recipe, carefully mixing our batter, then leaving it to bake at its own pace.

"I would like to own a 40-foot sailboat."

~Thomas W. Wood, Financial Planner, Edelman Financial Services

These lessons, indeed, comprise Ric's Recipe. But it's really not my idea; it's called Modern Portfolio Theory, and the recipe is, in my opinion, the most effective way to invest.[122]

Modern Portfolio Theory was invented (discovered?) by a fellow named Harry Markowitz in 1952. It was the basis of his master's thesis in economics and, at the time, ignored by Wall Street. But Markowitz's work earned him the Nobel Prize for Economics in 1990.

[122] But it's not the newest way. The latest craze in the planning community is the Stochastic Model, or Monte Carlo simulation. In footnote 72, I gave that idea as much due as it's worth. Other ideas, too, have come and gone (remember the Dogs of the Dow?). Some of these ideas are interesting, and some have valuable elements — but all fail and are usually quickly forgotten. MPT works, and works better than anything I've yet seen. So, other than wanting to show their clients the newest thing (craze?) in planning, I don't understand why so many planners migrate from model to model so often.

Markowitz's principles are perhaps best illustrated by a study published in August 1986 by *Financial Analysts Journal.* The Brinson study, as it's come to be known (having been written by Gary P. Brinson, L. Randolph Hood and Gilbert L. Beebower), is itself a controversial and oft-cited report — primarily because so many advisors misquote and misinterpret its findings.[123]

The Brinson study asked a simple but very interesting question: Why do the investment returns of institutional investors vary?

At first glance, this might not appear to be a very intuitive question. After all, it's obvious that different bakers obtain different results because they use different ingredients. Likewise, different investors obtain different results because they use different investments.

Yesterday is not ours to recover, but tomorrow is ours to win or lose.

~Lyndon B. Johnson

Or do they? Imagine that you manage the funds for the California Public Employees Retirement System. CALPERS is the nation's largest pension fund, worth $152 billion as of June 2001. Imagine a friend of yours handles the pension assets for the Ford Motor Company, worth about $55 billion. With all the money you each have, will you and your friend actually buy different investments?

Let me put it to you this way: Say you and I walk into a supermarket with $100 each. It's virtually certain that we'll walk out with completely different items. But if you and I each enter the store with $10 million, we'll both exit with identical holdings; with so much money to spend, we'll each be forced to buy everything the store has to offer.

So it is with institutional (rather than retail) investors.[124] And this is precisely what Brinson set out to discover: If institutional investors have so much money to invest that they inevitably own everything, why do their investment returns vary?

[123] For a more complete commentary on the Brinson study, read Rule 44 in *The New Rules of Money.*

[124] It's obvious what an institutional investor is. A retail investor is a typical consumer — like you and me.

To find out, Brinson examined the performance of 82 very large pension plans — plans that invest hundreds of millions or even billions of dollars. The study discovered that 93.6% of the difference in variation in performance[125] is due not to the stocks each plan buys (since they're all buying everything), but to how much of each they buy.

Why Is Bill Gates the Richest Man in the World?

Bill Gates isn't rich because he owns Microsoft. After all, millions of people own that stock.[126] No, what makes Bill Gates so wealthy is that he owns *a whole lot* of Microsoft.

This is an important[127] distinction. Even if you were brilliant enough to buy Microsoft in 1985, you wouldn't be rich if you only bought one share and left the rest of your money in the bank.

Thus, not only must you buy the right investment, you must buy enough of it: How you slice your cake — or rather, how much of each ingredient you place into each slice — is the key to successful investing.

This is where the financial press gets it wrong. Every cover touts stories like "Five Fabulous Funds for the Future" and "Six Sizzling Stocks for the Summertime." They never give you an asset allocation model — either because they haven't figured this out yet, or because they fear that if they give you their model, they won't have anything else to say.

And so, with each edition, issue and broadcast, the Marble Cake eaters in the financial press fill you with stories of how certain cupcakes have succeeded, while admonishing you to buy Today's Special. But as you've now seen, it doesn't matter whether you buy growth or value, large cap or small cap, or U.S. or international. What matters is how much of each you do buy and how long you keep them.

---

[125] Not performance itself, but the volatility of that performance. Again, see Rule 44 of *The New Rules of Money*. And that's the last time I'm telling you before I send you to your room.
[126] Probably including you. According to *Financial Planning* magazine, one-third of all large-cap stock funds hold shares in Microsoft, as of April 2001 — making it the 4th most commonly held stock by mutual funds. (Only Cisco, Intel and Citigroup are owned by more funds). If you own a stock fund, chances are you own Microsoft (and those other three, too!).
[127] And pretty funny.

Go Ahead: Slice Your Cake

No matter how much money you have, it always adds up to one hundred. Not one hundred *dollars*, one hundred *percent*. The amount of dollars you have in your pocket or purse fluctuates constantly, but the amount is always 100% of how much you have at any given time.

This is why it's easier to work with percentages. So let's use percentages when slicing your cake, er, building your investment portfolio.

As we begin, we see that, broadly speaking, there are nine asset classes:

- Cash and cash equivalents
- Government securities
- Bonds
- Stocks
- Real estate
- International securities
- Precious metals
- Natural resources and commodities
- Hedge positions

Within each asset class are sectors, as mentioned earlier. Your first task, then, is to decide how many of the above asset classes you want in your cake.[128] Your cake does not have to contain nine slices (one for each class) and some slices can be larger than others. For example, your chocolate slice might be much larger than your vanilla slice, and you might omit tutti-frutti altogether.

> ***"I would like to renovate an older home and operate it as a B&B. I'll start within the next two years."***
>
> **~JoAn Drake, 54, Telecommunications Consultant**

After you've finished, you'll be ready to move on to the next step: Decide the specific ingredients of each slice. Will your chocolate slice contain

[128] If you don't like working with percentages, try using pennies. You've got 100 of them, so divvy them up as you wish.

milk chocolate, dark chocolate or white chocolate? Perhaps all three. What about chocolate chips or sprinkles? By this illustration, you see that you've decided to place "x" percent of your portfolio into stocks, and that you've further divvied that portion of your money among the various sectors (value, growth, U.S., international, and so forth) of the stock market.

This is a very individual process, one that is based entirely on your personal circumstances, liquidity needs, family and financial obligations, goals, risk tolerance and experience. It is the one area of financial planning that is dynamic, not static, and therefore I cannot lay out on these pages what ought to be the specific ingredients of "your" cake.

But before you ask for your money back, I *can* do two things that make up for this shortcoming. First, I'll show you how to manage that cake of yours once you've baked it, and second, I'll give you some excellent[129] guidelines to help you avoid the mistakes most people make when baking a cake— I mean, building a portfolio.

First, let's manage that cake you've baked.[130]

Who am I kidding? Most people don't build a portfolio, any more than people decorate attics. People just go around buying investments, usually on a whim and with no plan or grand scheme involved, until one day they look at their statements piled up as they get ready to prepare their tax returns, and they say, "Whoa! How did I get all these investments?!" – just as you eventually express shock at seeing all that stuff in your attic.

Since I don't know what your cake looks like, we'll use the one in Figure 8-1 as a reference. This cake shows that we've invested in the four major asset classes — stocks, bonds, government securities and cash — and we've allocated equal amounts to each slice.[131]

If you were to invest money in this manner,[132] it would be reasonable for you to expect the

[129] Hey, no one else will call them that, so I figure I'd better.
[130] Since by now you've had an entire paragraph to do so. What's taking you so long?
[131] Hypothetical! Just an example! Not real! For discussion purposes only! This cake is not intended to represent an actual asset allocation model, and none of my firm's clients use a cake that looks like this one. So don't go blaming me when little Johnny can't go to college because you used the cake you see here.
[132] Hypothetical! Just an example! Not real! For discussion purposes only! You're not really supposed to invest money in this manner. Okay?

stock portion to make more money over time than the cash portion. You'd also expect the government securities and the bonds to earn more than the cash[133] but less than the stocks.

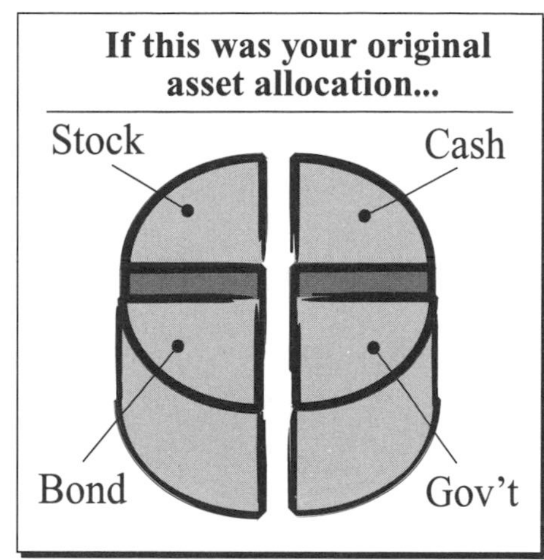
If this was your original asset allocation...
Stock
Cash
Bond
Gov't

Figure 8-1

Let's assume that, over time, this is indeed what happens.[134] If we were to bake a cake that reflects the current value of each of our slices, our cake might look like the one in Figure 8-2.

Clearly, our cake — the one we carefully made — no longer looks the way it did. What must we do so that each slice is restored to its original size?

We must sell some of the stocks (which currently comprise a bigger slice than we designed) and buy some of the cash (whose slice currently is smaller than our desired size). In other words, we must reduce the size of one slice so we can increase the size of another slice.

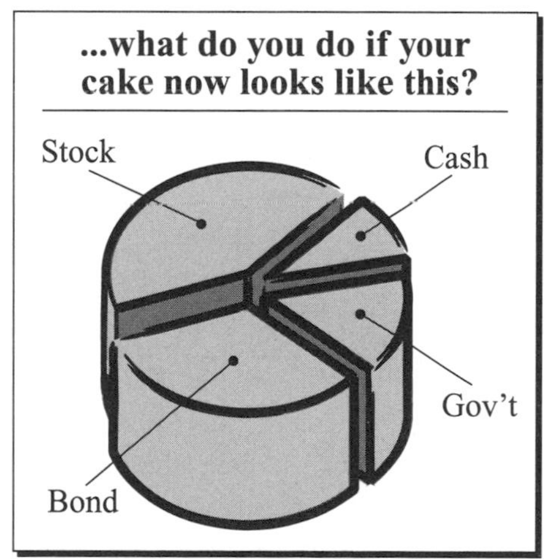
...what do you do if your cake now looks like this?
Stock
Cash
Gov't
Bond

Figure 8-2

Putting this in investment terms, we build a portfolio that consists of various assets.

[133] Because the cash is just sitting in your pocket or purse, not earning anything.
[134] It really might not happen this way because this is Hypothetical! Just an example! Not real! For discussion purposes only!

And although we want to maintain that portfolio for a long time, we notice that each asset earns a different return. This causes the overall portfolio to drift in size and shape. To counteract this phenomenon, we must periodically sell the asset that has made the most money so we can buy the asset that has made the least amount of money.

Indeed, we must sell the winner so we can buy the loser.

And yet, that is exactly the opposite of what you want to do. No, what you want is *more* of that stock slice! *"Look at that stock,"* you cry! *"It's doing fabulous! Wow! This is great! I want more!"*

And what about the cash?

"That dog? It ain't done nothin'! Get rid of that, and put that money into more stocks!"

Admit it. You want to buy the asset that has already gone up and you want to sell the asset that has already gone down.

You want to buy high and sell low.

But Wall Street warns you to "buy low, sell high." And that's exactly what I told you to do — except that I reversed the phrase. I said "sell high and buy low," and you thought I was nuts.

> Ignore fluctuations. Do not try to outguess the stock market. Buy a quality portfolio, and invest for the long term.
>
> ~Sir John Templeton

You thought I was nuts because you believe that past performance predicts future results. You believe that stocks will do well in the future simply because they did well in the past. That's why you want to *increase* the size of your stock slice, not *decrease* it.

You believe that past performance predicts future results, even though every mutual fund advertisement says:

PAST PERFORMANCE IS NO INDICATION OF FUTURE RESULTS. ANY ASSERTION TO THE CONTRARY IS A FEDERAL OFFENSE.

Want to know why you believe past performance predicts future results? Because you don't understand how the financial markets work. After all, no one has taught you about it, and you've at best had only limited experience. So, you do what seems to make sense: You apply all your experience, knowledge and education to the financial markets.

There's only one problem with that strategy: None of your experience, knowledge, or education has prepared you for Wall Street. As proof, consider your refrigerator door.

> ***"I want to learn Italian and tour the towns of Northern Italy — Lake Como here I come!"***
>
> **~Anonymous, Career Resource Specialist**

When you open that door, the light will come on.[135] That light has lit every time you have ever opened the door, so you know it will the next time you open the door. Your television operates the same way: If it has trouble tuning in channel 4, then it will always have trouble with channel 4.[136] When you pick up the phone, you know you'll get a dial tone — and you know what it will sound like. Past performance is very reliable with appliances and everyday products.

Past performance works in human relationships, too. We know how to make people laugh and cry, thanks to past performance. Medical science advances because it knows from past performance how the body can be expected to react. Past performance works with animals, too, who are probably even more predictable than people. Even the weather is discussed in the context of past performance: We know it won't snow in New York in July because the laws of nature are in command.

In fact, can you imagine a world that could not rely on past performance? Can you imagine turning the ignition of your car and having a piece of

[135] Unless your power is out. Duh.

[136] Especially if, in your area, channel 3 is the one you're supposed to tune in.

toast pop out of the CD player? Or opening that refrigerator door to remove your laundry? Washing your car to make it rain?[137]

Without question, and virtually without exception, we count on past performance for just about everything in our daily lives. But if you do that in the financial world, you will lose. That's because the laws of nature do not apply to Wall Street. Instead, economic theory applies — and theories aren't sure things. Besides, understanding "what happens if" is entirely different from predicting "what will happen next."

For example, we know what happens to bond prices when interest rates change.[138] But that is very different from predicting whether interest rates will rise or fall.

And that example explains it all. Although we know "what happens if," we have no way of knowing "what will happen next." Why? Because today's economic environment is completely different from the previous one. And the next one won't be the same as today's. Inflation rates are different. Tax rates are different. Interest rates are different. Unemployment levels are different. Currency valuations are different. The political environment is different. The social environment is different. Even the weather is different. With all these differences, how can we expect investments to perform the same as they did before?

An economist is the fellow who will tell you tomorrow why what he predicted yesterday didn't happen today.

— Laurence J. Peter

The answer, of course, is that we can't expect them to do so. That's why it's nonsense to invest in last year's winner. Because last year's winner thrived under last year's circumstances. And unless this year's environment is identical to last year's (which it won't be), it's folly to expect the same results.

This is why PAST PERFORMANCE IS NO INDICATION OF FUTURE RESULTS. And why any advisor who makes ANY ASSERTION TO THE CONTRARY is COMMITTING A FEDERAL OFFENSE.

[137] Okay, so that does happen every time you wash your car. Just as taking a shower makes the phone ring.

[138] Bond prices fall as rates rise, and vice versa. See Chapter 14 of *The Truth About Money*.

Yet, believing that the past predicts the future is precisely what virtually all investors do — including you.[139]

This is why people don't want to buy investments that have done poorly in the past. Instead, they only want to buy investments that have done well in the recent past. But do you now see why I want you to sell your winners and buy your losers?

It's not because I think your previous winner is about to become a loser.[140] No, I have a more serious concern. It's this: If you never sell the slice that holds the stock (the asset that has grown the fastest), eventually (if that trend continues) that slice will dominate your cake — to the point that all other slices will be mere slivers. As a result, you'll no longer have a diversified portfolio — for practical purposes, you'll have returned to a one-asset portfolio, just like the Pound Cake we tasted earlier. That is simply too risky — because, with your luck, the stock market will crash just as you need the money.

I'm not saying you need to sell what has been your most profitable slice because of market timing or sector rotation. I'm saying that you need to sell it in order to maintain a highly diversified portfolio.

If stocks have made more money over the past 75 years than any other asset class, why don't we just keep all our money in stocks?

Because although it's true that the overall stock market has done well over 75 years, it might not be true for any one year. Indeed, the stock market lost money in 23 of the past 75 years, or 30% of the time. We know that the markets are cyclical; we know that prices eventually recover.

But will you be around to enjoy the recovery? Are you willing to have your kids delay going to college because the market's down? Are you willing to delay your own retirement? Remember: The market is cyclical, but your lifeline is not.

It is said that stocks will do well in the long run. But in the long run, you'll be dead. This is why it is crucial that the only money you invest is money you believe you won't need for several years — preferably five years or more.

[139] Admit it: You objected to my idea of selling the stock slice, didn't you?
[140] On what basis could I make that statement? Past performance?

Here's something I haven't said in at least three paragraphs: Don't invest in last year's winning fund (or winning sector) in the hopes of achieving the same success this year.

Despite this oft-stated truth, too many investors insist on throwing money at last year's high fliers. To really understand how damaging this behavior is, let's return to 1999.

Last century's final year was an incredible one for tech stocks and the mutual funds that invested in them. Until 1999, no mutual fund had ever gained 100% in a single year. But in 1999, 182 funds managed that feat. It was an amazing year indeed.

So . . . how'd those 182 funds do in 2000?

According to Morningstar, 97% of them lost money in 2000, with many of them losing more than 50%! In fact, of the 182 funds, only six turned a profit.

The best — and worst — of them involved fund manager Ryan Jacob. In 1998, he managed The Internet Fund, the first fund to invest exclusively in Internet stocks. It earned an amazing 196% return that year. As a result, the fund attracted a lot of investor attention, and so did Jacob.

The Internet Fund gained another 216% in the first six months of 1999. Fund assets swelled from $1 million to over $700 million as investors poured money into the fund. Jacob then decided to leave and start his own fund, the Jacob Internet Fund. Investors went with him.

And they promptly lost 79.1% of their money. That's right — Ryan Jacob's new fund was the worst-performing fund of 2000.

Follow me on this. If you were invested with Ryan for both 1999 and 2000, an initial investment of ten grand would've grown to $31,600 after the first year. But then your money would have dropped 79.1%, leaving you with only $6,604 after the second year. And if you were among the unlucky ones who only invested at the beginning of 2000, your $10,000 would have been worth only $2,090 by the end of the year.

Don't invest in last year's winning fund in the hopes of achieving the same success this year. Personal experience can be a cruel teacher.

If you follow the strategy of periodically rebalancing your portfolio, you'll sell assets that have made money and buy assets that have not (or have made less).[141]

I hope this makes sense to you: It does not matter that you are buying an asset that lost money in the past (because the past does not predict the future). All that matters is that you are selling assets that have made money in the past (because it means you've made money on that investment). Thus, if your career consists only of selling assets at a profit, you will become wealthy.

Some people resist the idea of buying assets other than stocks because they know that stocks, over time, are the best-performing asset class. Why put your money into other assets if those assets are merely going to underperform stocks? Why bake cakes other than chocolate?

Ibbotson data show why. Although the S&P 500 Stock Index grew 12% per year from January 1972 through December 1994, a portfolio consisting equally of stocks, bonds, real estate, foreign stocks and cash[142] also grew 12% during that period. Thus, diversifying among many asset classes is not designed to reduce returns. Instead, it's designed to reduce risk: Based on the measurement of standard deviation,[143] the diversified portfolio was 39% less risky than the stock portfolio — yet its returns were identical.

In other words, a balanced portfolio is meant to lower risk, not necessarily returns.

"I want to write and produce a documentary film by age 42."

~Anonymous,
Freelance Writer

[141] For further discussion of when to rebalance a portfolio, see Chapter 44 of *The Truth About Money*.
[142] As represented by the S&P 500 Stock Index, Lehman Brothers Government Bond Index, NAREIT Equity Index, Morgan Stanley Capital International EAFE Index, and U.S. Government 1-year Treasury Bills, as reported by Ibbotson Associates.
[143] Which we'll explore later.

How Institutional Investors Slice Their Cakes

As people go about the process of slicing their cakes, they typically begin with a knife — and with no idea of how to proceed. As a result, they often slice their cakes in ways that are wildly inappropriate.

Although this might surprise you, you are not the world's first investor, and, unlike Captain Kirk, you are not going where no man has gone before.

Yet, that's exactly how most people regard their investment experience. They act as if their experience is the world's first experience, and they insist on experimenting with their own money instead of first considering the experiences of others.

If you had bothered to learn that bond prices always fall whenever interest rates rise, you wouldn't be surprised that your bond fund loses money when the Fed raises interest rates. If you had taken the time to study history, you would have realized that our recent obsession with Internet stocks was merely another in a long series of manic bubbles that was certain to eventually burst.

> Wall Street University charges high tuition.
>
> ~unknown

But so many investors don't do this. Instead, after losing money in stocks, they decide that stocks always lose money. After investing in a real estate deal that goes bad, they swear off real estate forever. They believe, because they've been investing for a whole 10 years, that they have extensive investment experience, and therefore they believe they are acting very reasonably when they say they expect stocks to grow 15% per year over the next 10 years.[144] They decide that *their* experience is the *only* experience, and they refuse to learn from others.

[144] It's true: According to a 2001 Gallup poll, 39% of those surveyed said they expect stocks to gain 15% or more per year for the next 10 years. No doubt they felt this way because the S&P 500 had averaged 21.5% per year from 1992 to 1999, according to Ibbotson Associates. Too bad they ignored the fact that the S&P's average since 1926 is only 13.3%, and never before in history has the stock market earned what it earned in the 1990s.

That's too bad, because slicing your cake without regard to how other cakes fared when similarly sliced can cause you considerable harm. And even if you don't give much credence to experience,[145] how about knowledge? Wouldn't it make sense to see how people who are much smarter than you[146] handle their money?

Sure it does. So, let's do that. But let's not get this information from reading personal finance magazines. All they do is write about how consumers like you are handling their money — that's little more than the blind leading the blind.[147]

Instead, let's see how the pros do it. Ever read, for example, *Institutional Investor* magazine? Probably not.[148] That's too bad. Because while rags like . . . well, you know their names . . . print stories about how the guy next door to you is managing his finances,[149] *Institutional Investor* and those like it tell you how the professional and institutional money managers are handling their assets.[150, 151]

"I will travel and enjoy the wilderness of interior Alaska — to satisfy my curiosity and challenge my senses!"

~Marty Corso, Financial Planner, Edelman Financial Services

---

[145] Since, after all, past performance is no indication of future results.

[146] Or at least, more educated in this subject.

[147] Did you ever read the "I Retired at 35!" stories? It always turns out that the people profiled moved from the suburbs and now are living on twenty grand a year in some Third World nation. Like you're going to do that.

[148] But why not? It amazes me that people who want to learn about personal finance read amateur magazines — the personal finance press — instead of publications written for professionals. Which physician would you rather consult: the one who reads *Playing Doctor*, or the one who reads the *American Journal of Ophthalmology*?

[149] Like you'll really get rich mimicking the actions of the guy next door. Hey, if he is so rich, why is he living next door to you?

[150] You probably think there's no value in your reading these magazines because their content won't be relevant to you, or because they handle their money in ways you cannot handle yours, if only due to the amounts involved. But did you conclude that after you read several issues — or before? I wonder if you've reached your conclusion after proper evaluation, or if you merely have a knee-jerk bias based on preconceived notions.

[151] It could also be that you've never heard of these publications, that you're put off by their costs (subscriptions to mags like this often cost $1,500 a year), or that you found that you don't need to read them because your advisor does so for you. If footnote 150 is applicable, you're guilty. If this one is germane, you're forgiven.

So, without further ado, let's see how the professionals slice their cakes, and contrast that with how individuals do it. As reported by *Pensions & Investments* magazine,[152] the managers of the nation's 1,000 largest pension funds allocate their plans' assets[153] as shown in Figure 8-3:

How Institutional Investors Do It

Average Asset Mix of the 1,000 Largest U.S. Pension Funds

	Corporate	Public	Union
U.S. Stock	52%	49%	47%
Bond	26	28	38
International Stock	15	16	5
Real Estate	2.5	4.5	5
Cash	4.5	2.5	5

Figure 8-3

"We want to build our new home in Williamsburg, then travel and show our dogs, starting in the summer of 2002."

~Charles and Elizabeth March, both 54, Consultant/Licensed Social Worker

[152] Hah! You thought I was going to quote *Institutional Investor.*

[153] The money these managers are investing isn't theirs, of course. It doesn't belong to their employers, either. The money constitutes the pension and retirement benefits of the companies' employees; thus, the managers are investing it on their behalf — and with them in mind.

As you can see, corporations, public pension funds (such as those for government employees) and unions all manage their assets essentially the same way. Thus, it is clear that the professionals are in agreement as to how their assets should be managed. I'd like to emphasize these observations about these data:

- **Although unions invest substantially fewer assets into international stocks than do corporations or public pensions, this is a political decision, not an economic one.** After all, the leadership of the United Auto Workers might have a difficult time explaining to its members why they're buying stock in Toyota instead of General Motors.

- **Due to the nature of its workforce, unions tend to invest slightly more conservatively than corporate and public pension funds.** This reflects the specific needs of its members. But even after doing so, the allocation model used by union pension funds does not differ much from its brethren.

- **Each group recognizes that real estate belongs in the portfolio.** However, because of the unique challenges of this asset class — primarily illiquidity and active management obligations — they keep their real estate holdings to a relatively small portion of overall assets.

- **Each maintains assets in cash, but only enough to meet its liquidity needs.** Since every pension fund knows that some of its employees will die, quit or retire in a given year, the funds maintain enough cash to handle those inevitable pay-out requests — but they keep in cash only enough to do so. The rest of their assets are fully invested, because the return on cash assets is so low that it places a drain on the performance of the overall portfolio.

- **Most importantly, but in a statistic not reflected in the chart, pension fund managers typically place no more than 1% of assets into any one security.** The only common exception, aside from cash equivalents, is U.S. government securities.

Now, let's see how individual consumers do it. Figure 8-4 shows how employees who are participating in the nation's 1,000 largest company retirement funds allocate their assets, according to the Employee Benefit Research Institute.

How Consumers Do It

Average Asset Mix of the 1,000 Largest U.S. Retirement Funds

	Corporate	Public	Union
U.S. Stock	70%	56%	60%
Bond	6	18	26
International Stock	4	5	1
Real Estate	0	0	0
Cash	20	21	13

Figure 8-4

"I want to build a house on Maryland's Eastern Shore by age 70."

~William C. Rolle, Jr., 67, Marketing Communications Consulting

We find similarity among consumers, although their cakes are not as consistent as they were among the professionals. Note these observations:

- **Corporate employees invest far too much money into stocks, and far more than either public or union workers.** Some will argue that corporate employees are more highly educated and therefore they understand better the superior profit potential of stocks. Some also will argue that corporate employees earn more money than public and union workers, and that they therefore have the financial ability to tolerate the greater risks found in the stock market. And some will argue that corporate workers are younger than those working for school systems, government agencies and unions, and with longer time horizons until retirement, increased allocations toward stocks therefore are appropriate.

  None of these arguments are legitimate: Those who are highly educated typically are not nearly as knowledgeable about investing as they think they are; such overconfidence is a common error among investors.[154]

  - It is also not true that the average income of corporate employees is higher than the average incomes for public and union workers. There is no study I know of that supports this claim, which appears to be little more than a conceit.

  - Finally, it is equally unproven that corporate employees are younger than public or union employees.

    Regardless of their motivation, rationale or justification, the undeniable truth is that corporate employees are investing substantially more of their assets into stocks than are other workers or professional money managers. This is highly dangerous, especially when we consider (as we will in the next bullet) what stocks those corporate employees are buying.

[154] This psychological phenomenon, explored extensively in the field of behavioral finance, is covered at length in *Ordinary People, Extraordinary Wealth.*

- **Although professional managers rarely place more than 1% of assets into any one stock, corporate employees, when permitted to buy employer stock in their retirement plans, typically place 34% of their assets there** — nearly half of their 70% cake slice. There is no reasonable justification for this; such action, to be blunt, is wildly speculative.

That figure is actually worse than it appears, for it refers to the average holdings of the 1,000 largest plans in the nation. But not all plans permit their workers to buy employer stock. If we reduce the surveyed universe to those employers that allow this practice, we find that 42% of all 401(k) assets are invested in employer stock, according to the Employee Benefit Research Institute. At some companies, employees have placed as much as 96% of their assets there. What could these people possibly be thinking?

"I would like to go fly fishing all over the U.S. and the world starting in 20 years."

~Anonymous, 33, Finance for U.S. Gov't

401(k) Plans That Offer Employer Stock

Company	18-month Performance of Company Stock	% of Plan Assets in Company Stock
Owens Corning	–93%	44%
Nortel Networks	–89	31
Corning	–87	25
Lucent Technologies	–86	37
Montana Power	–85	37
Hewlett-Packard	–75	29
Sprint	–64	25
Computer Sciences	–61	33
Dell Computer	–51	88

as of October 31, 2001

Figure 8-5

The only reason employees typically buy stock in their employer is this: *Because I work there.* The only reason they buy stock in Coca-Cola is because they don't work for Pepsi. The only reason they buy Ford is because they don't work for General Motors.

That's a lousy reason to own a stock — and certainly an indefensible reason for owning so much of it.[155]

One of my clients was an executive with W. Bell & Company, a local retailer. By working there for 30 years, he had accumulated $500,000 in Bell stock. But the month he retired, the company filed for bankruptcy, and he lost the entire $500,000. No one could have predicted that a 41-year-old company might suddenly close its doors.

The New York Times **ran a page-one story detailing the tribulations at Lucent. One employee profiled was Stephen Gilligan, who worked at the company (and its predecessor, AT&T) for 21 years. His grandmother, father, two sisters and two uncles also worked for the company.**

But when Lucent experienced financial trouble, Gilligan – a manager earning "in the six figures" according to the ***Times*** **– was laid off. He's now receiving a $600 monthly pension. And what of Gilligan's 401(k)? He had placed most of that money into Lucent stock, and it fell 91% since 1999. Tens of thousands of Lucent workers are in the same situation.**

Lucent, spun off from AT&T in 1996, was considered rock-solid. It owns Bell Labs, among other assets, holder of 28,000 patents, including the laser and transistor. Who could have expected a company like this to experience such problems?

The same could be said for Braniff, Pan Am and Eastern Airlines. International Harvester, Wang and Woolworth, too. All these well-known companies have gone out of business.

Investing your money in the stock of the company that employs you simply is not diversified behavior.

[155] I am not referring to Employee Stock Ownership Plans, which are specifically designed to enable employees to become owners of the companies they work for, or programs that enable workers to buy company stock at a 15% discount (which is common). If you have the ability to participate in these programs, do so. Just make sure that you are not placing more of your total personal net worth into company stock than is prudent. My recommendation: You should regard company stock as its own cake slice, and do not let it constitute more than 10% of your cake — preferably less.

- **Compared to institutional investors, workers have far too little money invested in international stocks.** Although union workers can be excused for this on political grounds, public and corporate employees enjoy no such privilege. Remember, as I wrote in *The Truth About Money*, by failing to invest internationally, you prevent yourself from investing in:

    - 7 of the world's 10 largest financial companies
    - 7 of the world's 10 largest insurance companies
    - 7 of the world's 10 largest utilities
    - 8 of the world's 10 largest appliance companies
    - 8 of the world's 10 largest auto manufacturers
    - 8 of the world's 10 largest chemical companies
    - 8 of the world's 10 largest machinery companies
    - 9 of the world's 10 largest electronics companies
    - 9 of the world's 10 largest banks

Failure? I never encountered it. All I ever met were temporary setbacks.

~Dottie Walters

- **Individual investors own no real estate, although professionals do.** This can be excused because few company retirement plans offer real estate as an option, but that doesn't get you off the hook entirely. Do you own any real estate?

  Sorry, but your home doesn't count.

  Your home doesn't count because you have to live somewhere, and the fact that your home grows in value over time is serendipity, not investment strategy. Besides, when you sell it and move to another place, that next house will cost as much as your current one because it too will have risen in value.[156]

  No, what I'm talking about is rental property. Raw land. Real estate investment trusts. The stocks of mortgage lenders, builders and developers. And mutual funds that invest in real estate and the real estate industry. The pros place 3% to 5% of their assets into this asset class. Think about that.

- **Individual investors have far too much money in cash equivalents.** In fact, if you look closely, you'll see lots of Marble Cakes being baked: portfolios that contain lots of stocks and lots of cash — and practically nothing else. Cash — selected for its one attribute (safety) — earns such a low return that it reduces the overall return of the entire portfolio. Reduce your cash position, and get that money invested more effectively.

"I want to learn a foreign language, tour Italy, learn to scuba dive and hike the grand canyon."

~Kelsey Williams, Financial Planner,
Edelman Financial Services

---

[156] For more on why your home is not the best investment you ever made, see Chapter 18 of *The Truth About Money*.

Although the data shown are based on retirement plan and pension assets, they are not intended to apply solely to your IRAs, annuities, and company retirement plans. Instead, this conversation is meant to apply to your total assets — retirement assets and regular savings alike.

A too-common error is for people to handle their IRA differently from the rest of their money. "It's for my retirement," they say, "so I can't risk losing it." That lets them justify putting their $400,000 IRA into bank CDs while they invest $200 a month into a stock fund.

Don't make this mistake. Money is money, no matter how it's titled or registered. Most people have money in a variety of accounts — IRAs for him and her, joint accounts, trust accounts, sometimes separate accounts in just his name or hers, separate retirement accounts at each place of employment, and often, separate accounts for the kids. None of that matters. What matters is how all that money is invested — and each investment must be made with regard to the rest of the assets. In other words, you need to create just one cake, not seven, and this one (large) cake will comprise your total investments.

Once you've done this, you then can turn to the individual registrations that you've established for legal, convenience or other purposes.[157] As a result, you might end up placing your entire retirement plan's assets into bonds — simply because other accounts are holding so much in stock. Or the husband's IRA might be invested completely differently from the wife's — again due to the need to maintain proper balance in the overall cake.

Money is money. Make sure you stay focused on the forest, and not on each tree.[158]

If you suspect that divorce might be in your future, beware the above advice. Proper cake-slicing might place in your name all the safer, lower-return investments, while your spouse gets all the riskier assets that earn higher returns. Later, an unsuspecting spouse might agree absent-mindedly to the other's suggestion that "you keep your account and I'll keep mine" even though the performance of each has been wildly different — different intentionally, but different nonetheless. If you're in a questionable marriage, be on your guard against this.

[157] Such as preventing a fight with your in-laws.

[158] It is beyond the scope of this book to discuss where you should invest the money you contribute to your company retirement plan with each paycheck. For complete information on that, refer to Chapter 46 of *The Truth About Money.*

The above scenario also becomes an issue when spouses are competitive with each other. Some people don't like the fact that the other's account is growing faster – which can occur when his and her accounts are invested differently. As you allocate your assets within your cake, be cognizant of your (or your partner's) propensity to feel this way.

Likewise, good financial advisors will give you recommendations for investing the money you're placing with them only after they have reviewed how you're handling your 401(k) and other company retirement plans. If the size of your 401(k) plan dwarfs the rest of your portfolio, or if that money is invested in just one asset class, the advisor will have you invest in other classes the money you're placing with him or her. Since so many people emphasize stocks in their retirement accounts (as we've seen), many advisors therefore find themselves forced to recommend bonds for their clients' other holdings.

And those advisors often later discover that they've shot themselves in the foot. Their client complains to them that the advisor's recommendation (bonds) has failed to make as much money as the stocks that the client himself had previously selected for his own 401(k). "I've been doing better on my own than I have with you!" such clients complain.

Boy are they missing the point.[159]

[159] What would you do if you were the advisor? Would you try to explain (again) why you offered the recommendations you did — or would this merely sound like a weak attempt at rationalizing your underperformance? Do you think your client would accept your argument, or would he close his account with you and begin to manage his own affairs (meaning, open an account with a discount broker and buy his own investments — ones that will, surprise surprise, be identical to the investments he's got in his 401(k) plan)? And in the face of risking the loss of your client, would you simply give the client what he says he wants — which is more of what he's already got? After all, this might not be good for the client, but it's a great way for the advisor to win and sustain the client's account. With all this in mind, ask yourself: How has your advisor handled your account? Has he given you recommendations that take into consideration the assets you have elsewhere? Have you let him do this for you, or have you given him grief for having done so?

CHAPTER 9

The Four Ways You Can Buy Your Investments

CHAPTER 9

The Four Ways You Can Buy Your Investments

If you make your own investment decisions, you'll find this chapter to be of great interest. If you rely on an advisor, this chapter will help you understand the basis for your advisor's recommendations.[160]

You have discovered that goals form the basis of your financial plan, and that your plan helps you determine the combination of ingredients (investments) you'll buy for your portfolio (cake).

It's time for you to buy your investments.

You have four choices:

1. You can place your money into mutual funds, and let the funds buy your investments for you.

2. You can place your money into variable annuities, and let the annuities buy your investments for you.

3. You can place your money with a private money manager, and let the manager buy your investments for you.

4. You can buy your own investments, with or without the aid of a stockbroker or other advisor.

---

[160] Assuming your advisor isn't that New York stockbroker who calls himself a "professional psychic." His "psychically charged" newsletter and book offer stock tips based on tarot cards, astrology, numerology, psychometry (psychically communicating with inanimate objects) and pendulums. And *The Washington Post* called *me* "unconventional."

Let's examine the advantages and disadvantages of each. Remember: You're about to choose one of these four. So pay close attention!

Be forewarned that my biases will be revealed in the material that follows. As if I haven't been doing that all along!

Despite what anyone tells you, each of these four choices is a legitimate, viable way to buy and own investments. For most people, the choice[161] is merely a matter of personal preference. And yes, I have my favorite — which will become clear soon enough.

Buying Mutual Funds

The Pros

- Mutual funds are managed by professional investors — often the same ones handling all those institutional assets. If you're like most people, you'll agree[162] that professional managers are likely to produce better returns for you than you might earn on your own, because they are more skilled and experienced, and because they devote more time and effort to the task.

- Each mutual fund invests in hundreds of securities, not just a few, and this diversification increases safety.

- Mutual funds are remarkably affordable to own. Most will let you open an account with as little as $500, or even just $25 if you invest monthly.

- Mutual funds make saving painless and easy. You can add money whenever you want, often in amounts as little as $25, and you can withdraw any amount at any time. You also can automatically reinvest all dividends and capital gains distributions, which further

[161] Yes, you're allowed to use more than one.
[162] Or put another way, be willing to admit.

boosts your savings. You can add to your account each month via automatically debiting from your checking account, and you can have monthly withdrawals transferred to your bank. There are no fees for these services.

More complete information on mutual funds is found in Part V of *The Truth About Money.*

- Mutual funds offer simplicity. You get a concise, one-page quarterly statement, making record-keeping easier. You also can see your fund's current value in the daily newspaper, and virtually all funds let you view your account online 24/7.[163] All funds also maintain cost basis data for you, which helps with tax reporting.

- Mutual funds can be very inexpensive, especially when compared to the other ways you can buy investments.

The Cons

- Although you can pick a fund that invests in any asset class or sector you wish, you have no say over the specific securities the fund will own.

- You also have very little control over the timing of tax liabilities, so little that it's fair to say you have almost no control.

"I would like to join a local club and start soaring (flying gliders) again."

~Diane Jensen,
Financial Planner,
Edelman Financial Services

---

[163] That's 24-hours-a-day, seven-days-a-week, for those of you who are still in the Stone Age. And "online" means . . . oh, never mind.

It's no secret that most stock mutual funds lost money in 2000, thanks to the stock market's dismal performance that year. It's also no secret that most of those same funds made a capital gains distribution, and their shareholders had to pay taxes on that distribution.

Huh? Why did shareholders have to pay taxes on a fund that lost money?

It seems bizarre, but this happened to almost every stock mutual fund shareholder in 2000. In fact, having to pay capital gains taxes on an investment that has lost money is the most common complaint of mutual fund shareholders.[164] But let me assure you: It's not as bad as you may think.

Let's start with an explanation of how capital gains taxes work. Say you invest $10,000 in a stock and it rises to $30,000. If you don't sell the stock, there is no tax. But if you do sell the stock, you will have to pay a tax on the profit. This profit is called a "capital gain." You can delay this tax for years — even decades — by holding onto your shares, because you don't pay the capital gains tax until you sell (assuming the asset appreciates).

Now, let's see how this tax rule applies to mutual funds. You buy shares of a fund, and the fund, in turn, buys stocks. If you sell your shares of the fund for a profit, you incur capital gains, just as if you had sold shares of stock (as in the paragraph above).

But say you keep your shares. No taxes, right? Not necessarily. Why? Because the fund is likely to sell some of the stocks it owns, for prices higher than it paid to buy them. When this occurs, the fund produces a capital gain. And since you are the real owner of the fund, you are the one who has to pay the taxes. That's why the fund issues Form 1099 to you; this form reveals your share of the capital gains that the fund incurred on your behalf during the year.

That's the key point: If the fund sells for a profit any of the shares of any of the stocks it owns, those sales trigger the capital gain — *even though you have not sold any of your shares of the fund.*

But how can a fund incur a capital gain if it has lost money? Say six months ago, you invested in a fund that's 10 years old and you paid $10 for each share. Further say that, at the end of the year, your fund's share price is only $8 — meaning you've lost money. But soon after, you receive a Form 1099 in the mail, declaring that you owe taxes on capital gains. How can this be?

It's simple: Even though you recently bought shares of the fund for $10 per share, the fund itself owns stocks that it purchased many years ago. It has now sold some of those stocks for a profit. Thus, even though you didn't enjoy that profit, the fund you own did, and as a current shareholder, you now must pay your share of the taxes on that capital gain.

[164] Those who own mutual funds inside their IRA or company retirement plan do not complain, because they pay no taxes unless they withdraw money from their account.

This certainly doesn't seem fair.

Now here's the good news. When you sell your shares in the fund, the tax you will be required to pay at that time will be lower than it otherwise would have been, because you have, in essence, prepaid your tax. And if you sell your fund for a loss, you'll actually get a refund for the tax you already paid.

In other words, mutual fund shareholders pay a little bit of their capital gains taxes each year, whereas stock investors pay all their taxes at one time. Some people argue that stock investors have the advantage because, by delaying the tax, their money can grow faster. But I'm not sure this is true, because most fund investors reinvest their capital gains distributions into more shares, and in many cases this enables them to compound their growth more effectively than stock investors can. Furthermore, when it's time to pay that tax, fund investors happily discover that their tax bill is quite small, because they've already paid some or most of the taxes due. (In fact, when our clients sell a fund they've owned for years, it's not uncommon to see them sell the fund for a substantial profit, yet owe nothing in taxes!)

Investors who don't periodically pay taxes also tend not to rebalance their portfolios as often as they should, because they fret that rebalancing might trigger a capital gains tax. Thus, they let tax considerations interfere with more important investment considerations, to their own detriment.

Finally, investors who pay capital gains taxes annually — as mutual funds typically cause them to do — usually pay those taxes out of pocket, instead of liquidating fund shares. This lets more money stay invested, which can lead to greater long-term wealth.

So, for all these reasons, don't let mutual fund taxes annoy you too much. Remember: There are worse things than paying taxes . . . like not having any money!

"I would like to indulge my creative urges, i.e. decorating, designing clothing, and quilting. I would like to fly in 1st class or business class."

~Anonymous, 69, Retired Auditor

Buying Variable Annuities

Annuities have all the benefits of mutual funds, plus:

The Pros

- Some annuities offer a variety of mutual fund families, giving you access to many fund managers in just one investment.
- You incur no annual tax liability. This eliminates the #1 complaint of mutual fund investors,[165] and explains why so many fund investors move their money out of funds and into annuities.
- You enjoy total control over the timing of tax liabilities, because you pay no taxes on your annuity's profits until you withdraw money from the account. Thus, if you leave the money invested for 20 years, you pay no taxes for 20 years.[166]
- You can rebalance your portfolio inside annuities with no tax implication, because transfers between annuity subaccounts are tax-free.
- You can let your money grow tax-deferred for even longer than you could with an IRA or company retirement plan. While those accounts usually require you to begin making distributions at age 70½ (forcing you to pay taxes), annuities let you keep your money invested well into your 80s and 90s.

More information on variable annuities is found in Part V of *The Truth About Money.*

"Start and run a viable small business for retirement income, running profitably by retirement, at age 62."

~Anonymous, 52, Fund-raiser

---

[165] Who haven't read the preceding two pages.
[166] Mutual fund investors go gaga when they discover this.

The Cons

- Withdrawals prior to age 59½ are subject to taxes plus a 10% penalty, making annuities appropriate only for retirement savings.

- When you finally do withdraw money from an annuity, the profits are subject to ordinary income tax rates, not the lower capital gains tax rates. But this is not as bad as it sounds, especially if you maintain a diversified portfolio. That's because some of the money you earn from mutual funds or individual securities would be subject to ordinary income tax rates anyway — meaning the annuity poses no new disadvantage in that regard.

- If you die while owning an annuity, your estate (or your heirs) will pay income taxes on the profits that you didn't pay during your lifetime. With mutual funds (and all other investments), the profit is passed tax-free at death, something called a "step-up in basis."[167]

> **Thus, you avoid annual taxes but ultimately pay potentially higher taxes with annuities than you would with mutual funds. Which one, then, offers a superior after-tax return? Our research shows that annuities always win if you leave the money invested for at least 15 years (which makes sense, since annuities are intended to be used for retirement savings). They sometimes win even in shorter periods, too, depending on the variables used in the analysis.**

- Although annuities issue quarterly statements just as mutual funds do, and although many also provide 24/7 account access, their prices are not usually found in newspapers.

- Annuities typically cost more to own than mutual funds.

> **Our research shows that the long-term benefits of tax-deferred growth more than compensate for this higher cost. But again, this presumes that the money remains invested for many years.**

[167] The 2001 tax law seems to change this. But the change doesn't take effect until 2010 and is valid for that year only (in 2011 we return to the law that was in effect in 2001). Since there will be five new Congresses and perhaps three presidents between the time the law was passed in 2001 and the time this provision goes into effect in 2010, it's impossible to state what the future tax rules will be. Stay tuned.

Hiring a Private Money Manager

The Pros

- When you hire a private manager, your money is placed into a "managed account," often called a "wrap account." Your professional money manager — often the same folks who manage mutual funds and institutional assets — uses your money to buy investments for you. As with mutual funds and annuities, the theory is that they will generate better performance for you than you'd get on your own.

- When hiring a private manager, your money is invested separately from all the manager's other clients. As a result, you have limited ability to affect your manager's investment decisions. For example, if you want to avoid tobacco stocks (on moral or economic grounds), the manager will comply. You cannot give such instructions to managers of mutual funds or annuities, because they pool all client assets into one account.

> ***"Learn to play the mandolin well."***
>
> **~John Davis,**
> **Financial Planner,**
> **Edelman Financial Services**

- Accordingly, you have extensive influence over the tax results of your account. You can tell your manager to delay selling profitable assets until the following tax year, or accelerate the sale of losses to offset other gains or take as a deduction on this year's tax return. You have no such control with mutual funds (and it's unnecessary with annuities).

The Cons

- Each of the above benefits, in my opinion, actually is a negative. Why? Because it's absurd to hire a professional manager only to tell her what stocks you do and don't want to own, or when to buy or sell. Either you're better at this than she is, or you're not. If you're better than she, skip to the next method, and if you're not, don't tell your manager how to do her job. That's just plain stupid.

People have told me that they would never dream of interfering with the management of their account — and then they call to ask that a trade be delayed until January. "But I'm only doing that for tax purposes!" they say. "I'm not trying to tell my manager when to buy or sell." But it's the same result, and making tax-motivated investment decisions, rather than economically motivated decisions, is a great way to lose money. See page 177 for my January 2001 example.

- If you hire a private manager, you can forget about simple statements. Instead of displaying just the account's value as mutual funds and annuities do, private managers issue multipage statements filled with line-by-line listings of every holding in your account and every transaction executed. You'll see how many shares you own, when you bought them, what you paid, and what they're currently worth — making it very difficult to resist the tendency to micromanage the account.[168]

- Although some managers offer online access, many don't yet offer this service.

- You can expect to receive a lot of mail, because you will receive a notice any time the manager buys or sells any asset within your account. Get a bigger mailbox and a larger filing cabinet to store all that paper.

[168] Indeed, one of the biggest problems private managers tell me they have is fielding phone calls from clients who want to talk about specific stocks that are in the portfolio, rather than on the overall performance.

- The above creates the need for massive record-keeping, much more so than with mutual funds or annuities. When you report your profits and losses on your tax return, you must report the results of each specific holding, not just the account's overall results. Expect your tax prep fees to rise.[169]

- Private accounts often are more expensive than mutual funds.

- Unlike mutual funds and annuities, whose fees are hidden, private and wrap fee managers debit your account each month or quarter, and this debit is reflected on your statement.

- Some argue that the mutual funds' practice of hiding fees is anti-consumer and that the private manager's method is fairer for consumers. But my experience is different: When people in wrap accounts see that their manager has charged his fee just as the account (coincidentally) has fallen in value due to recent market volatility, they begin to question the value of the manager. This can cause investors to close their accounts — selling low, as it were. Therefore, in my opinion, not throwing the fee in your face every quarter can help you maintain a big-picture, long-term focus — to your advantage.

  I admit that this is more of a psychological issue than an economic one, but when it comes to money, it's all about the psyche. And on this issue, as with so many others, private accounts lose.

"I someday will sail around the world by my own seamanship, with only my wife and my dogs. In 18 years."

~Anonymous, 27, Retired

[169] Can you say the word "cumbersome"?

Private accounts lose on this issue for another reason, too: Since the managers know that their clients will see their accounts debited each month or quarter, some managers engage in trading simply to justify their fee. After all, they worry, if they don't trade, their client might think they don't deserve their fee. This is called "reverse churning."[170]

No matter how you look at it, private managers' fees are a big negative.

- To establish a private account, you must invest at least $50,000, usually $100,000 and (with some firms) as much as $5 million. This puts private managers beyond the reach of most people.[171]

In case you haven't figured it out, I'm not a fan of hiring private money managers. But that's just my opinion.

"My personal goal is to become a freelance web designer, in order to enjoy what I do for a 'living' as well as enjoy the reason that I do so . . . life. Immediately — starting today."

~Carol E. Pope, 33, Systems Analyst

[170] Which, as the name implies, is the opposite of churning, an illegal activity where stockbrokers execute lots of trades in a client's account because they earn commissions on every trade.
[171] Guess I should have mentioned this first and saved you a lot of time, huh?

Buying Investments on Your Own

The Pros

- By picking your own investments (with or without the aid of a stockbroker), you enjoy total control over them. It is the only way to obtain a truly customized portfolio.
- Therefore, you also enjoy total control over the timing of your tax liabilities.
- I honestly can't think of any other advantages.

The Cons

- Picking your own stocks and bonds constitutes the most complex way to manage your money, for the burden is entirely on you (although a good stockbroker can absorb some of the workload). Because you will do your own research, you not only need the time to do it but also the time to learn how. You'll pay constant attention to the markets and stay in frequent contact with your brokerage firm — the former to learn what's happening and the latter to place your trades.
- Because those who pick their own investments tend to trade often, they often spend more on commissions, transaction fees and taxes than those who rely on mutual funds, annuities or private managers.

> The only thing that interferes with my learning is my education.
>
> ~Albert Einstein

My Preference

Which of the four methods do I recommend? Well, let's put it this way: With about $2 billion in client assets, I operate the nation's fifth-largest independent financial planning firm.[172] That certainly makes us large enough to manage client assets whichever way we deem best for our clients.

Our choice? We recommend mutual funds about 85% of the time, using variable annuities for the remainder.

This surprises people sometimes, because most envision that advisors like me are busy researching stocks and recommending them to our clients.

Let me tell you why we recommend mutual funds to our clients instead of stocks, so you can better understand the basis for my bias.

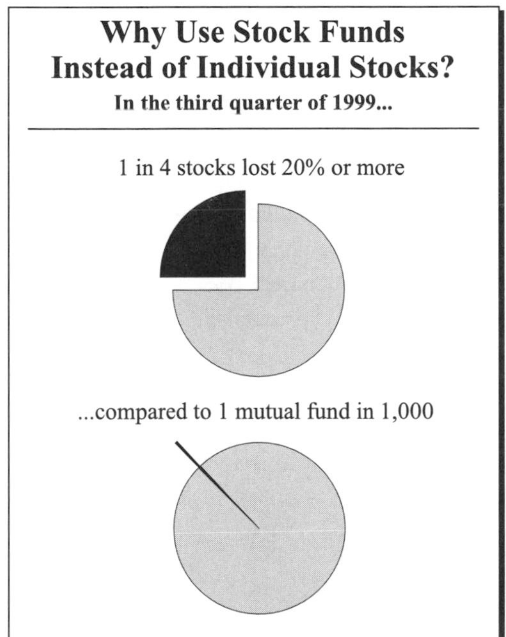

Why Use Stock Funds
Instead of Individual Stocks?
In the third quarter of 1999...
1 in 4 stocks lost 20% or more
...compared to 1 mutual fund in 1,000

Figure 9-1

First, buying individual stocks is a riskier approach. Take, for example, the third quarter of 1999 — "the beginning of the end" of our 1990s bull market. In those three months, according to Morningstar's Don Phillips,[173] of the 8,692 publicly traded stocks in the U.S., 25% of them — 2,173 stocks — fell 20% or more in value. That's an astonishing statistic: One in four!

But during that same period, the ratio of stock mutual funds that lost 20% or more was one in a thousand, or just 0.1%.

[172] According to the 2001 rankings of independent financial planning firms by *Bloomberg's Wealth Manager*.
[173] In a speech he gave at the *Baltimore Sun*'s Dollars and Sense Conference.

Stock funds didn't suffer the fate of individual stocks for two simple reasons: They are both professionally managed and extensively diversified. Although all stock funds owned some stocks that fell sharply in value, none of them owned *only* those kinds of stocks. That's because the funds are professionally managed, and the managers were successful in steering their shareholders' money away from many of the stocks that lost money. Furthermore, by owning hundreds of stocks, the funds were able to provide their shareholders with a cushion against the massive wave of declines that were then occurring in the marketplace. This illustration well explains why stock funds are safer to own than individual stocks.

The second reason we tell our clients to buy stock mutual funds instead of individual stocks is because stock funds often are more profitable than individual stocks. This is a shocking statement, because most believe that diversification, which lowers risks, also lowers returns.

"I want to take two trips per year so that by the time I die I will have seen most of the world."

~Vince Kiernan, 43, VP Finance

But it ain't necessarily so. Consider a study by the University of Missouri, results shown in Figure 9-2, which examined the performance of stocks and stock funds in the most recent and, more importantly, the best decade for stocks in U.S. history.

Craig L. Israelsen, Ph.D., associate professor at the University of Missouri in Columbia, compared the returns of individual stocks to mutual funds. His study's conclusion: Over the three-, five- and 10-year periods ending December 31, 1999, stock mutual funds made more money than individual stocks. Indeed, the study, published in *On Wall Street*, found that mutual funds not only reduce the risk of loss, they improve returns for investors.

The study found, for example, that in 1999, 54% of all stocks lost money, compared with only 13% of stock funds. In the three-year period ending December 1999, an amazing 46% of stocks — almost half of all stocks in the U.S. — lost money. But in this same period, only 2.5% of mutual funds lost money.

Individual Stocks vs. Stock Mutual Funds

1 year 1999	Stocks	Stock Funds
number in existence	6,242	2,448
median annual return	–4%	18%
highest return	1106%	494%
lowest return	–99.97%	–29.6%
standard deviation	229	37
number with negative average returns	3,343	311
percentage of total with negative average returns	54%	13%

3 years 1997–1999	Stocks	Stock Funds
number in existence	5,323	1,877
median annual return	2%	19%
highest return	476%	119%
lowest return	–91%	–18%
standard deviation	37	13
number with negative average returns	2,432	46
percentage of total with negative average returns	46%	3%

5 years 1995–1999	Stocks	Stock Funds
number in existence	4,122	1,414
median annual return	9.5%	21%
highest return	220%	58%
lowest return	–80%	–17%
standard deviation	25	8
number with negative average returns	1,280	5
percentage of total with negative average returns	31.0%	0.35%

10 years 1990–1999	Stocks	Stock Funds
number in existence	2,397	737
median annual return	9%	15%
highest return	97%	38%
lowest return	–43%	–9%
standard deviation	14	5
number with negative average returns	521	3
percentage of total with negative average returns	22%	0.4%

Figure 9-2

And this is even more dramatic: Of the 2,397 stocks in existence from 1990 through 1999, an eye-popping 22% had negative annualized returns. That means one stock in five lost money over a 10-year period.[174] In con-

[174] So much for that fabulous bull market you kept hearing about.

trast, of the 737 U.S. equity mutual funds in existence during that period, a minuscule 0.4% had negative annualized returns. In plain numbers, that's just three funds.

But if one in five stocks are losing 20%, doesn't that mean one in five stocks inside stock funds also are losing 20%?

Not at all. Remember that funds are professionally managed. So, even though one in five stocks might be losing money, fund managers could have been (and indeed often were) buying the four out of five that weren't doing so poorly.

Even if that weren't the case — even if four out of five of the manager's stocks were losers — he could still show a profit if the gains in that fifth stock exceeded the losses of the other four.

Diversification is a wonderful thing.

And the statistics get even more amazing. In this 10-year period — America's biggest bull market ever — the average annual return for individual stocks was 9%, while the average return for stock mutual funds was 15%. Compounding these returns over 10 years, a $10,000 investment in stocks would have netted you $24,782. Conversely, that same $10,000 in an average equity mutual fund would have netted you $40,455.

The third reason we use mutual funds in our financial planning practice is because there's more to a portfolio than stocks. People who buy stocks are often just fans of Marble Cake. They own bonds and stocks, but they fail to own real estate, international securities, oil & gas, natural resources, and so on.

Although it's rather easy to buy stocks and bonds, owning and managing real estate is a hassle. I doubt you want to fly to Tokyo to trade international stocks, and when's the last time you visited an oil well?[175] But you can own each of the other asset classes much more easily, conveniently and inexpensively via mutual funds. So with a basket of funds (more about which later) we can give each of our clients a well-diversified, comprehensive portfolio. You can't do this by just buying stocks.

[175] I did once, on a due diligence trip, just as a tornado arrived. Wasn't fun.

And that's a point worth stressing. Because when prices drop 30%, like many investments did in 2000 and 2001, it's not going to much matter which stocks you hold. That's because, when a market collapses, everything in that market falls. The solid players in the market will recover eventually, but in the meantime it's ugly for everyone in that market.

But you protect yourself when you properly diversify your assets among all major asset classes. That's because when stocks fall, bonds and real estate yawn — and maybe even rise. And vice versa.

Remember, you should not simply seek upside reward; you must also protect yourself against downside risk. That's why risk-adjusted returns are so important. It's also why those who consider return without also focusing on risk are making a big mistake.

Now you know why so many financial advisors (including me) recommend mutual funds for our clients instead of individual stocks. Because of this preference, the rest of this book is devoted to showing you how to pick mutual funds for your portfolio.[176] If you prefer to buy individual stocks, you can stop reading now.[177]

"Buy a really nice dollhouse in 2006 and start traveling to find unique to-scale furniture and accessories to decorate it."

~Anonymous, 54,
Speech/Language Pathologist

---

[176] Remember footnote 14 on page 21 that said we'd be digging 10 feet deep? Grab your hard hat, because we're about to tunnel 50 feet deep!
[177] And for those who are leaving, Bye!

PART III

How to Pick the Mutual Funds That Are Right for You

PART III

How to Pick the Mutual Funds That Are Right for You

With 8,171 funds to choose from, according to the Investment Company Institute, picking the right mutual funds is no easy task. So it's not surprising that many people do this so poorly. In this chapter, you'll see why others fail. You'll also learn how to do it correctly, through an in-depth examination of the six elements you should consider when selecting mutual funds.

"I want to learn to play the guitar reasonably well by the time I am 50. I have recently purchased a guitar and am in the process of finding an instructor. I have played the piano for years, but have always wanted to play an instrument I can take with me wherever I go."

~Jan Kowal,
Financial Planner,
Edelman Financial Services

By the time you're through . . .

. . . you'll know how to select funds . . .

. . . funds that fit within certain slices of your cake . . .

. . . a cake you want to bake based on the conclusions you reached in your financial plan . . .

. . . a plan you created so you can reach your goals.

Everything always returns us to our goals.

CHAPTER 10

How Most People Pick Their Funds

CHAPTER 10

How Most People Pick Their Funds

Because most people don't know what you now know, they pick their mutual funds based on just one criterion. You know what it is, too: past performance.

A survey of 3,300 mutual fund investors, conducted by Columbia University, proved that's how most people select their funds. And a joint study by the University of Illinois, Harvard University and the University of Chicago found that for every percentage point a mutual fund earns above average, new accounts the following year increase 2.6% and new assets increase 2%.

> ***"I want to visit Chile again — the home country of our daughter, who we adopted when she was six months old — in 2010."***
>
> **~Carolyn Conlan, 49, Gov't Manager**

Clearly, funds that have done well attract new investors, plus new money from old investors, because most people believe funds that have done well in the past will do well in the future.

And how do investors learn whether a fund has done well or not? Easy. They rely on the Star Ratings provided by Morningstar. I mean, that's how you pick your funds, isn't it?

Yes, it is. Don't lie to me.

I know you rely on Morningstar's Star Ranking System because the Financial Research Corporation says you do. FRC data show that, in 1998:

- 87% of all the money that people sent into mutual funds went to 4-star- and 5-star-rated funds.
- Of the 25 best-selling funds, 22 had 4 stars or 5 stars.
- Even though Fidelity (the largest mutual fund company) has 229 stock funds, only 33% (75 funds) had 4 stars or 5 stars, but those 75 funds got 94% of all of the money sent to Fidelity that year.

Morningstar's power and influence in the mutual fund industry is undeniable. If you're a fund manager and you don't have 4 stars or 5 stars, don't expect any new assets. Indeed, FRC examined net new money for 1998,[178] and guess what?

- 100% of all the net new money invested by mutual fund shareholders in 1998 went into 4-star and 5-star funds, and
- all 3-star, 2-star and 1-star funds incurred net withdrawals.

It might appear that I am bashing Morningstar, but I really am bashing the investors who select funds based solely on the Star Ratings. In fact, we occasionally use Morningstar data in our practice, so the problem isn't merely the data or Morningstar. Unfortunately, too many consumers — and too many advisors — don't understand how Morningstar works, and their misinterpretations cause them to make big investment mistakes. So, as you read on, keep in mind that my opinion about Morningstar is not necessarily the same as my opinion about the people who misuse it.

FRC's findings were confirmed by a separate study conducted jointly by the University of Oregon and the Federal Reserve Bank of Atlanta, which examined the cash flows of newly rated mutual funds. The study discovered that when new, unrated funds receive their first rating, those that are awarded 5 stars collect from investors an average of $26 million, or 53% more than normal. The study also found that funds that rise from 4 stars to 5 receive an additional $44 million in assets, or 35% above normal flow.

[178] Net new money refers to money sent into a fund minus withdrawals made by shareholders.

I suppose all this is understandable. After all, can you imagine a guy telling his wife he just bought a 1-star fund?

Would anyone buy the latest issue of *Money* magazine if the cover featured the fund manager of a 1-star fund?

Would you tune to CNBC or Louis Ruykeser (wherever he's airing these days) to see an interview of a 1-star manager?

This explains why, according to Strategic Insight Simfund, 90% of all the money in mutual funds — and that's $6.9 trillion as of June 2001, says the Investment Company Institute — is in 4-star and 5-star funds. All the other funds hold only 10% of all mutual fund assets.

So, go ahead. Tell me again that you don't rely on Morningstar to pick your funds.

Even if you don't, your advisor does – because he knows that if he doesn't recommend 4-star or 5-star funds to you, you'll go to another advisor who will!

Since everybody's relying on Morningstar, I have just one question: Do the star ratings work? I mean, will you enjoy superior performance by picking 4-star and 5-star funds? Look at the following data, produced by Financial Research Corporation and Strategic Insight Simfund, and decide for yourself:

- ✦ Of the stock funds rated 5 stars in 1991, 65% had fallen to 3 stars by 1993.
- ✦ Of the stock funds rated 5 stars in 1993, 44% had fallen to 3 stars by 1998.
- ✦ Of the stock funds rated 4 stars in 1993, 56% had fallen to 3 stars by 1998.

"In my latter 60s, I would like to volunteer at a national park to help protect our wild resources."

~Anonymous, 60, Teacher, Middle School

Does this phenomenon apply only to stock funds? Let's look at taxable bond funds to see:

- ✦ Those rated 5 stars at the end of 1997 earned an average of 0.5% in 1998.

- Those rated 4 stars at the end of 1997 earned an average of 4.4% in 1998.
- Those rated 3 stars at the end of 1997 earned an average of 6.5% in 1998.
- Those rated 2 stars at the end of 1997 earned an average of 7.2% in 1998.
- Those rated 1 star at the end of 1997 earned an average of 8.1% in 1998.
- And then, in 1998, of the 365 rated funds studied by FRC, the 5-star funds averaged 0.5% while the 2-star and 3-star funds averaged 7.5%.

These statistics are kinda backwards from what you'd have expected, aren't they?

It goes on.[179] In June 1999, the *Journal of Investment Consulting* released a study analyzing the performance of every growth and value stock fund that existed in the 7-year period of 1991-1997. As Figure 10-1 shows, both one year later and two years later, about half of the funds in each star rating

How Do the Stars Do in the Future?
a study of all value and growth funds 1991–1997

Year-end rating	% of funds performing above median one year later	% of funds performing above median two years later
★★★★★	52%	51%
★★★★	52%	48%
★★★	50%	50%
★★	49%	56%
★	42%	60%

Figure 10-1

[179] Just in case you're not yet convinced that the stars have no predictive qualities.

performed above average — and the other half performed below average. This was as true for 5-star funds as it was for 1-star funds. As you can see, two years later, there were more 1-star and 2-star funds performing above average than there were 4-star and 5-star funds performing above average!

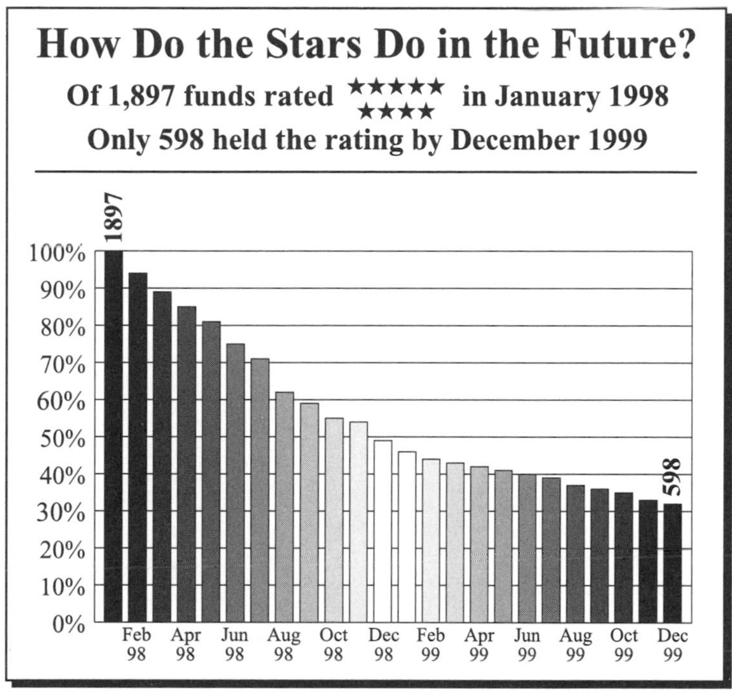

Figure 10-2

Morningstar's own data (see Figure 10-2) show that, of the 1,897 4-star or 5-star funds as of January 1998, only 873 retained a 4-star or 5-star rating as of 1999, and only 598 — or 31.5% of the original 1,897 funds — retained such ratings in 2000.

Let's continue to beat dead horses,[180] as we review the September 2000 issue of the *Journal of Financial Planning*. It contained a study that examined all the 4-star and 5-star funds in a variety of categories as of February 1999. The study reported that one year later, an average of 45% of the funds in each category failed to retain their ratings.

[180] Thought I didn't know that's what I was doing, eh?

One more, then I'll stop. Because this one is my favorite. In August 1995, Morningstar itself publicly recommended "Ten Terrific Funds — Morningstar Style," in a report it acknowledged as "our most blatant fund recommendation ever."

The performance of the 10 funds over the next two years went like this:

- five were above average
- one was average
- four were below average

Okay, I'll stop now.

Clearly, past performance does not indicate future results.[181] If you won't believe me,[182] consider the comments of others:

> Despite the focus on the stars, there is scant evidence that the stars accurately identify future top-performing mutual funds . . . the results of the study suggest [that] the stars are not useful in identifying future top performers within asset classes.
>
> ~*Journal of Investment Consulting,* June 1999

> Over-reliance on the stars — that is, considering only four-star and five-star funds — gets in the way of building a sophisticated, global portfolio.
>
> ~Morningstar Senior Editor Jeff Kelly, June 1996

> Probably the single most potentially dangerous action a mutual fund investor can take is to pay attention to "top performance" lists.
>
> ~John Markese, President, American Association of Individual Investors, February 2000

> If you ask us, star ratings are overrated.
>
> ~Morningstar's *Fund Investor,* Morningstar's own newsletter, February 1999

[181] Now do you believe me?
[182] Since I figure you still don't.

Has Morningstar failed? Not at all.

You see, Morningstar itself acknowledges that its star ratings are not intended to predict the future, but rather (and merely) to report on past performance. There is nothing in any of Morningstar's literature that suggests the stars will be helpful in predicting future results.

Indeed, what Morningstar's literature does say is, "Our system doesn't lay claim to some magical methodology for predicting future returns . . . as we see it, our job is to offer an objective measure of each fund's historical performance and risk."

> ***"I want to play contract bridge well. In 5 years."***
>
> **~Hugh Mason, 79**
> **Retired Military**

Notice the word *historical* in that statement. Morningstar's Star Rating System is designed to tell you how funds performed in the past; Morningstar makes no claims about the future, and it doesn't pretend to, either.

This contrasts sharply with the message you get from all those mutual fund ads that appear in the personal finance press — and sometimes in mainstream media, too. Since many of those ads brag about the stars a fund has earned — see examples on the next two pages — consumers are misled that the stars are a recommendation, like a *Consumer Reports* rating on toasters.

DILBERT © UFS
Reprinted by Permission.

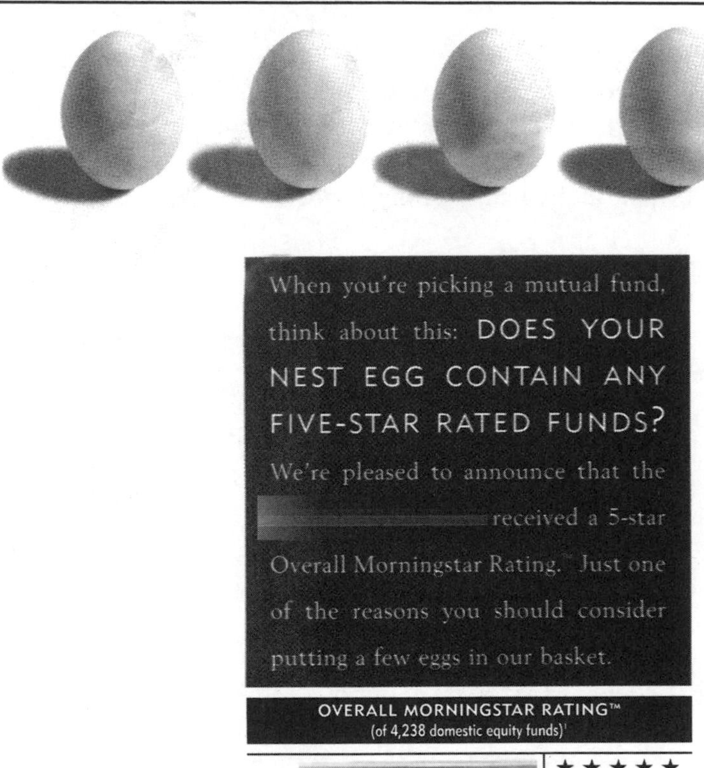

Three-year period ended January 31, 2001.

[1]Morningstar proprietary ratings on U.S.-domiciled funds reflect historical risk-adjusted performance as of January 31, 2001. The ratings are subject to change every month. Past performance is no guarantee of future results. Morningstar ratings on U.S.-domiciled funds are calculated from the funds' three-, five-, and 10-year average annual returns (if applicable) in excess of 90-day U.S. Treasury bill returns with appropriate fee adjustments, and a risk factor that reflects fund performance below 90-day U.S. T-bill returns. The Overall Morningstar Rating™ is a weighted average of a fund's 3-, 5-, and 10-year (if applicable) risk-adjusted performance. The top 10% of the funds in a broad asset class receive 5 stars, the next 22.5% receive 4 stars, the next 35% receive 3 stars, the next 22.5% receive 2 stars, and the bottom 10% receive 1 star. Fund was rated against 4,238 domestic equity funds and exclusively against U.S.-domiciled funds. The Fund commenced operations on December 31, 1997 and therefore its 3-year Morningstar Rating™ is the same as its Overall Morningstar Rating.™

Call or go online to get a prospectus, which contains more complete information including charges and expenses. Read the prospectus carefully before you invest or send money.

This ad strongly implies that your portfolio is supposed to contain 5-star funds, perpetuating the myth.

Give Your Portfolio a Wake-up Call

Have your mutual fund returns seemed a bit tired lately? Maybe your portfolio could use a gentle nudge. Funds aren't known for performance that will lull you to sleep. But our disciplined investment approach has delivered solid returns over the long term. Of course, to do that we take some risk. But Fund combines the aggressive approach to investing with the relative stability of larger, more established companies. Don't reach for the "snooze" button again – time is ticking toward your investment goals – call today and wake up your investment results with

Overall Morningstar Rating™ as of 1/31/01

★★★★★

out of 4,238 domestic equity funds

The Morningstar Rating™ reflects historical risk-adjusted performance as of 1/31/01 and is subject to change every month. Past performance is no guarantee of future results. The Fund's Overall Morningstar Rating™ is the weighted average of its three- and five-year ratings. Morningstar ratings are calculated from the Fund's overall average annual returns in excess of 90-day Treasury bill returns with appropriate fee adjustments, and a risk factor that reflects Fund performance below 90-day T-bill returns. For the three- and five-year periods ending 1/31/01, the Fund received ratings of five stars out of 4,238 and 2,598 domestic equity funds respectively. The top 10% of the funds in the broad asset class receive five stars.

Mutual fund investing involves risk including possible loss of principal. An investment in technology companies involves greater risk and price volatility. Products of technology companies may be subject to severe competition and rapid obsolescence.

For more complete information, including information on charges and expenses, call for a free prospectus. Read it carefully prior to investing or sending money.

Read this ad carefully. It does not state that it will earn high returns in the future, but that's the conclusion a reader is likely to draw. And the stars are the most dominant graphic element in the ad.

Before you invest – investigate.

~Salmon P. Halle

It's easy to understand why consumers are misled by these ads. After all, ratings are everywhere. Zagat's rates restaurants, Consumer's Union rates products, *Car & Driver* rates cars, and Ebert rates movies. But there's a huge difference between all those ratings and the stars issued by Morningstar: Watch a movie 10 times and each performance will be the same; it's not affected by external influences. But a mutual fund's performance changes constantly because its environment is changing constantly.

"Be able to retire by 55 so I can then be a student/ teacher in ancient Egypt and Israel."

~Stephen H. Pauley, 45, Information Technology

The press doesn't help matters, either. The magazines and financial shows are happy to interview the guy who managed last year's #1 fund. Many of them — including *Money*, *Forbes*, *Business Week*, *SmartMoney*, *Mutual Funds*, *Worth*, and *Kiplinger's* — release their own rankings, and most issues are filled with reviews of funds that have done really well. Although no one outright says so, they all leave their readers with the clear impression that, since the past performance of all these funds are being mentioned, these funds ought to be the ones that you're supposed to buy now. Right?

Now you know that that is Wrong.[183, 184]

If all this isn't enough reason for you to ignore Morningstar's Star Ratings, here are four more reasons.

Don't confuse activity with productivity.

~B.W. Lusher, Jr.

[183] And another thing. Have you noticed that the personal finance press tells you to "invest for the long term" while publishing a list of how mutual funds have done in the past three months? That short-term performance information has no value for consumers — but it gives the press something new to talk about each month.

[184] I'm starting to feel better now that I'm getting all this off my chest.

Problem #1: The Rating Formula Gives Newer Funds an Advantage Over Older Funds

No fund is assigned a rating until it is three years old. At that time, its three-year performance is averaged to produce a total return — the basis for its new rating. If a fund is four years old, only the most recent three years are considered.

But when funds are five years old, all five years are considered, and the most recent two years receive higher consideration than the original three years, on the belief that the fund's more recent performance is of greater relevance than its more distant performance.

When a fund is six, seven, eight and nine years old, only the most recent five years are considered, using the above methodology. But when a fund becomes 10 years old, all 10 years are considered.

"To own a boat large enough to live comfortably on year-round and travel from port to port. In 2025."

~Anonymous, 34, Federal Government Public Affairs Specialist

Morningstar's philosophy thus contains an unfortunate (and perhaps unavoidable) side effect: It favors newer funds over older ones. You see, if your fund is only three years old, those last three years constitute 100% of the results, but if the fund is 10 years old, the performance of all 10 years affects the rating. But do the events of 10 years ago matter to the person who's investing in the fund now?

This is not a rhetorical question. It's important that you answer it, so I'll ask you again:

Do the events of 10 years ago matter to you if you're investing in the fund now — yes or no?

Your answer is: ________

- If you said, "Yes, the events of 10 years ago do matter," that's too bad. Because when a fund is nine years old, the fund's first four years are ignored. Therefore, your philosophy does not match Morningstar's.

- If you said "No, the events of 10 years ago don't matter," that's too bad. Because when a fund is 10 years old, the fund's first four years constitute 20% of the fund's performance score. In fact, the most recent three years comprise only 53% of Morningstar's calculation. Therefore, your philosophy does not match Morningstar's.

Thus, no matter which viewpoint you hold, you can't always be satisfied with the way Morningstar produces its Star Ratings. That's because Morningstar sometimes says old performance matters, while other times it says it does not. Thus, there's an inherent inconsistency in the way Morningstar calculates each fund's total return.

Morningstar is making no error here, by the way. It appears to err because I rigged the examples: I used funds of different ages. If the two funds considered above were of equal age, Morningstar's approach would be fine.

"I want to learn how to make fine pastries and open a pastry shop in October 2011."

~Anonymous, 39, Human Resources Generalist

And that is the real problem: Some mutual funds are older than others. This makes it difficult to compare them. That's why Morningstar publishes, in addition to its overall Star Rating, the three component ratings (3-year, 5-year and 10-year) that comprise it. Indeed, no matter how Morningstar (or anyone else, for that matter) designs their system, that system will work better for some comparisons than others. I mention this to help you understand the danger of comparing newer funds with older ones merely by comparing the Star Ratings that have been assigned to them.

So, go ahead and compare three-year-old funds with other three-year-old funds, but be careful when comparing funds of different ages.

Notice that 10-year-old funds can be punished — and rewarded — merely for being 10 years old. Here's how: If they lost money eight years ago simply because the nation was in a recession, that poor performance of eight years ago will be factored into their overall return. Funds that are only three years old, which weren't around back then, are not held similarly accountable. This is simply unfair to older funds.

But older funds can benefit from this system, too. After all, funds that existed in the late 1990s will get credit for how they did during the tech boom, while funds created after that boom ended will not be able to boast about such returns.

Does all this make some funds better than others, or are some funds simply luckier than others because they happened to exist (or not) during some given historical period?

Such are the challenges faced by Morningstar (and other rating services) when trying to establish formulas for ranking mutual funds. It's too easy to criticize the rating services; it's much more effective instead to understand them, so you can improve your ability to effectively evaluate the funds they rate.

Another fact worth noting is that Morningstar ignores all performance beyond 10 years. This means no fund is held accountable today for how it performed during the crash of 1987 or the recession of 1991, and soon the interest rate crisis of 1994 will be removed from statistical memory. By the same notion, Morningstar does not restart the ratings when a fund changes its style, or when a fund's manager leaves — and we'll talk later about both those issues. Observers cite all these issues when cautioning investors about Star Ratings.

During the 10-year period 1987-1996, which includes the crash of '87, the S&P 500 produced an average annual return of 16%. But advance that interval just one year, 1988-1997 (which skips the crash of '87), and the average jumps to 19%.[185]

Ditto for the bursting of the Internet bubble of the 1990s. From 1995 to 1999, the NASDAQ grew 32.5% per year. But if we rotate forward just one year, to the period 1996-2000 (so the dot-com crash is included), NASDAQ's annual gain falls to 15.3% per year — or less than half.

What a difference a year makes.

[185] What's the difference made by those three percentage points? Well, on an investment of $10,000 over the 10 years, it amounts to a difference of nearly $13,000!

As if Morningstar's star rating didn't have enough problems, some fund companies manipulate the rating's methodology by engaging in deceptive or unethical practices.

One tactic involves "pooled trading." Say a fund family with 50 stock funds pools at its central trading desk all the buy and sell orders issued by each of its fund managers. Since it's not known until later which trades will be profitable, the company assigns the profitable trades to the funds that have the best records. It then assigns the less profitable (or even losing) trades into its funds that merely have average (or even poor) records.

Through such manipulation of trade reporting, fund companies can make sure that some of its funds receive (or sustain) high Morningstar ratings. The rationale is that it's better to have some funds that are great even it if means having some funds that are terrible (instead of having nothing but average funds), because great funds attract investor capital; average and terrible funds don't. The problem for investors is that they may have invested in a fund whose excellent trades are credited to a different fund. Although it's deceptive (and prohibited), it's alleged that some fund companies engage in this practice.

Another tactic involves "incubated funds." Fund companies know that new funds are not rated by Morningstar for three years. So when they launch new funds, they don't make them immediately available to the public. After all, why bother? As we've seen, investors tend to buy only 4-star and 5-star funds. Thus, new funds usually don't attract much attention — or investor capital. So, the fund company invests a few million of its own dollars into the fund to get it started, and it then manages the fund internally.

After three years, the company makes the fund available to the public — provided that its track record during the incubation period has been good enough to earn a high Morningstar rating. If the fund hasn't done well enough, the fund company quietly buries the fund with nary a word to the outside world.

It's bad enough that only good funds ever see the light of day. What's worse is when fund companies fill these small young funds with profitable trades diverted from their trading desks, as described above. The result is an incubated fund that makes its public debut with a fabulous three-year track record — a record that it almost certainly will be unable to sustain. Unsuspecting investors buy these funds only to discover that the funds do not duplicate the performance they enjoyed during their incubation period. Such trade diversion is a prohibited practice.

A third tactic has led to the name "survivorship bias." Say a fund company has 50 funds, but several of them have poor track records. How would it improve its company's overall reputation? Well, it could try harder to

improve the lackluster funds — or it could merely close the bad funds and merge their assets into the others within the family that have much better track records.

Does this really happen? Consider these statistics from Dreman Value Management: In March 1998, there were 220 equity-income mutual funds, according to Lipper Analytical Services. As of August 2001, only 30 still exist. The other 190 haven't survived.

When funds disappear, their performance records disappear, too. Their stats aren't included in the historical performance data people keep referring to (because no one bothers to report on funds that are no longer available) — and that includes all the data found throughout this book. It begs the question: Is a given fund family good, or does it merely look good because it has proverbially swept its bad funds under the rug? Critics of the mutual fund industry cite survivorship bias as a major reason historical performance data looks better than it really is. After all, they argue (with more than a little legitimacy) that the statement, "Only three equity funds lost money in the 10 years ending 1999" is true only because all the others that lost money have been merged away.

Want to hear about another tactic fund companies use to make themselves look better than they really are? Stay tuned, for later on you'll learn about "window dressing."

Problem #2: Fund Performance Is Unfairly Adjusted for Loads

Some funds levy a "load" or sales charge. This is in addition to the annual fee that all funds assess.[186] Buyers of load funds incur this cost, while buyers of no-load funds do not. Since paying a load lowers a fund's return, Morningstar reduces a fund's performance by the amount of its load. That might seem reasonable, but it's not. Let me explain why.

Loads exist for one reason, and one reason only: to provide compensation to the advisor who's helping you. If you're not using an advisor, there's no reason for you to invest in a load fund, for there are ample no-load funds

[186] You'll find a complete explanation of mutual fund fees and expenses in Chapter 27 of *The Truth About Money*.

from which to choose (and as data from Morningstar and others show, equally outstanding funds can be found among both loads and no-loads).[187]

But if you need or prefer assistance with researching, evaluating, selecting and monitoring funds, if you want help with executing the transaction, managing the paperwork and tax record-keeping obligations, and avoiding mistakes as you make critical life decisions, you could benefit from hiring an advisor. This explains why Investment Company Institute data show that two-thirds of all investors work with advisors.

And advisors demand to be paid for their services.[188] There are four ways they earn income:

- Some send you an invoice based on a flat fee or hourly rate, and you pay by check;
- Some recommend no-load funds (or private managers, usually via wrap accounts) and assess you a fee (typically 1-2% per year) based on the amount of money you invest. Often, they debit your account on a quarterly basis;
- Some recommend load funds, in which case the fund collects the "load" and passes part of it on to the advisor; and
- Some do a combination of the above.

Although there's no question that some consumers buy load funds without obtaining the services of an advisor, they are a minority. Therefore, when Morningstar reduces a fund's performance because it charges a load, it actually is punishing the fund because it is primarily purchased by investors who choose to hire advisors who earn their pay in this fashion.

"Make a return visit to Istanbul and other cities in Turkey as soon as we end the war in Afghanistan."

~Betty O'Lear,
Financial Planner,
Edelman Financial Services

[187] For evidence of this, see again Chapter 27 of *The Truth About Money.*
[188] Trust me on this one.

But Morningstar does not assess advisory fees for no-loads, even though a large percentage of those who buy no-load funds pay such costs. Thus, advisors who use load funds argue that the playing field is not level, for Morningstar's methodology clearly gives no-load funds an advantage.

I will visit Italy, Ireland, Russia and Loire Valley, France, in three years.

~Anonymous, 68, Systems Engineer

Even if you are among those who believe that this advantage is justified, the advantage is bigger than it deserves to be due to the way Morningstar does its math. You see, when Morningstar subtracts a fund's load from its return, it subtracts the maximum possible load. But this is unrealistic.

For example, Figure 10-3 shows a typical load structure for Class A (front-load) mutual funds. When investing in a Class A fund, you pay the load at the time you invest, and the amount charged is based on the amount you invest. If you invest less than $50,000, for example, you pay a load equal to 5.75% of your investment.

With front-load funds, the more you invest, the lower the load. But Morningstar assumes that all investors of front-load funds always pay the highest load.

Investment Amount	Load
Under $50,000	5.75%
50,000 but under 100,000	4.50
100,000 but under 250,000	3.50
250,000 but under 500,000	2.50
500,000 but under 1,000,000	2.00
1,000,000 and above	NONE

Figure 10-3

And that is exactly the amount that Morningstar debits from such funds' performance calculations. But this arbitrarily assumes that everyone is investing a (relatively) small amount of money. Investors with larger assets, who might really pay only 2%, could dismiss a fund from consideration because it has a lower Morningstar Star Rating than it otherwise might have — a rating lower because Morningstar's formula thinks the investor will pay a fee he actually will not incur.

> Science is a wonderful thing if one does not have to earn one's living at it.
>
> ~Albert Einstein

The same problem exists for Class B (rear-load) funds. When investing in a Class B fund, you do not pay a load when you invest; instead, you pay a fee when you sell. But as Figure 10-4 shows, the fee you'll pay depends on when you sell, and if you hold your shares for seven years, you'll pay no withdrawal fee at all.

With rear-load funds, the longer you keep your funds, the less you pay to sell them. When calculating the three-year rating, Morningstar assumes all investors of rear-load funds pay half the highest cost.

Year after purchase	1	2	3	4	5	6	7+
Charge	5%	4%	3%	3%	2%	1%	0%

Figure 10-4

But when calculating the three-year performance of Class B funds, Morningstar assumes you're paying the charge. (Interestingly, Morningstar only debits half the charge, rather than the entire amount, as though it couldn't decide whether to assess the fee at all.) Still, this is unrealistic for most Class B investors, since the majority holds their shares for many years.

Problem #3:
Morningstar Gives Too Many Funds a 5-Star Rating

Morningstar grades on a bell curve: Of the nation's 13,112 funds: [189]

- 10% receive 5 stars
- 22.5% receive 4 stars
- 35% receive 3 stars
- 22.5% receive 2 stars
- 10% receive 1 star.

Thus, nearly one-third of all rated funds receive the highest two ratings. How special can a "top-rated" fund be when it's merely one of 13,112 funds? How could such a huge list possibly help you select the right investment?

"I want to cycle across America at my 45th birthday. From San Francisco to Washington, D.C. —3,000 miles."

~Reynold Roy,
Financial Planner,
Edelman Financial Services

Problem #4:
Morningstar Changes the Ratings Too Often

You'll probably be shocked to discover that Morningstar does not change its ratings annually, semi-annually or even quarterly. No, Morningstar changes ratings on a monthly basis.[190]

All this explains why you should pay little attention to the Stars when investing. In fact, this explains why Morningstar itself pays little attention to the Stars. Indeed, Morningstar's 401(k) plan uses 16 mutual funds from 14 fund families:

[189] Sharp readers might note that I earlier said there are 8,171 mutual funds. Why now 13,112? Because the former number is provided by the Investment Company Institute, the trade organization that represents the mutual fund industry. The latter figure is provided by Morningstar. The discrepancy is due to the fact that many funds are available in multiple share classes, and while Morningstar counts each as a separate fund, the ICI does not. Just another example that statistics are only as valid as the statistician.

[190] When people tell me they want a 5-star rated fund, I ask, "Do you want one that was rated that way in September or in October?"

- Only three are 5-star funds
- Eleven are 3-star or 4-star funds
- Two are 2-star funds

This wide dispersion of stars should be expected. After all, of the six criteria it uses to select its own funds, Morningstar says consideration of "risk-adjusted performance rankings" (i.e., the stars) is dead last.[191]

Clearly, Morningstar is well aware of the problems with choosing funds based on its Star Rating system. And now, you are too.

"I would like to buy and live in a nice house on the Chesapeake Bay near Washington, D.C. I would like to be able to enjoy boating on the Bay and share in my wife's enjoyment with horses. In 2004."

~Anonymous, 54,
President, Consulting Firm

"Do a driving tour of the U.S., starting in Maine and driving through each of the lower 48 states at age 64-66."

~David Johnson, 49,
Government Worker

[191] It's also worth noting that four of the 16 funds are load funds, proving my point that you shouldn't refuse to invest in funds simply for that reason.

CHAPTER 11

How to Pick Mutual Funds

CHAPTER 11

How to Pick Mutual Funds

If you skipped
— or rather, fled —
the Morningstar
chapter, welcome back!
We now return you
to our regularly
scheduled reading.

By this point, you've either agreed to follow Ric's Recipe or you're still reading simply because you find this to be the most ridiculous book on personal finance since *Dow 36,000*.

In the futile hope that it's the former and not the latter, let's home in on our efforts to pick mutual funds that will conform to our freshly sliced cake.

I'm going to assume that you want a cake with many slices, each representing a separate asset class, and that you want to own a variety of market sectors within each asset class. You don't just want a chocolate slice, you want different kinds of chocolate in that slice.

"Visit Machu Picchu and the Galapagos Islands, by Sept. 2003."

~Mary Davis, Financial Planner, Edelman Financial Services

This means you're going to buy a bunch of mutual funds, each one investing in a specific sector. (There's another way to do this: You can buy hybrid funds, and we'll discuss that method later.)

Down through the ages, mankind has pondered many deep questions. We'll now consider the six questions that can lead us to the right mutual funds. These questions are:

1. Is it just me, or is it hot in here?

2. Are you always this wacky?

3. Why does B come after A in the alphabet?

4. Am I good or just lucky?

5. Is that a diamond ring, or a cubic zirconia?

6. Do you always get what you pay for?

The rest of this book is devoted to the subject of picking mutual funds. Maybe you have no intention of picking your own funds. If so, give this book to someone else, and go read, "How to Choose a Financial Advisor" — it's Part 13 of *The Truth About Money*. Because if you're not going to do this yourself, you'll need to hire someone to do it for you.

1. Is It Just Me or Is It Hot in Here?

We've all asked this question at one time or another. Why are we relieved when told, "Yes, it *is* hot in here." After all, we're still hot! But at least we realize that others are hot with us, and we find this comforting.

In the world of mutual fund analysis, this is called Relative Performance. It means you should examine investment returns in the context of "all things considered" rather than absolutely.

Let me present you with three scenarios:

Scenario One:	Your fund loses 20%.
Scenario Two:	Your fund loses 20% while all its peers lose 30%.
Scenario Three:	Your fund loses 20% while all its peers gain 10%.

Surely, the first scenario makes you unhappy. But does the second scenario make you feel a little better? It probably does.[192]

And without question, you feel worst under the third scenario.

> Being rich is having money; being wealthy is having time.
>
> ~Margaret Bonnano

Regardless of how each of these scenarios makes you feel, I'm saying that your focus should be on relative performance because I'm assuming that you've already chosen the slices for your cake, and you've accepted the risks associated with choosing certain ingredients for certain slices. I mean, if you're willing to go into the ring, you have no right to complain when you get bopped in the nose. But you have a right to complain if your nose gets bopped a whole lot more often than all the other noses that are in that ring with you. Make sense?

"How come Jasper's mutual fund is up twelve percent and mine's only up eight?"

[192] But I'm not sure why. After all, this is like saying you booked the best cabin on the Titanic.

I get emails from people all over the world, and some of them lament that they own a mutual fund that has lost money. These types of emails, largely absent in the 1990s, arrived with great frequency in 2000 and 2001, a period in which the stock market performed poorly.

"My stock fund is down," these emails typically would say. My reply (which I'd never actually send) was a sarcastic — "Oh, *your* fund is the one that went down?" — as though that emailer was the only one having this experience. I don't know if those emailers felt better when I told them that virtually all investors were losing money at the time — the Titanic cabin thing — but they should.

The point is that you cannot expect investments to make money all the time. At some point, and for some period, every investment will lose money. In other periods, those same investments will make money. So, what you want to know is this: Given the period studied, did the fund perform as you would have expected it to perform, and is that performance acceptable compared to its peers?

For example, as I've mentioned, rising interest rates cause bond prices to drop. Therefore, if you find that rates are rising, you should expect the prices of long-term bond funds to fall. So, when that scenario occurs, you should not be upset that your bond fund suffers a loss. Instead, you should be annoyed only if its loss is significantly larger than the losses suffered by most other long-term bond funds.

Similarly, when interest rates drop, making bond funds profitable again, you would expect your fund to increase in value, and your disappointment, if any, should be based on the degree to which this does not occur relative to other funds in its class.

Is each fund in your portfolio — each slice of your cake — performing in an acceptable manner (relative to its peers and the market's environment)? If so, you should not be upset at your funds if your overall performance is not meeting the goals you established waaaay back at the beginning of the book.[193] Instead, you need to change either the goals (meaning, start all over again — yuk) or change the portfolio allocation, by increasing the size of one slice while decreasing the size of other slices.

Unfortunately, this is not how most people handle their investments.

They typically begin with wildly unrealistic expectations (often because they've just now put money into a fund that gained 123% last year). Often, it never occurs to them that they might lose money. Later, when the gains are lower than expected or the losses larger, they bail out of the fund, threatening to sue whoever it was who told them about it in the first place.

Above all else, I choose funds that are consistent in their performance over a variety of time periods, relative to their peers.[194] This means doing (relatively) well in the last 3-year, 5-year, 10-year, 15-year and 20-year intervals.

The best way I can explain this is by referring to one of the nation's best stock fund managers. He once told me that his goal was to never be among the best 10% of performers in a single year. With so much competition, he reasoned, the only way to make the top 10% was to place big bets with large portions of the portfolio. If he bet right, the fund would make a lot of money and he'd make the top 10%. And no doubt he could bet correctly on occasion. But in other years, his fund would take a beating, sending him into the bottom 10%, and he didn't want to risk his shareholders' assets in that way.

"Right now I'm recovering from spinal surgery. My goal is to tour Australia and really enjoy it and walk everywhere, within one year."

~Jean Barber, 68,
Retired Federal Employee

[193] Remember them? Goals? This is a book about achieving goals, remember?
[194] That statement might sound like it's got a built-in contradiction of terms, but it doesn't.

Instead, he told me, his goal was to be in the top 25% each year. By being merely in the top quartile — not nearly as challenging a goal — and doing it every year for three years straight, his 3-year record would be in the top 10% — the very place he said he wasn't trying to be. He's been able to do this consistently because so few of his competitors manage their accounts in this fashion. It's the kind of slow-and-steady approach that I prefer. So, let's explore that approach further.

This is why the funds we use for our clients typically are older than most others. All other factors being equal,[195] we like 20-year-old funds more than 5-year-old funds, because the long track records enable us to review how the fund performed during a variety of market environments. We can't rely solely on this data, of course, because past performance does not predict future results . . . but it is more helpful to be able to review the data and minimize their importance than not have the data at all.

Another reason we prefer 20-year-old funds is because the 10 years ending December 31, 1999, featured only one segment of the market cycle. You see, throughout most of the 1990s, most stocks did only two things: They went up, or they went waaaaaay up. That environment tells us nothing about how a fund might do in a period of high inflation, weak dollar, civil unrest or other problematic times such as the ones we've had since September 11. Trouble is, there weren't many funds in the 1970s or 1980s, and not many of them are around today.[196]

All I ask is the chance to prove that money can't make me happy.

~Spike Milligan

[195] And they never are.

[196] In a weird way, this is really a benefit, because it dramatically reduces the universe of fund candidates, making our search efforts easier.

2. Are You Always This Wacky?

My prior comments about relative performance notwithstanding, consistency is important. After all, knowing that I'm always wacky helps you more than if I were wacky only some of the time.

Here's an example to illustrate this.

You are considering two investments. The Gopher Fund has a standard deviation of 18, while the Eagle Fund's deviation is zero. But both have an average annual return of 10%.

"I want to produce a successful documentary film with wide theatrical release by the time I'm 40 years old."

~Anonymous, 31, Internet

Since both have the same return, does it matter which you pick? Indeed it does. Because even though their historical returns are identical, standard deviation tells us that they used very different routes to get there.

Standard deviation refers to the degree to which your *annual* returns deviate from your *average* return. In the Eagle Fund's[197] case, it has earned a 10% return every year — never more, never less.[198] It never varied. Thus, its annual return is the same as its average return.

The Gopher Fund also enjoyed a 10% average annual return. But the Gopher's deviation is 18. This means that in some years, the fund's *annual* return was higher than its 10% *average* return, and in some years it was lower.

The question though, is: How much higher, and how much lower, did the Gopher Fund ever get, compared to its average? Statisticians tell us that annual returns fall within "one standard deviation" 67% of the time, and within "two standard deviations" 95% of the time.

In other words, although our Gopher Fund earned an average return of 10%, we might not be able to say that it really earned 10% in any one

[197]This is a hypothetical fund, as is the Gopher Fund, in case ya didn't know. My lawyer made me disclose that to you. Sheesh.
[198]Now you know why it's hypothetical — I couldn't find a real fund that did that!

year. Instead, all we might be able to say is that, for any given year, it probably earned somewhere between –8% and 28%, and that it almost definitely earned from –26% to 46%. For actual standard deviation statistics, refer to Figure 11-1.

Standard Deviations
1986–2000

	With a Standard Deviation of	and an Annual Average Total Return of	95% of the time, these funds earned somewhere between
U.S. Government Securities Funds	5	7.1%	–2.9% and +17.1%
Corporate Bond Funds — High Yield	12	7.9%	–16.1% and +31.9%
Balanced Funds	9	11.4%	–6.6% and +29.4%
Stock Funds	14	15.3%	–12.7% and +43.3%
International Stock Funds	19	11.9%	–26.1% and +49.9%

Figure 11-1

Imagine the mutual fund salesman who pitches the Gopher Fund to his neighbor. If he says, "This fund produced an average return of 10% per year," he'll probably be invited over for a barbecue. But if he says, "In some years, this fund lost 26% and in other years it gained 46%," he'll probably have to leave the neighborhood. See Figure 11-2.

When a fund's annual performance routinely deviates from its long-term average, this deviation becomes standard . . . hence the phrase "standard deviation."

Now you see the crisis that awaits the poor soul who buys this fund merely because she'd heard it has averaged 10% per year. You can be confident that such investors never imagine that they might lose 26% in a single year from such an investment — yet that's exactly what so many funds did in 2000, to the surprise and shock of their shareholders.

But those returns, in virtually every case, were well predicted by standard deviation.

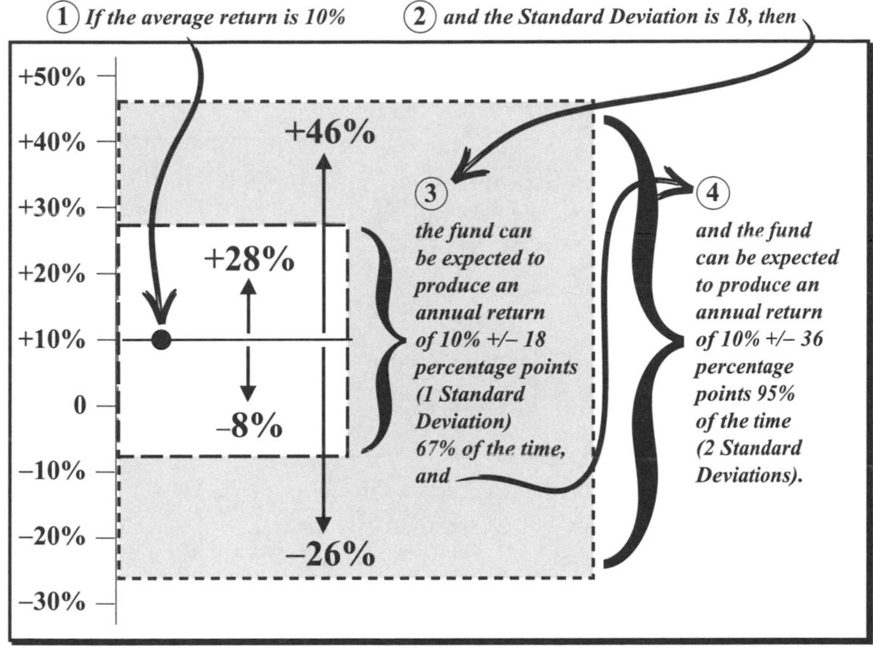

Figure 11-2

"O.K. The forward rate for marks rose in March and April, combined with a sharp increase in German reserves and heavy borrowing in the Eurodollar market, while United States liquid reserves had dropped to fourteen billion dollars, causing speculation that the mark might rise and encouraging conversion on a large scale. Now do you understand?"

You've already learned not to take at face value Morningstar's Star Rating and Category Rating. Now you know not to select a fund simply because it has a high average annual return. Look for funds with lower standard deviations than other funds, because the lower the standard deviation, the less volatile the fund. And if you find one with a standard deviation of zero, let me know.

Standard deviation data is available from Morningstar.

Why Standard Deviation Is So Important

You know how bad the stock market was in 2000 and 2001. What you don't know is that it was even worse than you realize.

That is, if you had investments that lost 50% of their value. Too many people faced horrible losses during the tech stock blowout, and too many of them still refuse to sell those investments. Instead, they're saying, "I'm hanging in there. I'm not going to sell with these big losses. I'm going to wait for these losses to recover."

Such sentiments are understandable. After all, stock prices recovered after the 1987 drop. They recovered after the '91 drop. And they recovered after the '94 drop. Heck, they even recovered after the '29 drop (though that one took a while).

So is it wrong for these investors to keep holding on? Indeed it is, and let me show you why. Through this illustration, you'll discover not only why it's silly to "hang on" but equally critical that you *never* allow yourself to suffer massive losses in your investments.[199]

Let's begin with this easy question. Is it possible for your investments to lose 10% in a given year?

[199] And the only way to avoid massive losses is to avoid exposing yourself to that possibility in the first place, which is the real point of this conversation. This is so important, I probably shouldn't have made this point in a footnote.

Well, sure it is. No matter what type of investment you own — stocks, bonds, real estate, gold, international securities, or mutual funds of those assets — you can lose 10% in a 12-month period.

Second question: Should that worry you?

No, and here's why.[200]

If your portfolio falls 10%, earning 10% will not return you to break-even. Instead, you'd need to earn 11.1% (try it with a calculator and see).

Now, this is not a big deal, for your investments can earn 11.1% in a year (almost) as easily as they can earn 10%. Thus, if you lose 10% in a year, it makes perfect sense to "hang on" and wait for your investments to recover, because they almost certainly will. This is the basis for my position that you should maintain a "long-term, buy-and-hold" strategy: Give your investments the time they need to recover from their occasional losses.

But this idea falls apart when the loss is 50%. In that event, you must gain 100% to break even. Think about it: If your $100 falls to fifty bucks, you've got a 50% loss. But that fifty must double to become one hundred again.

Although it's not a big deal that you must earn 11.1% after losing 10%, being forced to earn 100% is a much bigger challenge for those tech stocks that fell 50%.

"I will finish my book on pre–civil rights era southern white enablers, go to China, and establish a lectureship in my father's name."

~Elizabeth N. Shiver, 69, Editor/Writer/Businesswoman

And if you owned an Internet stock that fell 80% (many tech stocks did), you'd need to gain 400% to break even. Although those investments declined 80% in just one year (or less), will they gain 400% in as short a period? I doubt it, and I think you doubt it, too. In fact, assuming those stocks grow 10% per year from this point forward, it will take them almost 17 years (!) to reach their previous level. That is indeed a good reason to panic.

[200] This is very important, so pay attention.

And if you are one of the schmoes who lost 95% in MicroStrategy, you now must earn a whopping 1,900% to get your money back. You tell me: How long will it take for that stock — heck, any stock — to grow 1,900%?

If it grows 10% per year from now on, it'll take 31 years to get you back to where you started. How old did you say you are?

Check this out: You have $100. You lose 95%. You now have $5. That $5 now gains 95%. You now have $9.75.

Yippee.[201]

When it comes to investing, it's the percentages that count, not the dollars. And people just don't understand this. That's why it's misleading when the media report that, "stocks gained 2% today." Gee, if stocks fell 2% yesterday but gained 2% today, we must be back to where we started, right?

Wrong — you're losing money, and now you know why. Look at Figure 11-3 to see just how much of a problem you're facing.

How Long Will It Take You to Recover Your Losses?

(2) and if your stocks earn this return from now on

(1) If your stock lost	6%	8%	10%	12%	15%
20%	4	4	3	2	2
30%	6	5	4	3	3
40%	9	7	5	5	4
50%	12	9	7	6	5
60%	16	12	10	8	7
70%	21	16	13	11	9
80%	28	21	17	14	12
90%	40	30	24	21	17

(3) it'll take this many years for you to recover your losses

Figure 11-3

[201] This isn't mere theory. I described on page 218 how something like this really happened to fund manager Ryan Jacob and his investors.

The year 2000 was the worst year for the Dow since 1981, the worst year for the S&P since 1977, and the worst year ever for NASDAQ. No matter what stocks you owned, if you owned only stocks, it's highly likely that your portfolio fell in value. The only real question was how much. But there was some good news even in a year such as that one.

Despite the negative returns on stocks that year, you shouldn't have lost much money. In fact, you may even have made money (though just a little). Fred Barbash, then-columnist for *The Washington Post*, said it best: "You're a market outperformer if you lost less than 10% in 2000, a genius if you stayed even, and a true wizard at plus 5%."

As Fred correctly observed, people who were invested mostly in stocks probably learned a hard lesson in 2000. On the other hand, if you had sliced your cake (I mean, handled your portfolio) as I've been recommending – using a diversified approach, one that was well balanced among stocks, bonds, international securities, real estate, natural resources, oil and gas, and even some cash – then 2000 did you no real harm. In fact, not only did you avoid the losses of 60% or more that some investors suffered, you might have made money. Why?

Because as bad as the stock market was in 2000, the big untold story – something no one talked about – is the fact that 2000 was one of the best years ever for bonds; the Lehman Long-Term Bond Index was up 20% in 2000. It was also one of the best years ever for utility stocks; the Dow Jones Utility Index was up a whopping 45% in 2000.

This is why investors who faced those huge 50%, 60%, 70%, 80%, 90% and 95% losses in the tech fallout are now decades away from seeing again the money they once had. This is a genuine financial crisis for them.

Now you see why you must make sure that your overall portfolio does not incur losses of this magnitude. And the only way to do that is to maintain a highly diversified portfolio — a cake with many slices. That doesn't simply mean owning 200 stocks instead of one (or many varieties of chocolate). It means flavors and ingredients other than chocolate — owning asset classes other than stocks — because if all you own is one asset class, you face the risk of experiencing a sudden and unpredictable loss of such huge magnitude that it could take you years — even decades — to recover.

Now you understand why NASDAQ's 52% crash (from its high in March 2000 through December 31, 2000) was so horrible for some people, and why, if you didn't suffer those massive losses, you should be thankful. And make sure you always maintain a diversified portfolio to help you avoid such losses in the future.

2000's relatively great performance for bonds and utility stocks reinforces the need to maintain balance and diversity in your portfolio. Investors began to realize this only after they lost a lot of money in 2000.

Think back to January 1, 1999. Most investors weren't invested in dot-com, technology, telecommunications, or biotech stocks. In fact, most investors had not heard much about those stocks. But when NASDAQ started making headlines at the end of 1999 (after posting an amazing 87% return), and with tech stocks soaring 100%, 200%, or even more, many investors started to take notice.

> ***"I want to buy a condominium in New York City."***
>
> **~David Savage, 33, VP, Marketing**

As a result, hordes of investors rushed into these investments in early 2000, with little more to go on than stories of how other people had made huge profits doing the same thing. And sure enough, these new investors bought those stocks at their highest prices, just in time to see them begin their drastic declines.

This is why I emphasize slicing your cake into many pieces. It's impossible to tell which stock, sector, or asset class is going to be this year's big winner. So, by owning a little bit of everything, you have a better chance of enjoying more consistent returns. Here's why.

Let's pretend you rode the dot-com stock wave. On January 1, 1999, you put 100% of your money into an investment that mimics the NASDAQ index. You know this is volatile, but you think aggressive investing is the only way to make big profits. So, you bet your kid's college fund on January 1, 1999.

Lucky you, the NASDAQ gains a whopping 87% in 1999 — the NASDAQ's *best ever* one-year performance. With the Internet in full swing, you let your money ride.

Then comes 2000, with its 39% loss — the NASDAQ's *worst ever* one-year performance. As disappointing as this is, it's not tragic, right? After all, a gain of 87% followed by a loss of 39% still leaves you with a profit, doesn't it?

Sure, but how much of a profit?

Figure 11-4 shows that a $10,000 investment in NASDAQ on January 1, 1999, would have grown to $22,414 at its peak in March 2000. But by December 31, 2000, your account would only be worth $11,407. That's a total two-year profit of just $1,407 — or an average annual return of just 6.8%. That's nowhere near the 10% annual return that a well-diversified portfolio of stocks and bonds might have netted you — without forcing you to take any wild rides, either.

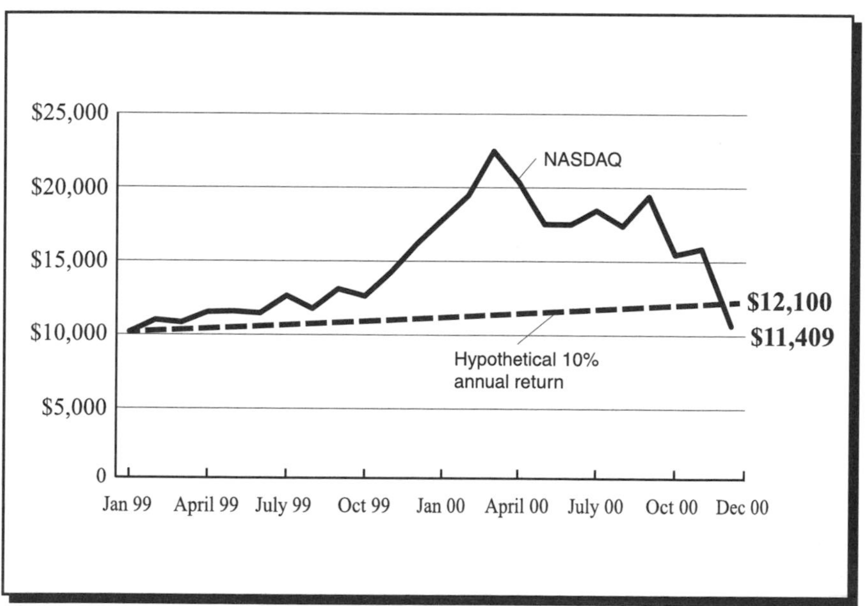

Figure 11-4

Similarly, no one in 1999 wanted to own mutual funds that invest in value stocks or real estate. After all, those funds languished while the tech stocks, and the mutual funds that invested in them, skyrocketed. But in 2000, value and real estate funds were the top performers.[202]

3. Why Does B Come After A in the Alphabet?

It doesn't in my book. That's why we're turning to Beta, the second letter of the Greek alphabet, not Alpha.

Beta is a measurement that compares a mutual fund's volatility with the volatility of the overall stock market. Since it's a comparison, knowing your fund's beta doesn't help you unless you compare it to other betas.

No matter how volatile or serene the stock market, its beta is always equal to 1. Therefore, a mutual fund whose beta is 2 is twice as volatile as the stock market, while a fund whose beta is 0.5 is half as volatile.

Morningstar provides this information, as it does most vital statistics that fund investors find useful.

Please note that beta does not predict fund performance. Like all financial measurements, beta reflects historical data. It simply says that when the stock market's value changed in the past, a 2-beta fund changed twice as much, and that a 0.5-beta fund changed half as much.

By comparing the average returns and betas of different funds in a given cake slice (asset class), or by comparing different cake slices to each other, we can identify preferable investments.

For example, from 1985 to 1999, the average annual return of the average stock fund was 16%, according to Morningstar. During the same period,

[202] You might conclude from all these examples that, since last year's winners don't sustain their success, you ought to invest in last year's losers — on the premise that they are about to become winners. Be very careful about pursuing this idea. It's called the Contrarian Theory — buying investments no one else wants. The danger is that this is really just a variation of market timing and sector rotation, and contrarians have not demonstrated any better long-term investment success than anyone else. The better approach is to own everything all the time, not just those you think are poised (for whatever reason, contrarian or otherwise) to do well.

the average balanced fund[203] earned 12% per year. If we looked no further, we might conclude that the stock fund was a superior investment. But an examination of beta reveals that stock funds averaged a beta of 1, while balanced funds averaged just 0.56.

This means that balanced funds earned 73% of the return of stock funds, but took only 56% of the risk to do it. I regard this as an excellent risk/reward ratio, and that's why my firm frequently recommends balanced funds.

I'm showing more of my firm's philosophy here, and it's easy to disagree with it.

After all, wouldn't you rather earn 16% per year for 15 years instead of 12% per year? To put that into economic terms, the average stock fund would have turned $10,000 into $92,655, while the average balanced fund would have netted only $54,736. That's a big difference.

No, that's a huge difference. Why, then, do my colleagues and I often prefer balanced funds?

Because we know our clients. Most people say they want high returns, but the investments that produce them suffer from high volatility, as beta demonstrates. And despite their claims to the contrary, most people simply cannot stomach wild swings in portfolio value, any more than they can tolerate the wild roller coasters found in today's amusement parks. Thus, when those stock funds occasionally suffer large drops in value (that's when, not if), most people bail out. By selling low, they assure themselves of losses.

Therefore, we prefer to give our clients funds we know they'll keep — netting $54,736 — rather than funds that might earn $92,655 but which they'll never see because they won't hold onto the funds long enough to enjoy the profits. Furthermore, we are more concerned with helping our clients achieve their goals within an acceptable risk level than in helping them seek the highest return.

Indeed, our expertise (if we have any!) is in knowing our clients. If you don't know who you are, Wall Street can be a very expensive place to find out.

And yes, just for the record, we often do recommend stock funds for many of our clients. It's always based on each client's individual circumstances.

Like all investors, you must decide how you feel about risk, because more than anything else, risk will determine your return. Ideally, as I've been preaching throughout this book, you'll take only as much risk as necessary to achieve your goals — but no less, either.

[203] Balanced mutual funds invest in a combination of stocks, bonds and cash. We'll discuss them more later.

Are you willing to invest a small portion of your savings into some high-risk opportunity? Many people are willing to do this. They think it'll be fun and exciting — and maybe even profitable! Besides, they say, they're willing to lose the money they're investing.

My response: Go right ahead. Add a slice of jalapeño pepper to your cake, and see how it turns out. It might work, but the odds are against you. But please don't call what you're doing baking (or investing). Because what you're really doing is speculating. There's nothing wrong with that, provided (a) you realize that's what you're doing, (b) you know you'll likely wind up with indigestion, and (c) you understand that doing this could delay or even destroy your chance to enjoy your cake (i.e., achieve your goals).

Investors are found in the offices of financial planning firms. Speculators — just so you know the difference — are found in casinos and day-trading offices.

4. Am I Good or Just Lucky?

I bet that even the greats ask themselves this question from time to time.

But not Joe. He manages a mutual fund. He's good at it, and he knows it. Over a period of years, he's averaged 20% per year. Then Joe is hired away by a competing firm to manage another mutual fund. When the new fund announces that Joe is now their manager, can it brag about Joe's track record at his old fund?

If you have trouble deciding, you're not alone. The U.S. Securities and Exchange Commission, which regulates investment companies (such as mutual funds), says yes. After all, a great baseball pitcher will be a great pitcher no matter whose jersey he's wearing. Therefore, since the SEC has jurisdiction over mutual fund *prospectuses*, Joe's new fund is permitted to disclose, in his new fund's prospectus, his former fund's performance record.

But the regulatory arm of the National Association of Securities Dealers disagrees. The NASD-R says no.

After all, no pitcher ever pitched a no-hitter without getting critical help from his team's fielding — and when Joe joined his new firm, he left his teammates (the fund's analysts and researchers) behind. Besides, players do not take their team's win-loss records with them when they are traded.

Therefore, since the NASD-R has jurisdiction over mutual fund *advertising*, the fund is prohibited from disclosing the old fund's track record when promoting Joe's new fund.

These conflicting jurisdictional actions have created a schizophrenic environment. But although the regulators haven't been able to reach agreement as to the value and relevance of a fund manager's prior track record, academic studies are less ambiguous.

"My goal is to learn to play a guitar after I retire."

~Judith Chinn, 59, Executive Admin. Asst.

A study reported in *Financial Analysts Journal* examined the records of all mutual funds that experienced manager changes from 1983 to 1991, to see what impact the change had. Since fund managers change funds about as often as ball players change teams, this is no insignificant study.

The results show that, in funds that suffered poor performance, introduction of a new manager boosted performance by 2 percentage points per year, but if the fund's performance was good, then the new manager's performance was unlikely to be as good.

This might seem obvious, but these findings are really quite important. It means that the most important thing is to determine *why the manager left.* If he left because his performance was bad, it may not be necessary for you to leave as well. But if he left because *the team* was bad, then you may have something more to think about. And if he left because his good record got him noticed by other funds and they've hired him away, you almost certainly want to reconsider your position in the fund.

The only problem is that it is often difficult for retail investors (that means you) to learn on a timely basis that a manager is leaving. Usually, they discover this months later, if ever. Worse, most fund shareholders are rarely able to learn the real reason a manager is leaving. This is the water cooler scuttlebutt to which retail investors rarely have access. But financial advisors often have this access — not just because we pay closer attention to these types of things, but because the fund companies know that we influence how hundreds of millions of dollars are invested. That gives us access to fund personnel that most investors could never match. In my opinion, it's one of the little-known benefits of working with an advisor.

But there's more to the study's findings. Importantly, it found that, regardless of whether the old fund was managed well or not, the fact that the fund was experiencing a change in management caused risk to increase. Furthermore, 65% of those funds experienced a shift in style.

These are important, and related, findings. It means that when there's a new kid in town, he's going to show everyone that he means business. He doesn't do this merely by selling many of the holdings selected by the prior manager, but in the majority of cases by changing the entire fund's profile. Here come style drift and cap creep!

Therefore, be on the lookout for manager changes. When they occur, you can expect:

- A change in style
- High turnover, which will increase both fund expenses and, potentially, capital gains distributions
- Increased risk

Years of Experience	Average Return
Fewer than 4 years	–21.9%
4–9 years	–14.9%
10–19 years	–8.1%
20 years or more	–5.4%

Figure 11-5

Morningstar also weighs in with an interesting study. It has found that management experience is critically important. For the year ending March 2001, the S&P 500 lost 21.6%. By ranking funds based on the years of experience of fund managers, shown in Figure 11-5, Morningstar found that the less experienced the manager, the worse his performance.

Morningstar also notes that the average tenure of a fund manager is four years. Although the study does not break out the funds by sector, it's fair to assume that managers of all experience levels can be found in each asset class and sector type.

"I always wanted to own lots of horses when I turn 50."

~Marguerite Thompson, 37, Stay-at-Home Mom

Star or Team

Most funds hire a star — or at least, someone they hope will become a star. You know the names of these stars[204] — Fidelity's Peter Lynch, Mutual Shares' Michael Price, Templeton Funds' Sir John Templeton and others — and their reputations and track records are magnets for investor capital. But what happens when the stars stop managing the funds that made them famous — as Peter, Michael and Sir John have all done?

What's an investor to do?

Fret, that's what. Enter manager turnover, with all the problems described above. To avoid this problem, a few fund companies use a team approach. It surprises me how few do this, for many that do have remarkably good track records.

I am not providing a list of team-managed funds because the list changes periodically, and would quickly become out of date. It's best to investigate this as part of your research. Or just ask any good financial advisor.

Through the team approach, a lead manager divvies up the fund's portfolio among several — perhaps as many as 20 — comanagers. In some organizations, each comanager is solely responsible for his or her small piece of the cake. In others, each comanager must win the consensus of the group before buying or selling any security.[205] The most extreme ideas are tossed

[204] That's why they're stars — get it?
[205] Investment clubs operate in much the same way.

out — good and bad — and what's left (in theory, anyway) are the prudent, solid ideas that lead to more consistent, above-average performance.

By working as a unit, the fund can avoid the whims of a wildcat, and if one comanager leaves, the others provide much-needed continuity. This can reduce or even avoid the problems inherent to manager turnover, and it's one reason why funds using the team approach often experience less volatility, style drift and cap creep.

In our experience, we have found that team-run funds tend to have greater consistency than those run by just one person. So pay attention to how your fund is operated, for if it's team-run, a manager's departure is not as significant as it otherwise might be.

Most fund families do not use the team approach, and several have had poor results trying it. The team approach, as its name suggests, requires a disciplined and unique corporate culture, and in a business based on egos, this is not something that always works best.

My firm recommends funds that are managed by both stars and teams. But when all other factors are equal,[206] we prefer the teams.

5. Is That a Diamond Ring, or a Cubic Zirconia?

Appearances can be deceiving. This means you need to study that ring carefully before you buy it or place it on your finger.

The same is true for a mutual fund's holdings. Consider the following example.

> ***"I want to buy a vacation home in 15 years."***
>
> **~Anonymous, 38, Attorney**

The average balanced fund posted a 12-month return of 4.4% for the year ending June 30, 2000, according to *The Wall Street Journal*. Figure 11-6 shows how the top 10 balanced funds performed in that period.

[206] And they never are.

As you can see, the top balanced funds earned returns ranging from 21.6% to 33.6%. That's a fairly narrow spread.

Except for the #1 balanced fund. Its return is omitted from the chart, so I'll give it to you here: The #1 fund earned 116.5%.

That's not a typo. That's one hundred sixteen point five percent.

The Top 10 Balanced Funds for the 12 months ending June 30, 2000

Fund	Gain
1	———
2	33.6%
3	32.1
4	30.4
5	24.0
6	23.9
7	23.1
8	22.3
9	22.2
10	21.6

Figure 11-6

How did that manager produce a return so much higher than all its peers? Now, I'm certain that its investors were thrilled to have doubled their money in a year, and I'm equally certain that the fund enjoyed a substantial inflow of new assets.[207, 208]

But I think those investors should have been scared, not excited, because *something weird must have been going on at that fund.* I don't know what that was (because I didn't bother to check),[209] but if I owned that fund I would have been all over it.

I would expect that the fund started advertising its newfound performance record, and got its manager interviewed on CNBC and quoted in *Money* magazine.

[207] Indeed it did. Before the fund produced that incredible return, it had $25 million in assets (as of July 31, 1999, according to Morningstar). But one year later — after the fund gained 116.5% — it had total assets of $73.2 million. But based on its return, the fund should have had only $54.1 million in assets, not $73.2 million. Where'd the other $19.1 million come from? From investors, of course — who added money to the fund in apparent hopes that it would sustain, or repeat, its performance.

[208] Meanwhile, the worst balanced fund for the year experienced a net withdrawal by investors of 10%. No doubt they put some of their withdrawals into that #1 fund. Sell low, buy high. It happens all the time.

[209] Hey, I had other things to do, awright?

Too bad, because in the year following this stellar performance, according to Morningstar, the fund lost 14.8%. Was this a surprise? Shouldn't have been. It's *beta* was 1.21 (more than twice as high as the average balanced fund) and it's *standard deviation* was 50.7 (making it not just the most volatile balanced fund of all, but the 316th most volatile fund out of all 13,112 mutual funds tracked by Morningstar). Investors could have avoided this problem had they bothered to compare the fund against its peers — something called (surprise!) *relative performance.*

But statistics only give you a limited amount of insight. In the final analysis, nothing can replace a detailed examination of a fund's actual holdings.

Here's an example. As of April 5th, 2000, according to *The Wall Street Journal,* the Legg Mason High Yield Bond Fund had placed 25% of its assets in the stock of a Bermuda telecom company.

It often is difficult for retail investors (that means you) to get a list of a fund's current holdings. Morningstar and others publish data on fund holdings, but it's not as current as you might like. When asked for data, funds typically reveal only their top 10 holdings and a breakout of their sector allocation. It's not easy for retail investors (i.e., you) to get much more. But financial advisors often have this access. It's another benefit of working with an advisor.

I was certainly surprised to hear that. After all, this fund is supposed to buy junk bonds. Who would ever guess that the fund would use some of its assets to buy stocks?

> ... and not just to buy a small amount of stocks, but to use <u>25% of its assets</u> to buy stocks?
>
> ... and not just use 25% of its assets to buy stocks, but to place 25% of its assets <u>into just one stock</u>?
>
> ... and not just one stock, but an <u>international stock</u>?

How common is this practice?

You'll never know what your fund is investing in unless you examine its current holdings. The problem is that funds are required to disclose their complete holdings only twice a year — in their annual and semi-annual reports — and each is issued many weeks after the fact. Funds don't like to release this data because they consider the information to be proprietary, and they don't want to reveal their strategies to competitors.

As a result, funds may — and often do — deviate from their expected strategy. That's why it's important that you go beyond the prospectus, which merely tells you how the fund is permitted to invest, to the annual and semi-annual reports, which reveal how the fund actually does invest.

The irony is that funds are doing nothing wrong when they behave this way. The prospectus for the Legg Mason High Yield Bond Fund clearly stated that the fund could invest up to 25% of assets into investments other than high-yield bonds. I can imagine the reaction of a typical shareholder of the fund, who says, *"Yeah, but I didn't think you'd actually do it!"*

One of the reasons it's important to examine current holdings is to help maintain diversity while avoiding redundancy.

Let's again refer to Fidelity Magellan. I mention it solely because it is the world's largest mutual fund. As of June 30, 2001, it held $88 billion in assets and enjoyed 6.1 million shareholders — or one out of every 17 U.S. households. That's one big fund!

"Learn to play bridge within the next 2 years."

~Cindee Berar,
Financial Planner,
Edelman Financial Services

Window Dressing is another deceptive practice of fund companies,[210] and unfortunately all too common. It occurs when fund managers own assets they know their shareholders won't like to see — things like Bermuda telecom stocks in their bond funds — or holdings that recently have suffered bad press or large drops in value.

Knowing that a six-month reporting deadline is approaching, the fund manager sells the objectionable assets and replaces them with holdings more likely to garner investor favor. Then, after he reports the holdings on June 30, he rebuys on July 1 the assets he really wants the fund to own.

If many (or all) of your fund's holdings have been held by the fund for less than six months, there might be a whole lot of Window Dressing going on.

Funds no longer can do what the Legg Mason High Yield Bond Fund did. Shortly after the *WSJ* story broke, regulators changed the rules, requiring funds to invest at least 80% of assets in a manner consistent with the fund's overall objective. Before this change, funds had to invest only 65% of assets in that way. This is a big improvement in investor protection.

[210] For descriptions of other deceptive practices (trade pooling, incubating and survivorship bias) see page 272.

It's so big, in fact, that it has 317 stocks in its portfolio, as of June 2001. There's nothing inherently wrong with this[211] — unless[212] you happen to also own another fund that invests in U.S. stocks. That's because Magellan's holdings are redundant to 32% of all stock funds. That's based on data provided by Overlap, a nifty software program (and Internet site) that allows you to compare the holdings of any fund with any other fund (or even *many* other funds, as shown here).

Redundancy is a common problem among mutual fund investors.

I once got a call on my radio show from guy who said, "I'm really unhappy with my mutual funds. I have seven of them and they're all down 20%." It turned out that he had seven similar stock funds. So, of course, their prices all fell when the market dropped in 2000. After all, he didn't have seven funds — in essence, he had one fund seven times.

Is your portfolio truly diversified, or merely redundant?

If two funds are "redundant" when at least 15% of their holdings are identical, Overlap's data show that, as of September 30, 2001, it would be redundant to own both Magellan and nearly a third of all other stock funds. Overlap's data change monthly, so you'd have to keep your Overlap subscription current. Thus, this statistic may be out of date as you read this.[213] Also, many debate the point at which funds become redundant. Is it really 15%? Or is it 20%, or even 30%? You must decide this for yourself.

Of the 32% of funds that are redundant to Fidelity Magellan:	
15–19% of stock holdings are identical	19%
20–29% of stock holdings are identical	34
30–39% of stock holdings are identical	24
40–49% of stock holdings are identical	13
50% or more of stock holdings are identical	10

Figure 11-7

[211] Although some might argue that this is too many for one person to manage effectively, and that some holdings must constitute such a small percentage of the fund's total assets that the position itself is meaningless. Others would disagree, saying Magellan has no choice. With so much money to invest, it either must buy a huge number of stocks or wind up owning such large amounts of a few stocks it would begin to control the market in those stocks. Others argue it does that anyway. Well, with all this arguing going on (what else would you expect when talking about the world's largest fund?) I'm not offering my opinion. That's because convincing you to buy or sell Magellan is not the point of this illustration, which is where we're now going to return. Move your eyes back up the page, please. Thank you.

[212] And you knew there'd be an "unless" didn't you? Hey — get back up that page now, Young Grasshopper.

[213] Then again, maybe it's not.

6. Do You Always Get What You Pay For?

Finally, fees. And I do mean "finally." Fees belong at the end of the fund selection process because they are the least important criterion.

> ***"I want to take my wife on a world cruise for her 80th birthday."***
>
> **~James E. Steinmiller, 70, Retired**

All mutual funds charge a fee. It's called the annual expense ratio, and although the fee varies substantially between asset classes, there usually isn't much difference among funds within a given asset class.

For example, it costs very little to manage a U.S. government bond fund, and lots more to manage a portfolio of international stocks. Not only are trading expenses much higher for the latter, the research effort is more elaborate as well — what with offices and analysts stationed worldwide and the like.

Therefore, the fees of all government bond funds fall within a fairly narrow range, as do the fees of all international stock funds. But if you try to compare the costs of a government bond fund to those of a foreign stock fund, you'll be convinced that the latter is ripping you off. This is another example of the importance of comparing funds to their peers, and not to some broad or general figure.

And you'll always find exceptions in every fund category. In every case, some funds charge surprisingly little, while others charge substantially more than the rest.

The one mistake to avoid is this: Believing that lower costs automatically translate into higher returns. This simply is not true. Although lower fees allow the fund to invest more of your money for you, this does not mean the fund will produce superior results.

Indeed, the fund families that make low fees their primary marketing pitch often do so because their funds are not known for superior investment returns.

Let's put this another way. Which would you prefer:

Fund A, which charges low fees but loses money

or

Fund B, which charges high fees but makes money

It's a silly proposition, but the concept is sound: There is no correlation between fees and performance, a fact confirmed by every study conducted on the subject.[214]

Ditto for load and no-load funds. We've already discussed[215] how loads are as likely as no-loads to perform well. To that I add the point that the annual fees charged by load funds often are lower than the fees charged by no-loads. And vice versa — meaning that:

some load funds charge high annual fees, and some don't.

and

some no-load funds charge high annual fees, and some don't.

In fact, some of the very lowest-cost funds are load funds, while some of the very highest-cost funds are no-loads.

It amazes me when people insist on buying only no-load funds. There are 8,171 funds available, and only 32% of them are no-load. Why would anyone want to ignore two-thirds of the mutual fund universe solely for that reason?

The correct approach, then, is to go about sorting through the universe of funds using the guidelines provided for you in this book. After you've narrowed your search to a few acceptable funds, where all the other factors are equal,[216] choose the one with the lowest cost.

But if you insert cost as a sort criterion any earlier than last — including the notion of loads — you could omit some outstanding choices.

[214] Wanna see 'em? Read Chapter 27 of *The Truth About Money.*
[215] On page 273.
[216] And they never are.

I'm not a fan of limiting myself to just one fund family. Consider the Ford Motor Company: They make the Mustang, but they also made the Edsel.[217]

No manufacturer can be great at everything. Most fund families have expertise in a given segment of the investment marketplace. Some specialize in bonds, while others are known for their value funds. Still others have expertise in international markets.

Therefore, it's better to pick the best funds you can find, regardless of which fund family offers it. This is why our clients typically own funds from several families.

However, it's worth pointing out that placing most or all of your assets into one fund family might reduce expenses. As always, your approach should be determined by your individual circumstances.

So there it is. In case you missed it,we have resolved some of the biggest questions in the universe. Well, okay, maybe that's taking things a bit too far. Let's just say that we've explored how to evaluate mutual funds.

We did this by considering:

1. Is it hot in here, or is it me?	**Relative Performance**
2. Are you always this wacky?	**Standard Deviation**
3. Why does B come after A in the alphabet?	**Beta**
4. Am I good or just lucky?	**Management**
5. Is that a diamond ring, or a cubic zirconia?	**Current Holdings**
6. Do you always get what you pay for?	**Fees**

"I'd like to take a cruise around the world in 16 years."

~Anonymous, 50,
Antique Dealer

[217] Never heard of the Edsel? Go ask your grandparents.

CHAPTER 12

Should You Bake Cakes or Cupcakes?

CHAPTER 12

Should You Bake Cakes or Cupcakes?

So far, we've explored how to buy different mutual funds for each slice of your cake. But instead of baking one cake that has many slices, you could bake lots of cupcakes; each would feature an ingredient that would have been found in the bigger cake's many slices. We introduced this idea back in chapter 7, but let's explore it further here.

In investment terms, this is the difference between buying "sector-specific" funds (the cupcakes) or hybrid funds (the cakes). Many people — including many advisors — prefer the hybrids. These contain investments from two or more asset classes instead of just one. My colleagues and I are fans of them as well, and we often use them in our planning practice.

"I want to attend cooking school and begin a new career in the culinary field by age 40."

~Anonymous, 33,
At-Home Mom

Used properly, hybrids take maximum advantage of the mutual fund concept. The first advantage is convenience: Instead of selecting and buying several separate funds to invest in the various asset classes and market sectors you want, hybrids consolidate them into just one fund.

The second advantage is that a hybrid is less volatile than its individual components. If you own a stock fund and a bond fund, for example, you will see how each swings in value. But if you own a hybrid that invests in both stocks and bonds, the seesawing will be less severe. This can make it easier to stick with the fund during volatile periods (which these days seem to be just about always).

However, people often encounter two problems when using hybrids. First, it's easier to go beyond diversification and morph into redundancy. Second, because the funds themselves ultimately control how much of their assets they will place into any given asset class or market sector, you might lose some control over the slicing of your cake. So, be on your guard when using them.

"I'll go underwater in an oceanographic submarine within the next five years."

~James Baker, Financial Planner, Edelman Financial Services

Are hybrids for you? As Figure 12-1 shows, you should own the left column or the right, but in most cases, not both.

If you want to maintain a certain percentage of your assets in specific sectors of the U.S. stock market, for example, you should buy funds that invest in those types of stocks. But if you instead merely want to be broadly invested in U.S. stocks, a diversified stock fund can be sufficient, leaving the sector selection to the fund's manager.

Sector Specific Funds		Hybrid Funds
Growth Fund *and* Value Fund	OR	Diversified Stock Fund
U.S. Stock Fund *and* International Stock Fund	OR	Global Stock Fund
Bond Fund *and* Stock Fund	OR	Balanced Fund

Figure 12-1

If you buy separate sector funds, you'll likely have to manage them closely. But by using diversified stock funds, you can leave your money invested, with no changes even for decades, because the fund manager will be making any needed changes for you.

Global funds, which invest in the U.S. as well as overseas, frequently change their U.S./Foreign weightings — and they sometimes do so drastically. Therefore, when we want a client to own foreign stocks (something we don't always want to do), we usually invest separately in U.S. stock funds and international stock funds. This enables us to control more effectively the size of U.S. and foreign stock slices of the client's cake. But this point merely reflects our preference; others prefer to handle these classes differently.

People make a common error by owning both a U.S. stock fund and a global fund. That can create redundancy, because the global fund might have 60% of its money in the U.S., making it too similar to the U.S. fund.

A similar problem occurs when you buy balanced funds even though you already own stock funds and bond funds.

How Many Funds Do You Need?

Too much of a good thing is wonderful.

~Mae West

Would it surprise you that we have clients who have placed 100% of their entire life savings into just one mutual fund?

It's true, and it shouldn't surprise you — that is, if you've come to understand that even a single mutual fund can offer you extensive diversification.

For example, tell me if you think the following is a reasonably diversified portfolio — I mean, cake[218] (ignoring, for the sake of conversation, the particular needs and circumstances of the investor):

U.S. stocks	60%
U.S. government securities	20%
High-quality[219] corporate bonds	15%
Cash and equivalents	5%

[218] I'm trying hard to avoid jargon for you. It ain't easy.

[219] Limited to Investment Grade bonds, or those rated AAA to BBB. No speculative grade, or junk, bonds. For more on this, see Chapter 11 of *The Truth About Money*.

This allocation is illustrated by the cake in Figure 12-2.

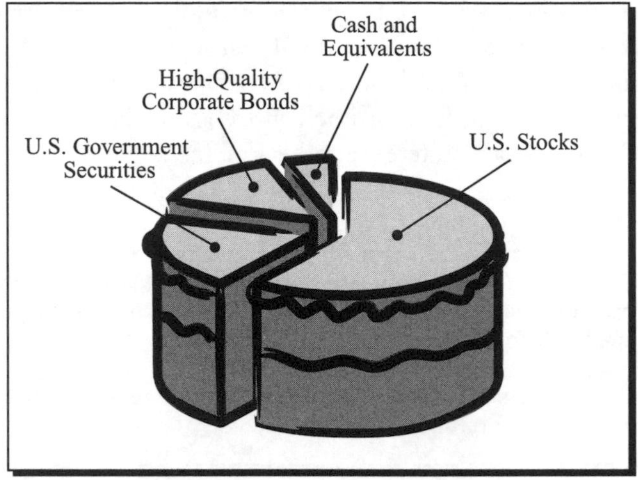

Figure 12-2

Let's look further at this portfolio to examine the stock holdings more closely. Tell me if you think the following is a reasonably diversified portfolio of stocks, which represent 60% of the total portfolio:[220]

Advertising	0.3%	Entertainment	5.8%
Aerospace	3.2%	Financial Services	8.2%
Agricultural Products	10.3%	Healthcare	7.6%
Apparel and Textiles	0.3%	Manufacturing	9.3%
Automotive	1.7%	Metals and Minerals	3.2%
Biotechnology	2.3%	Printing and Publishing	1.7%
Business Services	0.3%	Real Estate Investment Trusts	2.0%
Chemicals	2.0%	Restaurants and Lodging	2.6%
Computers and Electronics	5.5%	Retail	5.8%
Consumer Goods & Services	3.8%	Telecommunications	15.4%
Energy	7.1%	Transportation	1.5%
			100.0%

[220] Try this paragraph instead: Let's look further at this cake to examine the stock slice more closely. Tell me if you think the following is a reasonably diversified mix of stock ingredients, which represent 60% of the total cake.

If we were to display these holdings into the cake's stock slice, it would look like Figure 12-3 below.

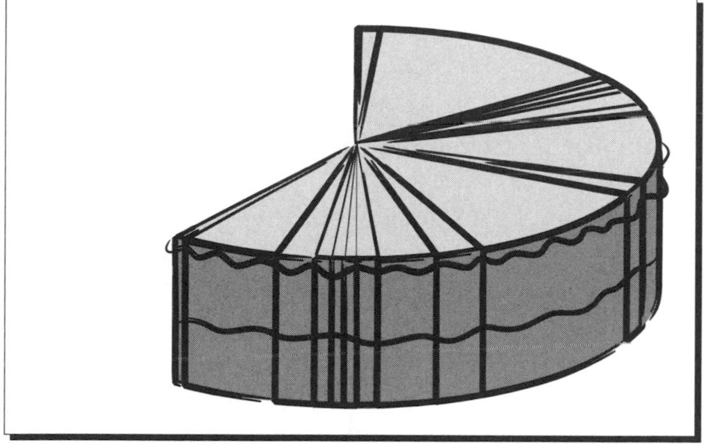

Figure 12-3

And if we were to display Figure 12-3 as part of the total cake, the overall portfolio/cake would look like Figure 12-4:

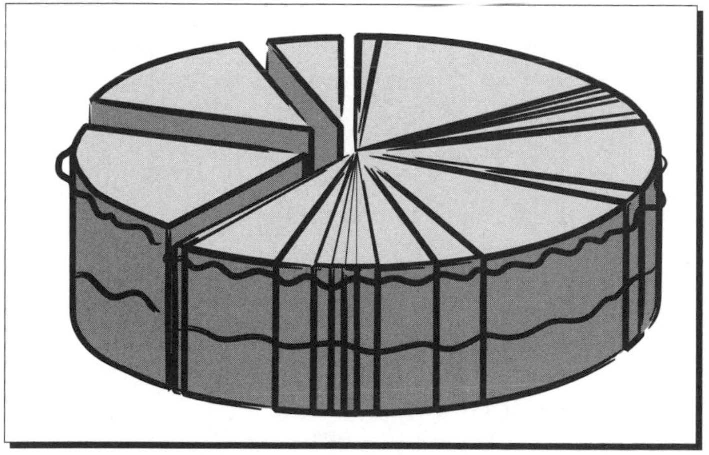

Figure 12-4

One could argue that the size of the cake's slices should be tweaked based on the goals of the individual investor, as well as the investor's economic outlook. But those comments aside, I'm sure you'll agree that this portfolio is reasonable.

To see if indeed you do agree, answer this question: Ignoring for the moment your particular goals, could you envision yourself investing in a portfolio that looked something like this one?

If you said yes — and I bet you did — then be prepared to invest 100% of your life savings into a single balanced mutual fund. Because the portfolio you're looking at is exactly how one balanced fund has allocated its assets, as of June 30, 2001.[221]

You see, whether you use separate funds, hybrids or a combination of the two, it takes remarkably few mutual funds to construct an extensively diversified portfolio. In fact, I've just shown you how a single fund can give you greater diversity than the overwhelming majority of American investors have — even more diversity than those who have brokerage statements that are pages and pages long.

But if you can't find a balanced fund with an allocation that matches the cake you've constructed for yourself, if you are uncomfortable with letting the fund do your cake slicing for you, or if you simply prefer the separate-fund route, here's an alternative for you. Instead of using just one balanced fund, you could instead buy six funds, as follows:

- 1 money market fund
- 1 government bond fund
- 1 corporate bond fund
- 1 U.S. value stock fund
- 1 U.S. growth stock fund
- 1 international stock fund

[221] And no, don't ask me for the fund's name. If I give it to you, you'll just throw money at it, and I can't let you do that without knowing whether the fund is appropriate for you, based on your goals and circumstances. Remember, I'm trying to give you an education, not a hot tip. But nice try.

Although this strategy creates more paperwork for you and involves more research and tax reporting, it offers several advantages. First, you can control more effectively the size of each cake slice, and the ingredients within each slice. Second, you'll end up with a cake that's more customized than the ones offered by balanced funds, because they tend to have value slices or growth slices but not both, and most exclude international securities.[222]

"I would like to tour Alaska within 2 years."

~Anonymous, 64, Retired on Disability

But this list assumes that growth (or value) and international positions are appropriate for you; if they're not, you'd exclude those two funds, leaving you with four — and buying four separate mutual funds instead of a single balanced fund is of questionable economic merit. You will undoubtedly increase paperwork, but increasing your return or reducing your risk is less certain.

There's another important, although completely noneconomic, reason for choosing several separate funds over a single hybrid: Doing so might make you feel more secure.

You wouldn't really be more secure, mind you – because what counts is what you own inside your funds, not how many funds you own – but owning several funds instead of one fund gives you the appearance that you're more diversified. But that's all it is – appearance.

Still, if that enables you to sleep easier at night, and if that makes you more likely to hold onto your investments for long periods, then by all means invest in that manner.

I have found that most people are indeed willing to place all their money into a single fund — to a point. At some psychological level, though, they decide that they have (or are considering to place) into just one fund "too much" money, and at this point, they prefer to add additional funds to their portfolio. They'll do this by adding a second fund within an asset class, and it provides them with further (perceived if not real) diversification.

[222] Which explains why we sometimes give our clients two balanced funds (one investing in value stocks, the other in growth) plus an international stock fund.

Thus, instead of using just four or six mutual funds as shown above, a more elaborate set of holdings would consist of seven to 10 funds, as follows:

- 1 money market fund
- 1 government bond fund
- 1 corporate bond fund
- 1 or 2 U.S. value stock funds
- 2 or 3 U.S. growth stock funds
- 1 or 2 international stock funds

How much money is too much to place into a single fund?

The answer is entirely subjective. You should handle the topic in a manner that's comfortable for you — while being ever on your guard against creating redundancy within your portfolio.

Notice that we continue to own just one money market fund, one government bond fund and one corporate bond fund. There is such little difference among the holdings of different funds in these asset classes[223] that it's really pointless to own more than one of each of these investments.

But the stock market is very different from the government bond market. Although the portfolio holdings of all government bond funds look a lot alike (and consequently, the range of returns among all such bond funds doesn't vary much),[224] this cannot be said of stock funds.

"By age 55, I want to buy a small ranch in Colorado, and spend half the year sailing my own 50-foot sailboat."

~Anonymous, 36, Physician Scientist

With 8,692 stocks traded in the U.S. alone (and another 27,526 traded outside the U.S.), stock fund holdings — and returns — are all over the map. In any given year, some post huge gains while others are stagnant or incur losses.

[223] All government bond fund managers get their bonds from the same place, after all.
[224] It's therefore a great example where fees are a more important consideration.

Because value funds typically invest in the largest of companies (remember, Morningstar says this constitutes only 5% of the entire U.S. market), owning two value funds can be sufficient to own an effective cross-section of these stocks.

But the growth sector is a lot bigger and more diverse. Therefore, owning three funds can be effective (and free of redundancy).

To expand our clients' diversification beyond the four major asset classes of stocks, bonds, government securities and cash, we often recommend a real estate fund and natural resources fund[225] to further diversify the portfolio and to serve as an inflation hedge.

Even after doing so, most of our clients still end up owning fewer than a dozen funds,[226] regardless of how much money they're investing. Often, they have far fewer than a dozen.

Notice what's missing:

- **No junk bond funds.**
- **No convertible bond funds.**
- **No international bond funds.**
- **No currency funds.**
- **No short-term or intermediate bond funds.**
- **No stock market sector plays.[227]**
- **No hedge funds.[228]**

These omissions merely reflect my personal bias. In our practice, we believe that such investments have excessive risks for their potential long-term reward. However, many advisors use funds in these asset classes, and no one's a crook for doing so. We simply choose not to do so (generally speaking, that is, for there always are exceptions based on an individual client's circumstances).

[225] These funds typically invest in hard assets (as opposed to the paper assets of stocks and bonds) such as oil and gas, precious metals, timber & lumber/paper products and commodities.
[226] That's a dozen different funds. Many times, a client will own the same fund four or five times — but in different accounts (his IRA, her 401(k), joint accounts, and so on).
[227] Funds that invest in a single sector, such as biotech, pharmaceutical or financial stocks.
[228] Hedge funds engage in "negatively correlated" investments — using strategies such as options, futures and short-selling. These funds are designed to rise in value when stock prices fall. They "hedge" the "bets" you made in the stock market.

With this information as a backdrop, let's see how one investor handled his own asset allocation model. For this example, I want to stress that:

- This is a real investor. I'm not making this up.
- He did this on his own. He wasn't our client when he showed us his portfolio (so don't laugh, at least not at me!).
- He's married, has no children, is in his late 50s, is employed and in good health. In other words, no unusual circumstances that would necessitate unusual money management strategies. Still . . . well, you'll see.

His overall allocation model looked like Figure 12-5:

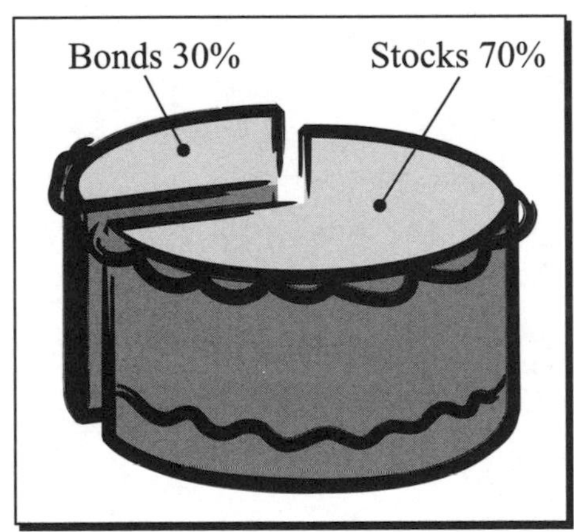

Figure 12-5

So far so good. Although we can argue over whether he's got too much or too little in stocks, let's assume that this allocation model is correct for his situation.

The 30% he allocated to bonds was split as follows:

- 5% cash
- 25% investment grade bonds (consisting of both governments and high-grade corporates)

Again, this is reasonable. You'll take over from here.

Using the worksheet (Figure 12-6) on the next page, split that stock portion (70% of assets) into large-cap, mid-cap and small-cap stocks. Then, allocate each of those into the growth and value styles. Finally, decide how many funds you'd use for each sector.

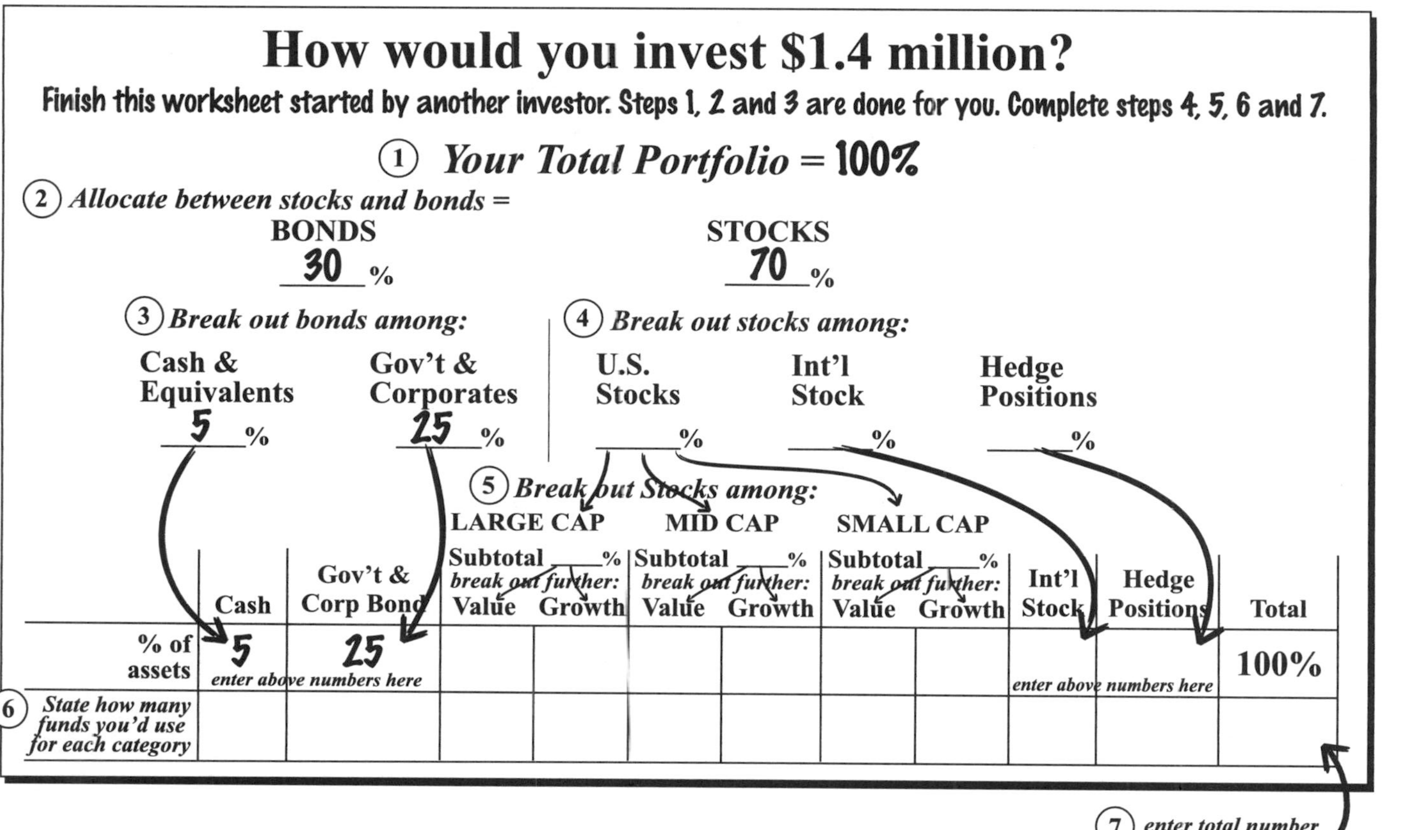
How would you invest $1.4 million?
Finish this worksheet started by another investor. Steps 1, 2 and 3 are done for you. Complete steps 4, 5, 6 and 7.
1 Your Total Portfolio = 100%
2 Allocate between stocks and bonds =
BONDS 30 %
STOCKS 70 %
3 Break out bonds among:
Cash & Equivalents 5 %
Gov't & Corporates 25 %
4 Break out stocks among:
U.S. Stocks %
Int'l Stock %
Hedge Positions %
5 Break out Stocks among:
LARGE CAP
MID CAP
SMALL CAP
Subtotal %
break out further:
Value
Growth
Cash
Gov't & Corp Bond
Int'l Stock
Hedge Positions
Total
% of assets
5
25
100%
enter above numbers here
6 State how many funds you'd use for each category
7 enter total number of funds used

Figure 12-6

How many funds did you end up owning? I wonder if you allocated the assets the same way he did, or if you used the same number of funds as he did. To find out, look at Figure 12-7, which shows how he filled out his allocation and how many funds he had bought.

How would you invest $1.4 million?

Your Total Portfolio **= 100%**

Allocate between stocks and bonds =

BONDS 30 % | STOCKS 70 %

Break out bonds among:

Cash & Equivalents 5 % | Gov't & Corporates 25 %

Break out stocks among:

U.S. Stocks 70 % | Int'l Stock 0 % | Hedge Positions 0 %

Break out Stocks among:

	Cash	Gov't & Corp Bond	LARGE CAP Subtotal 51 % *break out further:* Value		MID CAP Subtotal 15 % *break out further:* Value		SMALL CAP Subtotal 4 % *break out further:* Value		Int'l Stock	Hedge Positions	Total
			Value	Growth	Value	Growth	Value	Growth			
% of assets	5%	25%	33%	18%	8%	7%	3%	1%	0	0	100%
State how many funds you'd use for each category	8	23	21	10	8	6	3	1	0	0	80

Figure 12-7

Here are my observations about his portfolio:

1. He invested nothing into international stocks. This was unreasonable; it is appropriate for someone in his situation to own that asset class.

2. He allocated such a small portion of assets to small-cap stocks that the effort was pointless. If you're not willing to invest at least 5% into a given asset class, don't bother.

3. Diversification is one thing, but this is ridiculous! He used:

    - 8 money market funds
    - 23 government bond funds
    - 21 large-cap value funds
    - 10 large-cap growth funds
    - 8 mid-cap value funds
    - 6 mid-cap growth funds
    - 3 small-cap value funds
    - and a partridge in a pear tree (I mean, one small-cap growth fund).

"Eat an entire copy of Ric's next book, not merely the front and back covers like I did last time."

~Liza, 6, Ric and Jean's other weimaraner

4. And for all these 80 funds — a typewritten list that ran single-spaced to one and a half pages — he owned:

    - not a single real estate fund
    - not a single natural resources fund
    - not a single international fund
    - and for those inclined to use hedge funds, not a single one of those, either.

5. He had invested an average of just 0.125% of his assets into each fund. Can you imagine the mail he must be getting? Managing this portfolio must have been a full-time job for him. I shudder to think of the record-keeping and tax-reporting problems he's created for himself.

6. Not to mention incredible redundancy in his portfolio.

How many funds did you use?

We showed this client how to eliminate redundancy while preserving diversity by reducing his list from 80 funds to just seven. That's right — seven mutual funds. Not only did these seven preserve his preferred allocation, they actually increased his overall diversification, making his portfolio actually safer with seven funds than it was with 80.

Sometimes, people let themselves get carried away. You read about a fund in a newspaper or magazine article, so you buy it. A friend mentions some fund he's investing in, so you buy that, too. You see a manager interviewed on CNBC, so you open an account there as well.

"I want to become a cruise ship rabbi in my early 60s."

~Anonymous, 56, Lawyer

Suddenly, you've become an addict. Your funds are no good, you're missing out on great opportunities, you need more of them. Then, one day you notice that you need a larger mailbox. Where did all this stuff come from? You begin to realize that you're getting no economies of scale, because you've scattered your money among dozens of fund families, brokerage firms, banks and money management companies. Your mail is overwhelming. Your record-keeping obligations are massive. Your spouse is getting annoyed.

And it's all so completely unnecessary.

By refocusing on your goals — remember them? — and reminding yourself of the true power of mutual funds — their inherent ability to give you all the diversification and professional management that you need and want — you can eliminate the baggage caused by redundancy.

The downside, of course, is that by reducing his 80 funds to just seven, this guy needs to find a new hobby. Tracking just seven funds is not time-consuming. The paperwork is minimal. There's no longer a demand for constant attention.

He'll have to find something else to do.

And that's as it should be. Because you should not be getting excitement from your mutual funds. They should not offer you a fulfilling experience. That fulfillment is supposed to come from the attainment of your personal goals.[229]

Oh, I know, it's kind of fun to track the market every hour. But, really, don't you think that planning your trip to Turkey would be even more fun?

If you get excited over your investments, you're missing the point. Get excited about life, not financial statements.

"Your mother called to remind you to diversify."

[229] Remember your goals? Those things we talked about for the first 121 pages of this book? You might need to reread all that, since we've spent so much time lately on the details of investment management.

CHAPTER 13

Should You Rely on Active or Passive Management?

CHAPTER 13

Should You Rely on Active or Passive Management?

With that simple question, we enter the hotly debated arena of index funds.

Most mutual funds are managed by professional money managers; they decide what investments to buy and when to sell them. Index funds don't do this. Instead, they consist of portfolios that are intended to mimic the holdings of some market index.

"Tour Austria to hear the organs; also see the Grand Canyon. It's beginning to happen now!"

~Mary Jo Hull, 68, Retired

There are thousands of indexes and hundreds of index funds, ranging from funds that mimic the well-known S&P 500 Stock Index to the little-known American Gas Index, a list of U.S. gas companies.

I've written extensively about my opposition to index funds, both in my second book, *The New Rules of Money*, and in my monthly newsletter, *Inside Personal Finance*. Others have written even more extensively on the virtues of index investing. So which should you pick?

I really don't care.

Oh, please, don't take that the wrong way. I don't mean that I don't care about you. Rather, I mean that I don't care whether you use index funds or not. Because, despite all the arguments both pro and con — and I'm about to levy a whole bunch of cons on you[230] — about index funds, the truth is that there is more than one way to get rich.

As I often say, you can spend your entire life investing in index funds, and I can spend my entire life investing in actively-managed funds, and in 40 years, we'll both laugh at the poor fellow who never invested at all, or who spent the whole time invested in bank CDs.

So, with that most important point in mind, let me now share with you some additional reasons[231] why you should use actively-managed funds instead of index funds.

If you're not really interested in the debate surrounding index funds, simply skip this chapter. But if you are even thinking about investing in index funds — let alone really doing it — do yourself a favor and read on.

To begin, let me remind you that I am not attacking index funds. I am defending active management. After all, I didn't start this conversation, they did.[232] If they — the index fund promoters — hadn't claimed that indexing is superior to active management, I wouldn't have found it necessary to say anything at all on the subject.

But the fact is that indexers don't merely say that index funds are good.[233] No, indexers go far beyond that, claiming that indexing is *better* than active management. And them's fightin' words.

Indeed, indexers offer only two reasons why they prefer index funds over actively managed funds. The first is that index funds are cheaper. Second is that index funds produce higher returns.

So, allow me to respond to these claims.

First, the claim that index funds make more money than actively-managed funds is false. You've heard the contention: *Index funds beat 80% of all actively-managed funds.* Actually, I've heard hundreds of variations of this

[230] Wait, that didn't come out right.
[231] Beyond those offered in *The New Rules of Money.*
[232] And that pretty well sums up the maturity level of everyone involved in this debate — me included!
[233] And they are. After all, there are many ways to get rich, and it is possible to do it with index funds.

claim — with figures ranging from 51% to 100%. But never has anyone ever been able to show me any academic, independent or third-party source supporting this wild claim.

The claim is so wild, in fact, that I find it hard to understand how anyone could actually believe it. If index funds *always* beat actively-managed funds, there wouldn't *be* any actively-managed funds.

What is true, however, is that in some periods of history, the performance of index funds has indeed been better than the performance of the majority of actively-managed stock mutual funds. Sometimes, in fact, they beat the vast majority of actively-managed funds. But this doesn't mean it's always true.

To allay your doubts about my objectivity — having been accused more than once of berating index funds solely because they are a competitive threat to my practice — let me state, for the record, that we have the ability to recommend index funds to the clients of our financial planning practice. We simply have concluded that doing so is not in our clients' best interests.

In fact, there is a set of institutional index funds available only to clients of advisory firms like mine; consumers cannot buy these index funds on their own. These particular index funds are widely regarded as superior to those available from mutual fund companies. They are cheaper than those offered even by the nation's largest promoter of index funds, no small feat considering that price is one of the two arguments favoring the index camp. They also are more comprehensive, offering an array of asset classes and investment strategies no other index fund organization can match. And like I said, you can get them only through professional advisory firms like mine. Yet my colleagues and I choose not to recommend them.

So there.

For example, the S&P 500 Stock Index outperformed just 25% of actively managed funds from 1977 through 1979. And from 1980 through 1982, it outperformed only half of all actively-managed equity funds. Furthermore, according to Evaluation Associates' study of five-year rolling returns since 1981, the S&P 500 Index beat the managers of large-cap stock mutual funds less than half the time, and it beat small-cap stock funds only once (in the five-year interval 1986–1990). For much of the middle 1990s, indexes beat most actively-managed funds. I acknowledge this. But that streak ended in 1998. Starting in 1999, and continuing through 2000 and 2001-to-date, the vast majority of actively managed funds have beaten the index. In fact, as shown by separate studies by Solomon Smith Barney and Callan Associates, the S&P 500 Stock

Index has performed miserably compared to actively-managed stock mutual funds since 1999. Their data show that, for the 12-month period ending June 30, 2001, 67% of stock funds beat the S&P 500. For the 18-month period, 73% of funds beat the S&P, and for the two-year period, a whopping 83% of all stock funds beat the index. So much for the claim that index funds are superior.

If we look closer at the 1994–1998 period, we begin to understand why index funds beat most actively-managed funds. In this five-year period, large-cap growth stocks were the best performing U.S. stocks. Most index funds, mimicking the S&P 500, benefited from this fact, but most actively-managed funds, which invest their assets elsewhere, did not. It is worth noting that this was the first time since 1975 that growth stocks outperformed value, as shown in Figure 13-1.

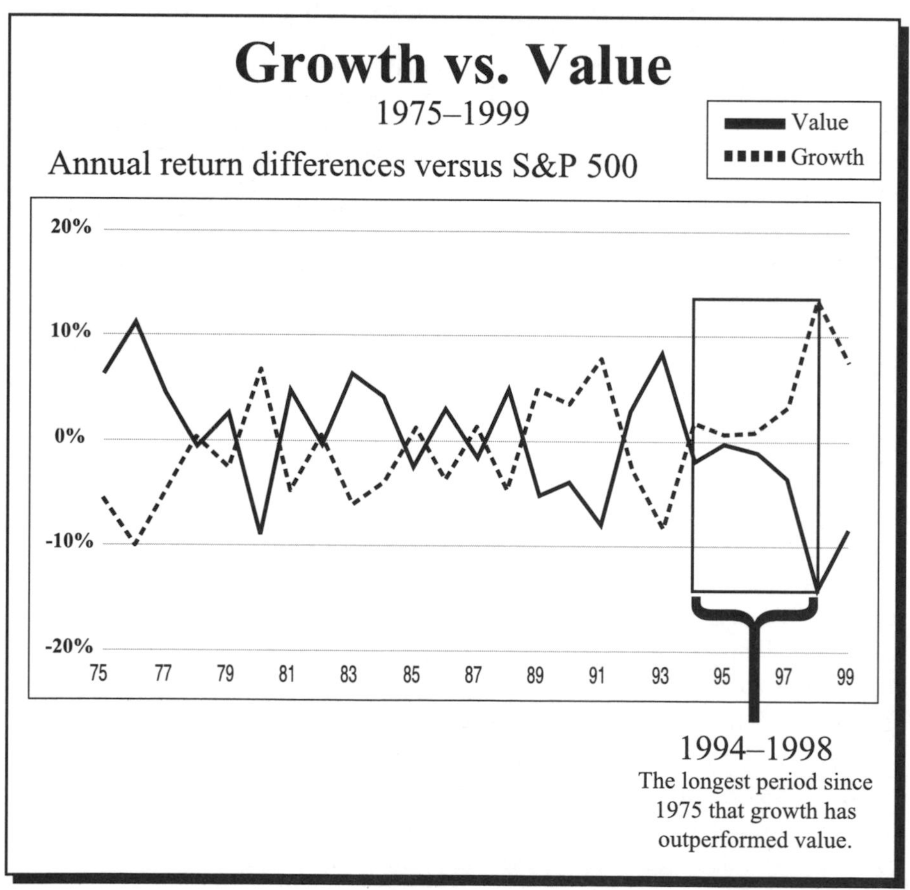

Figure 13-1

Let's look at what else was happening in the mid-1990s. This was the beginning of the tech boom, and the markets were being flooded by new investors and new investor capital. With little or no experience, these neophytes were basing their investment decisions on recent past performance and what the media told them to do. So when the media started reporting that index funds (something few had ever heard of before 1995) were a cheaper way to make more money than regular ol' mutual funds, investors flocked to them. And that's when the mantra began that index funds "always" beat those that are actively managed. "Always" really meant "within my personal experience."

The other claim, that index funds are cheaper than actively managed mutual funds, is true. It is also irrelevant. As we have already seen, paying lower fees does not necessarily produce higher returns. So although this claim is correct, it is also pointless.

The best way to demonstrate this is by referring to one of the most profitable mutual funds in history, one which has produced one of the best track records for the 15-, 20- and 25-year periods, according to Morningstar. *This particular fund also has the single most expensive fee schedule in the entire mutual fund industry.*

Thus, the claim that index funds charge less merely diverts your attention from what really counts.

And what really counts is . . .   is . . .

you think I'm about to say . . . performance, don't you?

You'd be wrong. What really counts is not performance, but risk-adjusted performance.[234] And this is where the indexers fall to pieces.

Nowhere have I ever seen any index promoter claim that index investing is an optimal way to invest. That's because it's not. Index investing is, by definition, always 100% invested in the assets of its index. But fund managers have the ability to shift assets based on market conditions. This is why index funds have higher betas than most other mutual funds — something indexers never talk about.

---

[234] As you'd know if you didn't skip the chapter on Morningstar.

If you won't believe what I have to say about index funds, will you believe William Faus? You ought to, because he invented index investing.

In 1969, Faus suggested to his bosses at Mellon Bank that they offer their clients a stock index fund. His premise: The bank's money managers wouldn't produce returns that were as good as the S&P 500. The bank responded to his idea by firing him. So Faus went to Wells Fargo where, two years later, he launched the nation's first index fund, exclusively for the bank's institutional clients. And the rest, as they say, is history: Today, there are 276 stock index mutual funds, according to Lipper Analytical Services.

Indeed, what was heresy in the late '60s has become a widely accepted way to invest. Of course, William Faus has been the indexers' biggest champion. Until now.

In a speech delivered in the summer of 1998 to — no, in a bombshell dropped on — a conference of the Association for Investment Management and Research, Faus said something for which no one was prepared, and few could believe. So astounding were his words that his speech was reprinted in *Financial Analysts Journal*. Here's some of what he said:

> Unlike the Reverend Billy Graham, who claims to have a lot of faith but no evidence, I had a lot of evidence but no faith in traditional asset management. My conversion to indexing came out of my work on common stock price formation, my research on market efficiency, and the negative implications of my findings for traditional stock-picking strategies. In my naiveté, I fully expected index funds to win and to win big. . . .
>
> But I stand here today, dejected, about what we index-fund proponents have accomplished, and less than certain about where indexers are going. I note in passing that Wells Fargo sold its indexing business a couple of years ago. Warren Buffett is apparently not upset about it. He remains a major Wells Fargo shareholder. . . .
>
> The bottom line is that although, comparatively, active managers could hardly have faced a more difficult environment in the past 15 years, or indexers a more favorable one, the index funds failed to fully capitalize on the opportunity. . . .
>
> And I doubt that they will so soon have another so favorable environment. Based on my analysis, I believe the S&P 500 is likely to under perform the broader markets in the foreseeable future. . . .
>
> For the next five years or so, actively managed portfolios may outperform the S&P 500 by 50% or more, which spells more trouble for the already sputtering institutional large-cap index-fund business.

He has been proven right: Compared to actively-managed funds, indexes indeed did sputter in 1999, 2000 and 2001.

Faus' comments created shock waves in the money management field, at both institutional money management firms and pension fund houses.

But I have not seen his comments published anywhere in the personal finance press.

The World's Dumbest Investor

I've got to tell you this story. It's hard to believe, but it's true. It's about an investor we'll call Stan, who has owned a stock for a very long time. Last month it dropped 17% in value.

So what does Stan do? He decides to sell this underperformer and buy another stock. The stock he wants to buy rose 77% last month.

> ***"I want to see as many national parks as possible before age 70."***
>
> **~Anonymous, 62, Attorney**

Does it make any sense to sell a stock after it has gone down to buy a stock that has already gone up? Of course not! It's the dumbest thing in the world. But even though we know to "buy low and sell high," Stan insisted on doing it backwards. That is how you self-destruct when investing.

Exactly who is Stan? He's your plain-vanilla S&P 500 Stock Index Fund. You see, the S&P Investment Management Committee decided to remove Venator, the company that owns Woolworth, from the S&P 500 list and replace it with America Online.

Shortly after the committee's announcement, funds that match the S&P had to change their portfolios accordingly. So if you own an index fund, your fund manager had to sell a stock that had lost a lot of money, and buy a stock at its highest price ever.

So look at what happened: S&P announced on December 24, 1998, that the change would be effective on January 4, 1999, giving everybody a week's notice. On December 24, Venator was trading for 6¼. The following trading day was December 28, but the index funds couldn't act because the change wasn't yet effective.

However, everyone else could act.

Since all the index funds would soon be dumping Venator onto the market, investors knew the price would drop. And since all the index funds would be buying AOL, everyone knew its price would rise. And that's exactly what happened. On December 28, Venator stock fell 3% on trading volume of 1.7 million shares — 150% more than normal.

As for America Online, well, AOL shares jumped 15% in a single day. Twenty-five million shares were traded — a 270% increase in volume.

"I want to complete my Ph.D. while living on campus."

~Judith V. Alsina, 56, Licensed Clinical Social Worker

Meanwhile, nothing had changed with either company's profitability, earnings potential or operating fundamentals. The trading was done merely because a committee said, "you're out and you're in."

As a result, "Stan" and all the other folks who own S&P 500 index funds sold Venator low while simultaneously buying America Online at its highest price of the year. Is this smart investing?

This is just another example showing why I dislike S&P 500 stock index funds. Index funds, due to their nature, are forced to buy high and sell low, which is clearly not in your best interest.

One reason index funds pay too much for the stocks they buy is that the S&P committee announces its changes before the changes actually take place. This gives investors time to buy the stock, knowing that all the index funds are going to have to buy it from them. In essence, this lets investors hold these stocks hostage.

Indeed, from January 1 to August 31, 1999, according to Standard and Poor's, the average daily gain for each stock on the New York Exchange was 0.99%. But the average daily gain for stocks about to be added to the S&P 500 Stock Index was 8.83%.

Clearly, investors held these stocks for ransom, knowing that index funds would be forced to buy them. And index funds did — paying far too much along the way.

And that reveals an unspoken truth: Index funds are a contradiction in terms.

It is alleged that index funds are better than "actively-managed" funds — implying that index funds aren't managed. Instead, it is argued, index funds simply buy the stocks that appear in some list.

But who created the list?

Aha! An investment committee decides what stocks belong in the S&P 500, and its members use subjective measures in making their decisions. As reported by *Money* magazine columnist Jason Zweig, more than 30% of the S&P 500's stocks have been added since 1991 — including 18 in 2000. So it's absurd to suggest that index funds aren't managed, because they are. So, who's kidding who?

Instead of pretending that the S&P 500 Stock Index is not managed, indexers ought to pay attention to *how* it's managed. Because it's really weird: First, the committee selects 500 stocks, and then decides how much of each stock to place into the index. Now, here's the weird part: Instead of placing the greatest emphasis on the stocks it feels have the greatest potential for growth, the committee simply lists each company according to its market value. Thus, buyers of index funds invest a lot more of their money into General Electric (the biggest stock in the index) than McDermott International (the smallest stock).

News flash! The EAFE Index is underperforming the EAFE Index!

Huh?

The Europe Australasia Far East Index, developed by Morgan Stanley Capital International, is an index of foreign stocks. Investors use the EAFE Index to gauge the performance of the international stock market.

So what do I mean that the EAFE is underperforming the EAFE?

It's this: On May 31, 2001, Morgan Stanley changed the stocks that comprise the EAFE; investors were informed that the "new" EAFE would replace the old one, effective in November, 2001. During the interim five months, Morgan Stanley released performance data for both versions.

And, sure enough, during that time, the new EAFE underperformed the original. If this is a permanent trend, it would be a bummer for mutual funds that mimic the EAFE. That's because these funds now emulate the new version — the version that didn't do as well as the original.

But if indexes are "unmanaged," why would there be any changes to the EAFE? And who would have made those changes?

So much for the claim that index funds are "unmanaged."

How much more? About 728 times more! It's true: If you were to invest $50,000 into the S&P 500 Stock Index,[235] a whopping $2,140 of your money would be placed into GE. Meanwhile, less than *three dollars* would be invested into McDermott. If you were investing fifty grand, would you bother to make a three-dollar investment? How could doing so have any impact on your wealth?

Does it make any sense to invest more money into GE simply because it's bigger than McDermott? Since when does being bigger mean its stock price will grow faster?

Yet this is how the S&P 500 works. Although you're buying 500 stocks, you're placing 40% of your money into just 25 of them. The other 475 stocks get all the rest. No wonder only three bucks finds its way into shares of McDermott.

What does all this mean for index investors? Simple: The performance of the S&P 500 is not based on how all the companies in the index do. Instead, the S&P 500's success is based on how *only the biggest stocks* in the index do. I warned you about this in *The New Rules of Money*, and my prediction came true in 2000. That year, the S&P 500 fell 9.5%. This occurred despite the fact that:

- 57% of the stocks in the S&P 500 rose in value.
- 51% of the stocks in the S&P 500 rose more than 10%.
- more than a third of the stocks rose more than 30%.
- the average return for all 500 stocks was 14.5%.

If you insist on buying an S&P 500 index fund, please don't kid yourself into thinking that you're buying "the market." Not only does the S&P own only about 7% of all the stocks publicly traded in the U.S., it owns only the very largest of all American companies. You'd be better off thinking of the S&P 500 as just another large-cap stock fund.

[235] As of September 2001.

How could this be? Simple. The stocks that did well were not high on S&P's list. The big stocks — the ones that got most of S&P's weighting and the ones that were responsible for the S&P 500's success in the 1990s — performed dreadfully in 2000, and their lousy performance dragged down the overall index.[236]

The S&P 500 is not just a managed portfolio of stocks, it's a poorly managed portfolio of stocks.

According to Aronson & Partners, which analyzed the performance of the voluntary substitutions[237] made to the S&P 500 by the S&P index committee since 1997, the committee consistently buys high and sells low.

Here's how it works: First, the S&P index committee decides to add a new stock to the index or delete a current stock from the index. Regardless of whichever action it wants to take, the committee must also do the other, because the index must own exactly 500 stocks. Therefore, any time it adds a stock, it must remove a stock, and vice versa. Simple enough.

But here's what Aronson found:

- **Looking first at the stocks not yet in the index, these stocks had gained an average of 65.8% in the 12 months before the committee added them to the list. Did the committee add these stocks because it believed that these winners would keep on winning? If so, the committee was sorely disappointed because, in the 12 months after these stocks were added to the index, they lost an average of 47.7%.**

- **Looking now at the stocks that were removed from the index, these had fallen an average of 12.0% in the 12 months before the committee removed them from the list. Did the committee kill these stocks because it believed that these losers would keep on losing? If so, the committee once again was sorely disappointed because, in the 12 months following their removal from the index, they gained an average of 16.7%.**

Nice going, S&P! The stocks they bought fell, while the stocks they sold rose.

Can you believe that people actually invest their money in S&P 500 stock index funds?

[236] I'm talking about Wal-Mart, which lost 23%; Cisco, which fell 29%; Intel, down 27%; and Microsoft, whose stock collapsed by 63%. These stocks, and others like them, contain so much of the total assets of the S&P 500 that their massive losses drowned out the gains made by the rest of the index's stocks. I warned you in my second book that this could happen.
[237] The study ignored changes due to mergers, acquisitions and bankruptcies.

The irony is that many of the people who screamed the loudest about the virtues of index funds no longer own them. Ask yourself: When's the last time you heard anyone talking about index funds? For a while — in 1995, 1996, 1997 and 1998 — indexing was all anyone talked about.

But when the S&P 500 stopped outperforming the field, everyone's attention moved on. Suddenly, tech stocks became the rage. Indeed, look at Figure 13-2 to see the net cash inflows of the Vanguard S&P 500 Stock Index Fund — the nation's largest index fund.[238]

The pattern is clear. Investors didn't think much of the fund until the S&P 500 Stock Index started producing double-digit returns in 1995 — that's when investor capital flowed into index funds in unprecedented amounts. And then, as soon as the index started losing money in 2000, net *inflows* became net *outflows*, as investors — including many of those who had previously argued that index funds are always the way to go — pulled their money out of index funds. Indeed, according to a study in *Financial Planning* magazine, investors from January 1, 2000, to April 30, 2001, withdrew $24 billion from 81 S&P 500 index funds.

Investors Like Indexing Only When Indexing Is Profitable

	Total Return of the Vanguard S&P 500 Stock Index Fund	Increase/Decrease in net new cash, in millions
1991	30.2%	$1,516
1992	7.4%	1,850
1993	9.9%	1,110
1994	1.2%	986
1995	37.5%	4,511
1996	22.9%	8,985
1997	33.2%	8,959
1998	28.6%	10,745
1999	21.1%	14,782
2000	–9.1%	–4,683
2001	–6.8%	–3,590

Figure 13-2

[238] Net cash inflows reflect increases in total fund assets minus withdrawals and market gains. Raw data provided by Morningstar.

It's obvious: Most indexers are not true believers of indexing. They are simply fair-weather friends, favoring whichever market sector or investment style is in vogue. I hope they don't treat people the way they treat their investments.

Even if it's true that index funds beat actively-managed stock funds — and as I've shown you, it's not true — so what?

I say this because (a) I didn't know it was a race, and (b) this doesn't mean other investments aren't doing just fine.

Consider this: Say you owned a mutual fund that gained 26% in 1998, compared to the 28% that was earned by the S&P 500. Are you upset? Angry? Annoyed?

I doubt it. And this is the point that people fail to acknowledge. It also explains why I really don't care if you insist on buying index funds.

Let's turn that question around. Say your mutual fund gained 30% last year, beating the S&P by 2%. Are you dancing in the streets over your victory?

Of course not.

And that's my point. If you didn't own an S&P 500 index fund in 1998, you didn't earn 28% that year. Instead, you did somewhat better or somewhat worse. But you certainly didn't earn zero. Yet, with their distorted perspective, that's what people who own the S&P think happens to everyone else. Of course, you know it's not true.

What does Standard & Poor think of the stocks in its own S&P 500 Stock Index? Well, as of June 30, 2001, it rated only 54 of those stocks a "buy." But if you own an S&P 500 index fund, you've got to buy the other 446 as well. Does that sound like something you really want to do?

S&P's own opinion of the stocks inside the S&P 500 Stock Index

Buy	54
Accumulate	156
Hold	251
Avoid	28
Sell	4
Non-rated	7

Figure 13-3

Index Fund Holders Could Be Hit With a Huge Tax Surprise

Some people claim to prefer index funds because they say index funds are tax efficient. They say that index funds are static portfolios — no trading. And since there's no trading, there should be no annual tax liability.

But there is. That's because portfolio turnover does exist in index funds. In 2000, for example, the S&P 500 experienced turnover of more than 25%. In the first six months of 2001, turnover exceeded 20%.[239]

> ***"I want to visit and spend time in each of the 50 states by the time I am age 60."***
>
> **~Ed Moore, Financial Planner, Edelman Financial Services**

But these figures, which are lower than you typically find among actively-managed funds, hide an additional risk: By not paying much in annual capital gains distributions, index funds are creating a massive buildup in capital gains. *Forbes* calls this "a ticking time bomb."

You see, indexers, like all fund owners, are going to pay taxes on their profits at some point. The big question is, when? In most mutual funds, taxes are paid on an annual basis. That's why you get IRS Form 1099 every year from your fund company, which discloses the amount of profit that's being reported to the IRS for the year. By paying this (rather annoying) tax each year, you reduce the amount of tax you'll owe in the year you actually sell your fund.

But because index funds generate smaller annual distributions, the annual tax bite is smaller. This doesn't mean your taxes are less — it merely means your taxes are less *for now.* Instead, the future for indexers will be an expensive one. And that's because of the huge hidden tax liability that's lurking inside index funds.

[239] Further proving my point that index funds are actively managed. Someone is making the decision to sell certain stocks and buy others.

As *Forbes* noted, if lots of investors "run for the hills" the next time the stock market drops, index funds will be forced to sell significant holdings to raise the cash demanded by those departing investors. Selling lots of shares will trigger a huge capital gain liability for the investors who remain. And when that happens (that's when, not if), it won't matter whether you've been in the fund for 10 days or 10 years: Everyone left will have to pay that whopping tax. Will you be among those facing that problem?

Meet Dr. Frankenstein

If none of these facts and statistics have convinced you to avoid S&P 500 Index funds, if the comments of William Faus, the inventor of index funds, haven't convinced you, perhaps you'll listen to John Bogle, the nation's loudest proponent of index investing. While chairman of Vanguard, Bogle created in 1975 the first S&P 500 index mutual fund, based on Faus' design for institutional investors. Bogle's fund has since become the nation's largest mutual fund[240] and Vanguard's name is now virtually synonymous with index investing. Yet here's what Bogle told *Boston Globe* financial columnist Charles Jaffee in August 2001:

> I have to take some responsibility for what's happening, and I don't like it much. Small-cap indexing, growth and value indexing simply don't work as well as I would have hoped. And they don't work as well not because indexing is a problem but because the indexes are a problem – there is too much turnover. As a result, I'm a bit troubled by my creation, like Dr. Frankenstein.

If I'm not mistaken, the townspeople in the film turned on Dr. Frankenstein when they discovered the truth behind his experiments. I suspect that John Bogle will, one day, face the same angry mob.

> ***"I'll go to the top of the Washington Monument at 2 p.m. on May 28, 2005."***
>
> **~Ric Edelman**

[240] Fidelity's Magellan Fund, still a bit bigger, is closed to new investors.

Chapter 14

Choosing Between Taxable and Tax-Deferred

CHAPTER 14

Choosing Between Taxable and Tax-Deferred

We've already talked about the pros and cons of mutual funds and annuities, but this issue deserves elaboration. Although Figure 14-1 compares the two, it doesn't answer the one question all investors have: Which vehicle generates the greater profit?

Conventional wisdom suggests that the mutual fund should produce a greater return than its annuity cousin, if only because it avoids a fee the annuity incurs. This logic makes sense, considering that most annuity subaccounts are managed by the very same folks who operate mutual funds.[241]

"I want to own a lake house and spend many hours there relaxing and enjoying my husband and our two children."

~Laura Welsh, 38, Manager—Healthcare

"I would like to create a charitable fund as a memorial to my father and my son to provide educational opportunities to the underprivileged."

~Jack Bubon, Financial Planner, Edelman Financial Services

[241] Indeed, almost every mutual fund is available in the form of an annuity. For practical purposes, the sole difference is the tax treatment of the two.

How They Compare

	Mutual Funds	Annuity Subaccounts
Managed By	Portfolio Managers	Portfolio Managers
Expense Ratio	Ranges from 0.2% to 3%	Industry avg. is 1.15% higher than funds
Annual Fees	Uncommon	Up to $50 per year for small accounts
Taxed Annually?	Yes	No
Tax Rates	Short-term gains and dividends taxed at ordinary income tax rates, as high as 38.6%. Long-term gains taxed at 20% or less.	No taxes due until withdrawal. Withdrawals subject to ordinary income tax rates, as high as 38.6%.
Tax Record Keeping Requirements	Extensive; dividend and capital gains reinvestments constitute separate trade lots and must be itemized on Schedule D when sold.	Minimal to none; no taxes due until withdrawal.
Are Fund Transfers Taxed?	Yes. IRS considers transfers to be a sell and a purchase, creating tax implications.	No. Tax law permits unlimited tax-free transfers, although many annuities limit fee-free transfers to 10 per year.
Do Assets Enjoy Step-Up in Basis?	Yes, although this benefit is threatened by new tax legislation.	No, creating a potential future tax liability for heirs that funds might avoid. New tax legislation appears to eliminate this concern.
Are Market Values Guaranteed in Any Way?	No.	Yes. Most contracts offer death benefit guarantees to protect account values for heirs.
Liquidity Restrictions	None, other than fund-imposed surrender fees, if any.	Withdrawals prior to age 59½ subject to 10% IRS penalty. There also could be annuity-imposed surrender fees.

Figure 14-1

But the data suggest otherwise. For reasons no one has been able to state definitively (though there are several theories), the fact is that data collected from Morningstar, Lipper Analytical Services and *The Wall Street Journal* show that variable annuity subaccounts often generate higher returns than their mutual fund counterparts, as shown in Figure 14-2.

	Category	Avg Return for Mutual Funds	Avg Return for Annuities	Winner
1 Yr Average Annual Returns	Aggressive Growth	15.8%	38.7%	Annuity
	Growth	47.8%	19.0%	Mutual Fund
	Growth and Income	–6.6%	0.6%	Annuity
	International Stock	24.5%	27.3%	Annuity
	Sector Fund	31.9%	11.3%	Mutual Fund
	Balanced	4.4%	5.3%	Annuity
	Government Bond	3.6%	3.1%	Mutual Fund
	Corporate Bond	2.8%	2.2%	Mutual Fund
	High-Yield Bond	2.3%	–2.4%	Mutual Fund
	Average	14.0%	11.7%	Mutual Fund
3 Yr Average Annual Returns	Aggressive Growth	–4.1%	22.1%	Annuity
	Growth	29.3%	21.2%	Mutual Fund
	Growth and Income	7.1%	12.1%	Annuity
	International Stock	11.8%	12.2%	Annuity
	Sector Fund	21.3%	10.6%	Mutual Fund
	Balanced	10.5%	10.5%	Tie
	Government Bond	5.1%	4.3%	Mutual Fund
	Corporate Bond	4.7%	3.6%	Mutual Fund
	High-Yield Bond	4.3%	1.7%	Mutual Fund
	Average	10.0%	10.9%	Annuity
5 Yr Average Annual Returns	Aggressive Growth	2.9%	19.7%	Annuity
	Growth	24.5%	21.6%	Mutual Fund
	Growth and Income	13.6%	16.6%	Annuity
	International Stock	11.8%	16.3%	Annuity
	Sector Fund	21.0%	10.6%	Mutual Fund
	Balanced	13.0%	13.0%	Mutual Fund
	Government Bond	5.2%	4.4%	Mutual Fund
	Corporate Bond	4.7%	4.5%	Mutual Fund
	High-Yield Bond	5.6%	5.9%	Annuity
	Average	11.4%	12.5%	Annuity

Figure 14-2

As previously discussed, annuities are intended for long-term investing, and you should not place any money into an annuity without intending to leave that money there until you reach age 59½.

Too often, people invest in annuities even though they do not intend, or cannot afford, to leave the money invested for a such a long time. Unless you do so, you probably would be better off investing in mutual funds.

This explains why only about 15% of our clients' assets are in annuities, with the rest in mutual funds. This does not mean that every client has 15% of assets in annuities, of course. Some — many, in fact — have no annuities, while others use them exclusively. It is, like all other investment decisions, entirely dependent on one's individual circumstances.

ARE YOU BUYING ANNUITIES WHEN YOU SHOULDN'T?

Sometimes, unscrupulous salesmen pitch annuities to consumers who might be better off buying mutual funds. As you've seen, tax deferral is a benefit only if you leave the money invested (a) for 15 years or more and (b) until you reach age 59½ (to avoid tax penalties for early withdrawal). In addition, annuities should be purchased only if the money is not being invested in a tax-deferred account (see next sidebar). And although annuities guarantee that heirs will inherit at least as much as you invest (something mutual funds can't promise), this benefit is of questionable value. That's because, according to Ibbotson Associates, stocks have not lost money in any given 15-year period since 1926 — meaning that annuities are "guaranteeing" something that probably doesn't need a guarantee.

So what's the problem? It's twofold. First, annuities sometimes pay higher commissions than mutual funds (which can entice advisors to sell them). Second, insurance companies that market both annuities and mutual funds often charge higher fees in their annuities than in their mutual funds (which can entice the companies to encourage their agents to sell their annuity products instead of their mutual fund products). For both these reasons, some firms and sales agents overhype the tax and death benefits as they encourage people to buy annuities even when they are not appropriate for the client's particular needs.

The National Association of Securities Dealers has had enough. And this is great news.

According to *Investment News*, the NASD (the chief regulator of investment sales practices) is targeting not just the agents who sell annuities inappropriately, but their firms as well. According to the story, the NASD has sent notices to "several brokerage firms" warning that the agency is likely to file charges against them

for their annuity sales practices. The charges, according to *Investment News*, include misrepresentation of variable products to consumers, failure to disclose pertinent fee information, and inappropriately selling variable annuities for tax-deferred retirement accounts.

Never before have regulators focused such widespread enforcement efforts against financial firms; they typically go after individual advisors. But now, the NASD seems to be saying that advisors are acting improperly because their firms are encouraging them to do so. In other words, we don't merely have a here-and-there bad soldier; we have an entirely bad army, led by generals issuing improper orders.

If the story is true, and if, indeed, the NASD holds these firms accountable, we could see a huge wave of class-action lawsuits on behalf of millions of investors. So, my message to you is:

First, pay attention to this. You are likely to hear about this in the media. Know the background, and understand how and if it applies to you.

Second, don't let the story lead you to believe that all annuities are bad, because they're not, or that all advisors who recommend them are bad, because they're not. Like any investment product, annuities are right for some people and wrong for others. If someone suggests that you buy an annuity, ask yourself if the money you're planning to invest is money that you won't need for 15 years. Only if that is the case should you consider the idea further.

The NASD is getting tough on unscrupulous sales practices, and I'm glad to see it. Maybe now annuities will be touted for all of the right reasons and will be recommended only to the people who can truly benefit from them.

"I would like to give back to my community by opening a small soup kitchen for those who are homeless — one particular homeless man comes to mind as I have watched him deteriorate and lose weight over the past 3 years while I attended grad school. He has walked the median strip for 3 years, looking hungry and weak. I'll do this at age 45."

~Donna Strait, 25, Physical Therapist

If you participate in a 403(b) plan at work, chances are you're one of the victims of abuse described in the previous sidebar.

Traditionally, 403(b) accounts only allowed you to invest in annuities. But Congress amended Section 403(b) so nonprofit and public employees could invest in mutual funds, too. This amendment is called Section 403(b)(7).

But rather than letting their workers invest in mutual funds instead of annuities, many nonprofit employers let their workers choose mutual funds in addition to annuities.

How do the workers choose? By listening to the sales pitches offered by the agents of the plan sponsors, often made at mandatory staff meetings. Often, sales agents are permitted to wander through the workplace, pitching any worker they can corral.

Agents usually earn higher commissions by selling annuities instead of mutual funds. Ordinarily, this could be excused, because investors who buy annuities get something — tax deferral — that mutual fund investors don't get.

Unfortunately, when a retirement plan is involved, this is not the case. That's because all 403(b) plans let your money grow tax-deferred — whether you choose an annuity or a mutual fund. Therefore, annuities don't give you any tax benefit that you're not already getting from the plan itself. And since mutual funds are cheaper than annuities, you're usually better off investing in mutual funds.

The NASD is concerned that agents are recommending annuities when there is no tax benefit for doing so. Thus, the NASD is seeking to protect millions of school, university, hospital, and other nonprofit employees.

That's good news. So, if you work in a school, hospital or other nonprofit organization, watch out for advisors who recommend annuities for your 403(b) plan. If that's the pitch, see what their reasons are. If the only reason is tax deferral, reject the idea.

"In 12–15 years, I would like to have season tickets to the Red Sox and maybe follow them around for a year. In my wildest fantasies, I would like to have the time, patience, and perseverance to write a book — subject to be determined."

~Anonymous, 48, Procurement Executive, Federal Gov't

CONCLUSION

Whew!

You made it through the grueling details about investing. You learned about taxable vs. tax-deferred investments, and active vs. passive investing. You learned more about Morningstar than you ever wanted to,[242] and you understand the nuances of mutual fund analysis and research. From now on, you'll shrug when someone touts past performance and you'll simply smile at the foolishness of people who offer you hot tips.

Many readers will use this information to choose their own investments. Many others, though, will just as reasonably conclude that they'd rather seek the aid of a financial advisor.

"I want to live the life of a country gentleman, carry a walking stick with a solid silver wolfhead and watch everybody else drive to work in rush hour traffic, starting this January."

~Joel Smith, 61

If you're the former, consider the following web sites listed in Figure 15-1. If you're the latter, visit www.ricedelman.com for a link to a referral list of financial advisors nationwide as well as the online investment management services we offer. The site also recaps the information found in Part 13 of *The Truth About Money,* called "How

[242] Go on, admit it!

Favorite Sites of Financial Advisors, according to a 2001 Study by *Investment News*:

advisor.com	moneycentral.com
bigcharts.com	Morningstar.com
Bloomberg.com	msn.com
cnbc.com	quicken.com
cnn.com	quote.com
cnnfn.com	sec.gov
etrade.com	smartmoney.com
financial-planning.com	stockquotes.com
forbes.com	thestreet.com
fpanet.org	usatoday.com
iarfc.org	wsj.com
money.com	Yahoo.com

Figure 15-1

to Choose a Financial Advisor." Whichever way you proceed, you're in a much better position to succeed than you were before, for you now know how to bake a cake. Whether you plan to bake alone or with the assistance of an advisor, you can already smell the wonderful scents that will soon be emanating from the oven. You can envision your cake in there, slowly rising, turning to a warm, soft brown, with an ever-so-slight spring to the touch. Soon, you and your family will be enjoying it immensely.

Because, although the second half of the book was devoted to teaching you how to bake a cake, in truth, you never really wanted to learn how to do that. You still don't. What you wanted was to eat a cake. And whether you go to a bakery for a professional's delicious cake, or whether you enter the kitchen yourself, you can envision the feast that is soon to come — a feast you've anticipated for a long, long time.

Soon, it'll be here. And you can't wait to taste it.

This is what financial planning is all about. It's about setting goals and showing you how to achieve them, so you can lead a more fulfilling, rewarding and enriching life. And when you're done with your journey, you will be able to say with great contentment, satisfaction and a smile . . .

I'm Full.

I've lived a life that's full.
I've traveled each and ev'ry highway;
But more, much more than this,
I did it my way.

Regrets, I've had a few;
But then again, too few to mention.
I did what I had to do
And saw it through without exemption.

I planned each charted course;
Each careful step along the byway,
But more, much more than this,
I did it my way.

~*MY WAY*, by Paul Anka, Jacques Revaux and Claude Francois

Sources

"Copy from one, it's plagiarism; copy from two, it's research."

~Wilson Mizner (1876–1933)

Figure 2-2:	Discovery.com.
Figure 3-1:	American Council of Life Insurers.
Figure 3-2:	American Council of Life Insurers.
Figure 3-3:	American Council of Life Insurers. Based on $100 daily benefit, 100% home health care, 100% nursing home coverage, 90-day elimination period and 5% compound inflation protection. Average costs based on composite policies from five large LTC companies. Actual prices vary by company.
Figure 3-4:	American Council of Life Insurers. Calculations based on a 5-year long-term care policy with inflation protection of 5%. Future cost of care represented in 2030 dollars. Annual savings assumes 8% return.
Figure 4-1:	Ibbotson Associates. Monthly performance of the S&P 500 Stock Index 1926–2000.
Figure 4-2:	Ned Davis Research. Figures based on the Dow Jones Industrial Average.
Figure 4-3:	Ibbotson Associates. Data reflect U.S. Inflation and Solomon Brothers Domestic 6-month Bank C.D. Total Return (annualized) 1980–2001.
Figure 4-4:	Ibbotson Associates. Monthly: Monthly performance of the S&P 500 Stock Index 1926–2001. Annual: Annual performance of the S&P 500 Stock Index 1926–2001. 5-Year: Performance of the S&P 500 Stock Index 1926–2001 based on rolling 5-year intervals. 10-Year: Performance of the S&P 500 Stock Index 1926–2001 based on rolling 10-year intervals. 15-Year: Performance of the S&P 500 Stock Index 1926–2001 based on rolling 15-year intervals.

20-Year: Performance of the S&P 500 Stock Index 1926–2001 based on rolling 20-year intervals.

Figure 4-5: Ned Davis Research.

Figure 5-2: Ibbotson Associates. Allocations based on 1926–1999 average annual returns of 13.3% for the S&P 500 Stock Index and 5.4% for the U.S. Intermediate Government Bond Index.

Figure 6-1: Ibbotson Associates.

Figure 6-2: Ibbotson Associates.

Figure 6-3: Ibbotson Associates.

Figure 6-4: Ibbotson Associates.

Figure 6-5: Ibbotson Associates.

Figure 6-6: Ibbotson Associates.

Figure 6-7: Ibbotson Associates.

Figure 6-8: Zacks Investment Research. Data for First Quarter 2001.

Figure 6-9: *Institutional Investor*.

Figure 7-1: Ibbotson Associates.

Figure 7-2: PrudentBear.com.

Figure 7-3: *Manias, Panics and Crashes* by Charles P. Kindleberger.

Figure 7-4: *A Random Walk Down Wall Street*, by Burton Gordon Malkiel.

Figure 7-5: Ibbotson Associates. Annual total return of the S&P 500 Stock Index minus the Small Company Stock Index from December 1925 through December 1999. The SCSI was developed by Professor Rolf W. Banz based on performance of the stocks of the New York Stock Exchange. Prof. Banz first created this index in 1925. Since 1981, the index has been maintained and updated by Dimensional Fund Advisors Inc.

Figure 7-6: Callan Associates. The S&P 500/BARRA Growth Index is a benchmark for large-cap growth stock performance. It is constructed of companies in the S&P 500 Index, which is a market-value weighted index for large-cap stock price movement, with higher price-to-book ratios than the companies in its value index counterpart. The S&P 500/BARRA Value Index is a benchmark for large-cap value stock performance. It is constructed of companies in the S&P 500 Index, which is a market-value weighted index for large-cap stock price movement, with lower price-to-book ratios than the companies in its growth index counterpart. The S&P 500 Index is an unmanaged index generally considered representative of broad stock market activity. Please note that indices do not take into account any fees and expenses of investing in the individual securities that they track, and that individuals cannot invest directly in any index. Data include reinvestment of all dividends and capital gain distributions.

Figure 7-7: Ibbotson Associates and Morgan Stanley Capital International.

Figure 7-8: *Business Week*. Data from January 1, 1997, to April 1, 2001.

Figure 8-3: *Pensions & Investments*, Employee Benefits Research Institute and Buck Associates.

Figure 8-4: *Pensions & Investments*, Employee Benefits Research Institute and Buck Associates.

Figure 8-5: Institute of Management and Administration.

Figure 9-1: Morningstar's Don Philips' keynote address at the *Baltimore Sun*'s Dollars & Sense Conference. Mutual fund results are at net asset value; if sales charges were reflected, performance would have been lower.

Figure 9-2: *Financial Planning.*

Figure 10-1: *Journal of Investment Consulting*.

Figure 10-2: Morningstar.

Figure 10-3: Typical Class A mutual fund prospectus.

Figure 10-4: Typical Class B mutual fund prospectus.

Figure 11-1: Morningstar.

Figure 11-4: Ibbotson Associates.

Figure 11-5: Morningstar.

Figure 11-6: Morningstar.

Figure 11-7: Overlap.

Figure 13-1: Callan Associates. The S&P 500/BARRA Growth Index is a benchmark for large-cap growth stock performance. It is constructed of companies in the S&P 500 Index, which is a market-value weighted index for large-cap stock price movement, with higher price-to-book ratios than the companies in its value index counterpart. The S&P 500/BARRA Value Index is a benchmark for large-cap value stock performance. It is constructed of companies in the S&P 500 Index, which is a market-value weighted index for large-cap stock price movement, with lower price-to-book ratios than the companies in its growth index counterpart. The S&P 500 Index is an unmanaged index generally considered representative of broad stock market activity. Please note that indices do not take into account any fees and expenses of investing in the individual securities that they track, and that individuals cannot invest directly in any index. Data include reinvestment of all dividends and capital gain distributions.

Figure 13-2: Morningstar and Vanguard.

Figure 13-3: Standard and Poor.

Figure 14-2: Lipper, Morningstar and *Wall Street Journal*. Data as of June 30, 2000.

Figure 15-1: *Investment News*.

About the Author

Financial advisor and educator Ric Edelman, CFS, RFC, CMFC, CRC, is the author of five books, which have collectively sold more than one million copies. *Ordinary People, Extraordinary Wealth* was a #1 *New York Times* bestseller; *The New Rules of Money* also was a *New York Times* bestseller; *The Truth About Money*, also a *New York Times* bestseller, was for 22 weeks #1 on the *Washington Post* bestseller list (70 weeks overall) and was named Book of the Year by *Small Press* magazine. His two most recent books are *What You Need to Do Now* and *Discover the Wealth Within You.*

Ric hosts weekly radio and television shows (for the former, he won the Washington, D.C., A.I.R. Award for Best Talk Show Host), writes a syndicated advice and news column for AARP's *Modern Maturity* magazine and other publications, publishes a monthly newsletter, and created the personal finance education web site RicEdelman.com. He also has produced a variety of video tapes and audio cassettes on personal finance topics.

For nine years, Ric taught personal finance at Georgetown University. He is a state- and AICPA-approved instructor for continuing professional education. He is also a member of the NASD Board of Arbitrators.

He has earned three Awards of Excellence by Royal Alliance Associates[1], was named Ace Advisor of the Year by *Ticker* magazine, named Financial Planner of the Year three times by World Invest Corporation, and named one of the D.C. area's top financial professionals by *Washingtonian* magazine.

Ric has been the subject of many feature stories in the media, has appeared on hundreds of radio stations and every major television network, and has been quoted by dozens of newspapers and magazines. He also has testified before Congress and provided services to many agencies within the federal government, including serving as a delegate to the 1998 and 2002 National Summits on Retirement Savings. Ric is a sought-after speaker, who is widely acknowledged as one of the most entertaining and informative experts in his field.

1 1999 #1 Group Manager, 1998 Outstanding Achievement, 1997 New Colleague of the Year.

Ric is the founder of Edelman Financial Services Inc., named three times by *Inc.* magazine as the fastest-growing privately-held financial planning firm in the country[2]. *Bloomberg Wealth Manager* in 2001 ranked EFS as the fifth-largest independent financial planning and investment management firm in the nation[3], with $1.7 billion in client assets. The firm has won more than 50 professional, business and community service awards, including Service Business of the Year by the Fairfax Virginia Chamber of Commerce and the Blue Chip Enterprise Award by the U.S. Chamber of Commerce and MassMutual. In 2001 Ric was named the Washington, D.C. Entrepreneur of the Year by Ernst and Young.

Ric is the founder of the Edelman Center for Personal Finance Education, a nonprofit organization. He also serves on the Board of Directors of the United Way of the National Capital Area, Junior Achievement of the National Capital Area, Boys & Girls Clubs of Greater Washington and on the Grants Committee of the Foundation for Financial Planning, where he is a major donor. He is also a full partner of the American Savings Education Council and the Jump$tart Coalition for Personal Financial Literacy.

Ric received an honorary doctorate from Rowan University in 1999. In 2002, the university named the school's new planetarium The Ric and Jean Edelman Planetarium in their honor.

12450 Fair Lakes Circle
Suite 200, Fairfax, VA 22033-3808
(703) 818-0800
FAX (703) 818-1910
redelman@ricedelman.com

RicEdelman.com

2 *Inc.* magazine's list of the fastest growing companies in America according to growth in net sales in the last 5 years.

3 *Bloomberg Wealth Manager* magazine, "Top Wealth Managers" June 2001. Based on a survey of 313 independent financial planning firms who offer comprehensive financial planning; more than 50 percent of client base are individuals; with client assets in excess of $25 million dollars.

Also Available from the Author

Ric's National bestsellers *Ordinary People, Extraordinary Wealth, The New Rules of Money, The Truth About Money,* and *What You Need to Do Now*

Also available on audio cassette by HarperAudio and in bookstores everywhere.

Seminars on Video

How to Choose a Financial Advisor

Ric Edelman shows you how planners are paid, what planners do, how to assess credentials, the 12 key questions to ask when interviewing planners, and more.

Protecting Against the Cost of Long-Term Care

Nursing homes cost $50,000 per year, but health insurance and Medicare won't pay for it. That's why half of all Americans hit poverty within six months. It's a crisis for children, too: You not only lose your inheritance, you wind up supporting your parents. Ric gives you the solution!

Why You Should Carry a Big, Long Mortgage and Never Pay It Off

Discover why most of what you've heard about homes and mortgages is wrong, which is why so many people squander tens of thousands of dollars on the biggest financial transaction of their lives.

How to Become a Successful Financial Planner

The video includes two hours of training showing you how planners are compensated, educational requirements and industry designations, federal and state licensing requirements, what types of companies are looking for planners, who the competition is, how you make money, and ethics and liability issues affecting the planning profession.

To Order Ric's Seminars on Video
Call Toll-Free 1-800-221-6597

Online with Ric!

RicEdelman.com

Financial planning in plain English! Advice on every topic from award-winning author and personal finance talk show host Ric Edelman. Sign up for Ric's free weekly newsletter!

Invite Ric to Speak at Your Next Conference

A long established educator in the field of personal finance, Ric Edelman is an entertaining, engaging, and informative speaker who wows audiences with the latest ever-changing financial topics, such as investments, insurance, taxes, real estate, retirement planning, wills and trusts, college planning, mortgages, and much more. Call 703-818-0800 for more information.

Ric on the Air

Radio MD, VA, DC & **Internet**

The Ric Edelman Show
Saturdays 10am-11:45 EST
Live at www.wmal.com
Call in at 202-432-WMAL

TV MD, VA, & DC

The Truth About Money with Ric Edelman
Mondays 8pm-8:30 EST
Call in at 703-912-1430

HarperCollins is not the publisher of, and is not responsible for the information contained in, Ric's Seminars on Video and *Inside Personal Finance.*

Subscribe to Ric's Award-Winning 12-page Monthly Newsletter

Get the Latest Financial Advice

You'll read the latest on investments, taxes, insurance, financial planning, estate planning, retirement, elder care, your IRA, 401(k), 403(b), and Thrift plans, debt management, mortgages, home ownership, ways to teach kids sound money-management practices, and even more.

It's the most comprehensive source you'll ever find on the topic of personal finance. Plus, you'll find everything explained in plain English … no gobbledygook.

What Others Are Saying

"*Your newsletter has some of the best financial advice out there.*"
– A. Hastings, Malden, Mass.

"*It is one of the best publications we get.*"
– A. Collins, Springfield, Va.

"*It's the first 'money' publication I've found that's fun to read!*"
– E. Ward, Evansville, Ind.

You Risk No Money

Try *Inside Personal Finance with Ric Edelman* completely risk-free. If for any reason you're not delighted with *Inside Personal Finance with Ric Edelman*, you can cancel anytime for a full, 100% refund of your subscription fee.

That means you can cancel on the 12th month of your one-year subscription and receive all your money back, every last nickel. No questions asked. Plus, you get to keep all your issues with our compliments. Order today and we'll get you started on your no-risk trial subscription.

43% savings
off the regular price

Order Today at (888) 987-PLAN

ONE-YEAR SUBSCRIPTION........$39.95

HarperCollins is not the publisher of, and is not responsible for the information contained in, Ric's Seminars on Video and *Inside Personal Finance.*

How to Give Your Child or Grandchild as Much as

$2,451,854 for only $5,000*

A small amount of money can grow into a small fortune, thanks to compound interest. But as simple and effective as it is, few people take as much advantage of this concept as they can. For example, few begin saving for college as soon as a child is born. And even if you were to set aside $5,000 for a newborn, it would grow over 18 years to just $27,800 (assuming 10% per year). That's hardly enough to pay for college today, let alone 18 years from now.

But imagine saving that same $5,000 for the child's retirement rather than college. With 65 years on which to compound the interest, again assuming a 10% annual return, the account would be worth not just $27,800 but more than $2.4 million!*

Although easy to understand, the tax, legal, and economic obstacles prevented most of us from creating an account that could let money grow like this. But now you can do this for the benefit of your loved ones!

Introducing the Retirement InCome – for Everyone Trust® So Innovative, It's Patented!

Your kids don't need a lot of money, and they don't need an astronomically high rate of return. All they need is a little money and an opportunity to obtain a competitive return—because time does the rest.

Through the RIC-E Trust®, you can put the power of compound interest to work for your children and grandchildren. You can establish a RIC-E Trust® for any child of any age. You don't have to be the child's parent or grandparent, and the child even can be

Index

HarperBusiness

Books by Ric Edelman:

ORDINARY PEOPLE, EXTRAORDINARY WEALTH
The 8 Secrets of How 5,000 Ordinary Americans Became Successful Investors—and How You Can Too
ISBN 0-06-273686-8 (paperback) • ISBN 0-694-52261-9 (audio)

Ric Edelman discloses the method of achieving extraordinary financial success by using eight unconventional but proven strategies for smart investing, culled from 5,000 of his most successful clients.

"If you follow these simple rules, you will not only accumulate wealth for yourself but you will enjoy a much happier and healthier life." —Dr. Paul B. Farrell, *CBS MarketWatch*

THE TRUTH ABOUT MONEY
Revised Edition
ISBN 0-06-095636-4 (paperback) • ISBN 0-694-51914-6 (audio)

A comprehensive, practical, "how-to" manual on financial planning, written for anyone concerned about their financial well-being. The book discusses investments, long-term care, planning for retirement, buying and selling your home, how to get out of debt, how to pay for college or your daughter's wedding, and much more.

"Conversational, clever . . . an easy read."—*USA Today*

THE NEW RULES OF MONEY
88 Simple Strategies for Financial Success Today
ISBN 0-06-272074-0 (paperback) • ISBN 0-694-51929-4 (audio)

Tailor-made for today's economy, Edelman's 88 strategies show how to achieve financial success, while making personal finance fun through easy, practical advice.

"He's unconventional. He's contrary. But when it comes to investing, people listen."

—The Washington Post

WHAT YOU NEED TO DO NOW
An 8-Point Action Plan to Secure Your Financial Independence
ISBN 0-06-009404-4 (paperback)

Returning to basics, Ric Edelman provides quick, practical, and sound advice for getting started on the road to financial freedom. Edelman's eight-point plan for financial stability shows how to preserve and protect financial assets, secure the financial future of loved ones, and ensure that our businesses and other sources of income are not compromised.

Originally published in hardcover as *FINANCIAL SECURITY IN TROUBLED TIMES.*

DISCOVER THE WEALTH WITHIN YOU
A Financial Plan For Creating a Rich and Fulfilling Life
ISBN 0-06-008130-9 (cassette) • ISBN 0-06-008131-7 (CD)

Want to receive notice of author events and new books by Ric Edelman? Sign up for Ric Edelman's AuthorTracker at www.AuthorTracker.com

Available wherever books are sold, or call 1-800-331-3761 to order.